FRONTLINE MEDIC – GALLIPOLI, SOMME, YPRES

Figure 1. Captain George Stephen Pirie, Royal Army Medical Corps. (© Peter Strasheim)

Frontline Medic –
Gallipoli, Somme, Ypres

The Diary of Captain George Pirie, R.A.M.C.

Edited by Michael Lucas

Helion & Company Limited

Helion & Company Limited
26 Willow Road
Solihull
West Midlands
B91 1UE
England
Tel. 0121 705 3393
Fax 0121 711 4075
Email: info@helion.co.uk
Website: www.helion.co.uk
Twitter: @helionbooks
Visit our blog http://blog.helion.co.uk/

Published by Helion & Company 2014

Designed and typeset by Bookcraft Ltd, Stroud, Gloucestershire
Cover designed by Paul Hewitt, Battlefield Design (www.battlefield-design.co.uk)
Printed by Gutenberg Press Limited, Tarxien, Malta

ISBN 978 1 909982 89 5

British Library Cataloguing-in-Publication Data.
A catalogue record for this book is available from the British Library.

For details of other military history titles published by Helion & Company
Limited contact the above address, or visit our website: http://www.helion.co.uk.

We always welcome receiving book proposals from prospective authors.

Contents

List of Illustrations

List of Maps

List of Abbreviations

A.D.M.S.	Assistant Director of Medical Services
A.D.S.	Advanced Dressing Station
A.P.M.	Assistant Provost Marshal
A.S.C.	Army Service Corps
C.C.S.	Casualty Clearing Station
C.O.	Commanding Officer
D.A.D.M.S.	Deputy Assistant Director Medical Services
D.S.	Dressing Station
D.S.O.	Distinguished Service Order
F.A.	Field Ambulance
F.O.O.	Forward Observation Officer
G.S.	General Service
H.L.I.	Highland Light Infantry
I.W.M.	Imperial War Museum
M.C.	Military Cross
M.D.S.	Main Dressing Station
M.G.C.	Machine Gun Corps
M.G.O.	Machine Gun Officer
N.C.O.	Non-Commissioned Officer
O.C.	Officer Commanding
O.R.	Other Rank
R.A.M.C.	Royal Army Medical Corps
R.A.P.	Regimental Aid Post
R.E.	Royal Engineers
R.F.A.	Royal Field Artillery
R.G.A.	Royal Garrison Artillery
R.M.O.	Regimental Medical Officer
R.N.D.	Royal Naval Division
R.S.M.	Regimental Sergeant Major
R.T.O.	Regimental Transport Officer
S.H.C.	Surrey History Centre
S.R.	Special Reserve
T.F.	Territorial Force
T.N.A.	The National Archives
T.O.	Transport Officer
V.C.	Victoria Cross
Y.M.C.A.	Young Men's Christian Association

Preface

The profession of medicine, and surgery, must always rank as the most noble that men can adopt. The spectacle of a doctor in action among soldiers, in equal danger and with equal courage, saving life where all others are taking it, allaying pain where all others are causing it, is one which must always seem glorious, whether to God or man. It is impossible to imagine any situation from which a human being might better leave this world, and embark on the hazards of the Unknown.
Winston S. Churchill *The Story of the Malakand Field Force*

I first came across the diary of Captain George Pirie, Royal Army Medical Corps (R.A.M.C.), in 2008. This was when I was researching 9th Battalion, East Surrey Regiment (9th East Surrey) a unit in which two of my great uncles served at different times, as did R.C. Sherriff, author of the most famous play on the Great War, *Journey's End*. Following correspondence, a member of Pirie's family in South Africa, most generously, sent me a photocopy of the transcript of the diary. I was immediately struck by its quality. It seemed to open a window into the past: it was so vivid.

The Captain's diary is a very special one. Not all diaries make good reading. Some are terse, some cover only trivialities, whilst with others the diarist is too absorbed in himself and his immediate concerns. Pirie's diary has none of these faults. He was a popular and gregarious man with a sense of humour; a keen and sympathetic observer of his fellow soldiers; and saw much frontline service, in both big actions and routine trench warfare. He kept a diary continuously (except for a period following discharge from hospital in autumn 1915) from late 1914, through his front line service at Gallipoli and the Somme, up to his death in action at Ypres in July 1917.

For the great majority of his service, Pirie was a Regimental Medical Officer (R.M.O.) with an infantry battalion. He was a brave and skilful medic, who was twice Mentioned in Dispatches (MiD) and those with a general interest in battlefield medicine should find his diary absorbing. The diary also throws light on the battles in which Pirie served and the day to day life of infantry battalions in and out of the line, specifically 2nd Hampshire and 2nd Royal Fusiliers, 29th Division, at Gallipoli and 9th East Surrey, 24th Division, on the Western Front.

Unlike so many accounts, written decades after the war and distorted by fading memories and hindsight, Pirie's diary is fresh: it tells how things were and, rightly or wrongly, how they were perceived at the time. Often fortunately, he did not know what tomorrow would bring for him and his companions. As Richard Holmes has written 'There is something unutterably poignant about a diary entry written by somebody who didn't know whether he would be alive to eat his supper that day.'[1] Like Pirie, a good number of those he wrote about did not survive the war. This diary is the Great War as it was experienced: the strain of unrelenting shellfire and sniper fire, with danger ever present in the front line; but also the comradeship and light relief in and out of the line, which helped to make things bearable.

Pirie's diary and his experiences can be compared with other diary-based accounts, published during and after the war. These include, most noticeably, Creighton and Davidson for 89th Field Ambulance at Gallipoli, and Hamilton of the artillery, Hitchcock of 2nd Leinster and, more briefly, R.C. Sherriff of 9th East Surrey, for 24th Division on the Western Front. There is also Ernst Jünger, from the other side of no man's land, for Guillemont.

I have provided introductions to Pirie himself and the background to the two diaries, as well as notes on the main characters, etc., whilst the index attempts to identify, as far as possible, all those mentioned in the diary. (Pirie met and mentions, an extraordinary number and variety of men, from privates to generals.)

Those who wish to delve further into the doings of 9th East Surrey are recommended to refer, in particular, to my previous book – *The 'Journey's End' Battalion – 9th East Surrey in the Great War.*

Michael Lucas
Birchington, January 2014

1   Holmes, *Tommy*, p.xxiv.

Acknowledgements

My greatest thanks must go to the family of Captain Pirie, who have given me permission to edit the diary for publication. Of them, I am grateful especially to Peter Strasheim, of Johannesburg, South Africa, for so generously sending me a copy of the diary some years ago, because of my interest in the Captain's service with 9th Battalion East Surrey Regiment. Furthermore, more recently, Peter drew Creighton's and Davidson's books to my attention, as well as supplying information about the Pirie family and most of the personal illustrations relating to George Pirie. Richard Kennedy provided much information about the Pirie family and also on a number of Captain Pirie's friends and colleagues, gave useful comments on drafts and contacted St. Andrew's College for me. Michael Hall suggested Helion as the publisher, helped with family information, gave helpful comments, provided the photograph of the memorial plaque and sponsored the illustrations from the Imperial War Museum (I.W.M.).

From my family, I am, as ever, truly grateful to my wife, Ann, for her technical help and tolerance towards yet more writing; and to my son Andrew for his continued interest and encouragement and much assistance with German sources.

At the Surrey History Centre (S.H.C.) I am especially grateful to Di Stiff who, knowing of my interest in all matters pertaining to 9th East Surrey, drew Private Cole's splendid set of caricatures of Pirie and his fellow officers to my attention.

I am thankful to a number of others for help with queries, etc. Ian Chatfield, curator of the Surrey Infantry Museum and David Cohen, an expert on Great War art, sought to throw more light on Edward Cole. Robert Gore-Langton replied on a quotation by R.C. Sherriff on Pirie. Nigel Lillywhite responded regarding George Pirie's letter included in the papers of his late father, Colonel G. Lillywhite, O.B.E., T.D. at I.W.M. Michael D. Robson helped with General Wolley-Dod.

My thanks are also due to Duncan Rogers, my publisher, who recognised the diary's potential.

For permission to quote from unpublished copyright material, I am grateful to: the Pirie family for the diaries and other writings of Captain George Stephen Pirie; The National Archives (T.N.A.) for various official documents in its care; to Kingston Grammar School for an excerpt from *Memories of Active Service* by R.C. Sherriff; and to St. Andrew's College, Grahamstown, South Africa, for a letter of condolence.

For permission to reproduce copyright photographs and other illustrations, I am grateful to: Michael Hall; the Trustees of the I.W.M.; Andrew Lucas; Peter Strasheim; and S.H.C.

I am also grateful to Jon Cooksey, editor of *Stand To!* the journal of the Western Front Association for agreeing to me reworking some of the material in my latest articles for his journal for this book.

Despite my best endeavours, I have not managed to trace all possible copyright holders. I apologise to them. If they will contact me through my publisher, I shall be delighted to ensure appropriate acknowledgement in any future edition of this book.

Introduction – Captain George Stephen Pirie, doctor and diarist
Family background and early life

Our diarist, George Stephen Pirie, was very conscious of his Scottish origins, but was born 24 July 1888 on his family's farm, *Leopards Vlei* (Marsh of the Leopard), thirty-five miles from Middelburg in the Eastern Cape, South Africa. He was the eighth of nine children (and the second son) of George Pirie and his wife Annie (née Paddison). George, the father, had been born into a farming family in Gamrie, Banffshire, Scotland in 1837. He emigrated to South Africa, where he met his wife, whose family had emigrated from England, and, over time, he established seven huge sheep farms in the Karoo. George's elder son William, born 1875, served in the Boer War and was a lawyer, who eventually took over his father's farms. The eldest daughter, Annie, died in 1914. The elder George died in 1915, whilst his namesake was serving at Gallipoli.

The family maintained its links with Scotland, visiting frequently, and this was reflected in George's education, which included a spell at Banff Academy. After attending St. Andrew's College, Grahamstown, South Africa, from 1904 to 1908, he read medicine at the University of Edinburgh. Although born and brought up in South Africa, he had a deep affinity for Scotland. He looks back in his diary for 15 September 1915 to his voyage in 1909 'to come home to start medicine'.

Whilst Pirie left no record as to why he chose medicine as a career, it seems likely that his brother in law, Gilbert Ormsby, was a key influence. Born 1876, Ormsby, whose father was a distinguished surgeon, qualified as a doctor in Ireland. He joined the R.A.M.C. in 1899 and saw much action in the Boer War. He married Alice, George's sister, in 1904. He continued in the Army and was to serve through the Great War.

George Pirie, after graduating, with distinction, in July 1914, continued to live in Edinburgh, at 14, Buccleuch Place, but became a senior house physician in nearby Leith.

In the meantime, following the German invasion of Belgium, Britain had declared war on Germany on 4 August 1914. Britain had a relatively small regular army, supported by a home service Territorial Force. Compared with the massive conscript armies of the Continental Great Powers, the size of the British Army could not be taken seriously, especially as nearly all commentators expected the war to be over within months. Britain's new war minister, Lord Kitchener, however, correctly

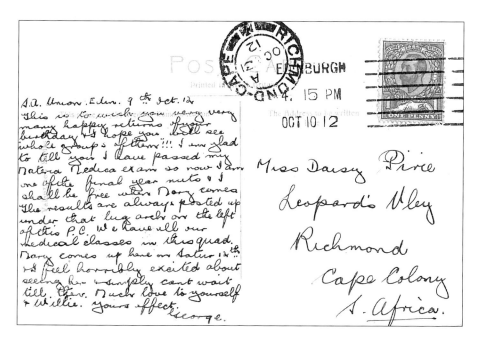

Figure 2. A postcard sent from Edinburgh University by George Pirie to his sister, Daisy, October 1912. (© Peter Strasheim)

Figure 3. The Pirie family at Leopards Vlei 1 August 1914 - left to right George, Mary (in the car), Charlotte, Willie. (© Peter Strasheim)

Figure 4. A 1914 German cartoon ridiculing British Arms - 'Now the Suffragettes will have to defend England'. (A.R. Lucas collection)

anticipated the war would last for years and planned a massive expansion of the British Army by raising 'New Army' or 'Kitchener' units, to serve for the duration of the war. In the meantime, the Regular Army units took grievous losses holding the line, supporting the French and Belgians.

South Africa, with the other dominions, joined the war on the British side. Whilst support for Britain among the English-speaking population, like Pirie's family, was solid, some Boers were pro-German and some even took up arms against the government. Most South African troops fought the Germans in Africa, but a brigade served on the Western Front, notably at Delville Wood on the Somme in July 1916.

Captain George Pirie and the R.A.M.C.

Pirie applied for a commission in the R.A.M.C., in mid-December 1914. In addition to his medical qualification, he had some military training as a sergeant in the College Cadet Corps in South Africa, and as a corporal in the medical section at University. Following an interview with Major Nicholls, commanding the Military Hospital at Edinburgh, he was granted a commission in early January 1915, in the Special Reserve, as was customary for many wartime volunteer officers, rather than a regular commission.

Pirie was to serve in a number of different units whilst with the R.A.M.C. and some explanation of the R.A.M.C's. organisation would seem appropriate. An infantry division in 1914 had an establishment of twelve battalions, with artillery, engineers and other services, totalling around 18,000 officers and Other Ranks (O.Rs.) The divisional commander had an Assistant Director of Medical Services (A.D.M.S.) – a colonel or lieutenant colonel. He had three Field Ambulances – effectively one for each infantry brigade. A Field Ambulance was a mobile medical unit. Its 1914 establishment was 10 officers and 224 O.Rs. – medical officers, stretcher-bearers, nursing orderlies, clerks and cooks. It had a 'stretcher-bearer division' and a 'tent division', providing an advanced dressing station and main dressing station, for the treatment of the wounded. A R.M.O., detached from the R.A.M.C. served each battalion. He was assisted by two orderlies and a number of regimental stretcher-bearers. In addition, a small number of R.A.M.C. O.Rs. were attached to each battalion to ensure adequate supplies of clean water.

Whilst he was to sail for the Mediterranean with No.15 General Hospital and serve with Field Ambulances and on a hospital ship, Pirie was to spend most of his service at Gallipoli, and later on the Western Front, as an R.M.O. This officer was, for his battalion, its general practitioner dealing with sickness, accidental injuries, inoculations, etc.; its Medical Officer of Health preventing disease by ensuring basic hygiene and use of clean drinking water; and its first line medic in dealing with battle casualties. He had a duty to the soldier as his patient, but also to the Army to minimise wastage of manpower, including through the detection of malingering. Casualties among R.M.Os. were high. During the Somme battles from 1 July to mid-November 1916 forty-three were killed or died of wounds, one hundred and forty nine were wounded and four were missing.[1] The most famous R.M.O. was Captain Noel Chavasse attached to 10th King's (Liverpool). He was to be awarded the Victoria Cross (V.C.) twice. His first award was for Guillemont, August 1916 and the second for Ypres August 1917, where he died of wounds. Whilst there is no reason to think they ever met, curiously Pirie was at Guillemont in mid-August 1916 and was to die, like Chavasse, through shellfire at Ypres, in the summer of 1917.

For the wounded, how far back they were evacuated would depend on the seriousness of their injury. The regimental stretcher-bearers would offer immediate assistance to them and convey them to the Regimental Aid Post (R.A.P.) There the R.M.O. would assess the casualties. He would not be in a position to give operative treatment, except in the most exceptional circumstances, such as emergency amputations to free trapped casualties. His priority would be to ensure that those requiring early treatment arrived in as good a condition as possible, and as quickly as possible, at the Field Ambulance. The wounded, unless only slightly injured, or moribund, would then be transported to the Field Ambulance's Advanced Dressing Station (A.D.S.) or Main Dressing Station (M.D.S.) by its R.A.M.C. stretcher-bearers, where immediately life saving operations, only, would be carried out. From there, casualties would be evacuated, usually by ambulance, to a Casualty Clearing Station (C.C.S.), normally beyond the range of enemy artillery. Here many operations were performed, as the early days of the war demonstrated improved outcomes for early major surgical intervention. (During the period of static warfare on the Western Front, Casualty Clearing Stations came to specialise in particular types of injury.) After the C.C.S., casualties would, as necessary, be conveyed to a Base Hospital or to a hospital ship and evacuation to a hospital in the U.K. or elsewhere.

During a major battle, the numbers of wounded to be treated were enormous. With the heavily contaminated soil of France and Belgium, even minor wounds could become serious through infection. Whilst the number of wounded and sick were roughly equal in France and Belgium, there were higher sickness rates on other fronts. During the course of the war, there were important developments in treatment which substantially improved survival rates for particular types of injuries.[2]

After training, Pirie was sent to the Mediterranean and tended the wounded from the first Gallipoli landings, which he had observed from a hospital ship. He then served on Gallipoli, primarily as an R.M.O. with units of 29th Division, from May until he was wounded in September. He was mentioned in dispatches for his good work on Gallipoli:

'For devotion to duty on every occasion in action, he has been indefatigable and is the most useful and hard-working medical officer one could possibly have.'[3]

1   McPherson, *Official History Medical Services* Vol III, p.53.
2   See Scotland & Heys, *War Surgery 1914-18*.
3   Quoted in Pirie's diary 31.8.15.

When recovered from his wound, Pirie was sent to the Western Front, where he was to serve until his death nineteen months later. From December 1915, except for a brief transfer to a Field Ambulance in early 1917, Pirie was R.M.O. to 9th Battalion, East Surrey Regiment. He was promoted to captain after a year's service and, in January 1917, was granted a permanent commission in the R.A.M.C. as a lieutenant, with the temporary rank of captain.

Pirie was clearly a conscientious R.M.O. Most of his superiors recognised his great value and he was mentioned in dispatches again, posthumously, for his work on the Western Front. He was a frequent visitor to the front line. Not all R.M.Os. were as conscientious or as popular. As he records in his diary for 26 March 1916, taking over from his Canadian predecessor at Wulverghem, 'I wanted to go up and have a look at the trenches but the Doctor …said "he didn't hold with going up to the trenches."'Lodge Patch, whom Pirie mentions, was R.M.O. to 8th Queen's. For much of his service he was unsympathetic to his men and unpopular with them.[4] Pirie, on the other hand, seems to have been quite the reverse. Perhaps Pirie's greatest trial as an R.M.O. was on the Somme and especially at Delville Wood, where he, his orderlies and stretcher-bearers and the rest of the battalion had to endure shelling of the heaviest and most unrelenting kind for four days and five nights. For 29 May 1917, Pirie records his Commanding Officer (C.O.), Lieutenant Colonel de la Fontaine, telling him that he was disappointed that Pirie had not been awarded the Military Cross (M.C.) for his work on the Somme, and that if he, himself, had not been badly wounded at Delville Wood, he would have ensured Pirie had got one. He would be recommending him strongly for one at the first opportunity.[5]

It was not to be. A week after returning to the front, after leave in Edinburgh, George Pirie was killed in action on his 29th birthday, 24 July 1917, near Hill 60, Ypres. He is buried in the Commonwealth War Graves Commission Dickebusch New Military Cemetery Extension. The inscription on his gravestone reads 'And this is the promise that he has promised us even eternal life.' He is also commemorated in a number of other ways, in both South Africa and Scotland. These include on his parents' headstone in Maitland Cemetery, Cape Town, and on the war memorials in the Anglican church at Middelburg, in Banff, Scotland and at St.Andrew's College, Grahamstown. His family donated a pair of silver vases in his memory, to the College.

Pirie's diaries

At the beginning of the first diary, Pirie, like so many, could not wait to see action. It was all to be a great adventure. On 3 March 1915 he was disappointed to be sent to the

---

4   I.W.M. 66/304/1 and P191.
5   Another 24th Division R.M.O. – who was awarded an M.C. – was Charles Wilson, the future Lord Moran. He was later to be Winston Churchill's physician and used his Great War experiences in writing his *Anatomy of Courage* in the 1940s.

Mediterranean rather than the Western Front – 'we may not see fighting'. He reread his diary on 2 August at Gallipoli and was amused by such naïvety. Similarly, he was excited by the drama of the Gallipoli landings and described that first day, 25 April, as 'The most wonderful day, I should say, that I have ever spent!!', although he was briefly unnerved by the ghastly sights of boatloads of badly wounded men. He was, however, soon all but overwhelmed by the suffering he had to deal with. But in spite of seeing war for what it was, he was determined to see it through. He was clearly a very brave man and managed to keep going under enormous strain, although repeatedly having to witness the death of his friends. Fear was something he had to control: he found the heavy shelling on 21 August 1916 worse than before, because with few casualties he had little work to occupy his mind. What seems to have helped him keep functioning on top of his training, was his sense of duty, his religious faith and the comradeship of his fellows.

Pirie seems also to have been a very popular and likeable character. One of his fellow officers in France and Belgium was R. C. Sherriff, who later achieved fame as an author and playwright: *Journey's End,* based on his wartime experiences, being his best-known work. The service of both men and their unit is described at length in my *The Journey's End Battalion: The 9th East Surrey in the Great War.* A letter of Sherriff's says: 'One day Captain Pirie – the Doctor of the Battalion, came down to see us, bringing a ray of sunshine with him. He was a dear, lovable little man, sympathetic, kind, human, everything a good man could be'.[6] Pirie frequently describes happy occasions socialising with others. He is also full of praise for his fellow soldiers, whether officers or O.Rs. He often refers to the bravery and stoicism of the men. It seems that he was instrumental in obtaining decorations for a number of his orderlies and stretcher-bearers.

It is extremely rare for Pirie to criticise others in his diary. The notable exception in the Gallipoli diary is 1 June when the 'C.O. and Adjutant of the Hants insulted me grossly'. They blamed Pirie for failing to get some wounded men away. Pirie saw the Adjutant as responsible and the C.O. seems to have subsequently seen it as sensible to discuss arrangements with Pirie beforehand. As for the Western Front diary, he clearly had a bad relationship with Lieutenant Colonel Swanton, a martinet, who, according to Sherriff's unpublished *Memories*, made himself quickly unpopular with 9th East Surrey after taking command in November 1916. By early January Pirie was describing him as a 'swine' and arranged a transfer out of the battalion in which he had previously felt so much at home.

Pirie generally wrote his diary every day or so, unless there was little going one, but during intense periods of action he was often unable to write up his experiences until days later, when out of the line. For example, after writing up 8 August 1916, he does not resume writing again until 18 August, when he writes after 'some strenuous days', which included the attack on Guillemont which cost the battalion such

---

6   Noted by Robert Gore-Langton in Sherriff papers at SHC – date not given.

heavy casualties. Another big gap comes after 31 August 1916, when he only resumes writing on 6 September – after the terrible days in Delville Wood. When on leave he also leaves gaps – six days, for instance, in July 1917 – making no mention of what he has done.

Sadly, only one of his wartime letters is known to have survived. This is included in this book as Appendix III. Although written ten days or so after Delville Wood, Pirie's emotions are clearly still raw from the experience of seeing many of his comrades and friends killed or seriously wounded in the Somme fighting. It is in stark contrast with the light-hearted letters from fellow officers, written at other times, retained in Sherriff's papers.

Pirie tries to keep his emotions in check in the diary, but sometimes they burst through, as with 28 April 1916 describing the funeral of his friend Howell, and the mortal wounding of his orderly, Corporal Halliday, on top of the deaths of a number of friends in the doomed attack on Guillemont, on 16 August 1916.

Why did Pirie keep a diary and for whom? Diary-keeping at the time was very common, although the Army disapproved for security reasons. Pirie seems to have intended that his diary be read by others – presumably friends or family -as he quite often takes the trouble to explain military terms, etc. On occasions, he even seems to be taking the reader on a guided tour of the front line. To what extent, therefore, does he self-censor the diary? He does not shy away from recording some of the horrible sights he sees, but does not dwell on them. He sometimes lets slip confidential information, as for example for 1 May 1916, that he has had to send an officer away because of nerves and names him. As for his inner life, whilst he expresses deep emotion at times, over the loss of friends, and makes mention of the comfort he finds in religious practice, he says nothing, for instance, about breaking off the engagement to his fiancée.

Whilst it is always possible that whoever made the transcription of the diary, or commissioned it, could have made cuts, there is no internal evidence to suggest this.

A note on the text

Pirie's manuscript diary has long since disappeared. It is unclear if it was in the form of bound books or loose sheets, and whether or not sent home at intervals. Fortunately, however, a member of the family had a typed copy made at an unknown date. This has quite a number of obvious spelling errors. It is very possible that many of these are the transcriber's. I have, therefore, felt free to correct these, wherever the errors are obvious, without comment. Pirie, himself, seems to repeatedly misspell the 9th East Surrey's Adjutant's name as 'Clarke' and Captain Agassiz of the 89th Field Ambulance as 'Agassy'. Again, I have corrected such errors without comment. Pirie occasionally follows Army practice of using capital letters throughout for place names, etc., sometimes in quotation marks and sometimes not. I have altered these, for consistency, to lower case, without quotation marks. It should be noted, however, that Pirie and the British Army of the time used French names for many places in Belgium which now use Flemish forms. I have retained the older forms. As for names of ships, Pirie sometimes puts these in quotation marks and sometimes not. I have put them all in italics, along with foreign words (unless names) and names of journals, in accordance with current practice. Pirie is sometimes confused about dating his entries. Where necessary I have put what appears to be correct in square brackets.

Pirie has his period slang, some rather outmoded spelling of words like tomorrow as 'to-morrow', his own abbreviations (which he does not always use consistently) and a number of other little mannerisms, such as use of repeated exclamation marks and putting what is reported speech, rather than the exact words, in quotation marks. He also uses C.O. (Commanding Officer) and O.C. (Officer Commanding) somewhat indiscriminately, when strictly speaking a C.O. commands a battalion and an O.C. a company or platoon. All of these idiosyncrasies, along with the odd grammatical error, his overuse of capital letters and his punctuation, I have respected. Only where there is significant lack of clarity have I felt obliged to complete words, insert words or comment on the possible meaning of the text and I have put these additions in square brackets.

I have broken up each of the two diaries with a small number of chapters, where there appear to be natural breaks, for ease of reading, but have left Pirie's long paragraphs untouched.

With the notes, I have tried to avoid repeating information already given in the Introductions. I have attempted to identify all those mentioned in the diary for the index. This has not always proved possible, especially with the O.Rs., with many men of the same surname. I have provided notes on some individuals. The choice and the extent of these has depended on their importance within the diary; the sources available; and space. Basic information on various men has been drawn from their medal cards (series WO 372) and for junior officers of 9th East Surrey, principally from their surviving War Office files (series WO339 and WO 374), all at T.N.A. For medical officers, obituaries in the *British Medical Journal* have been useful.

Part I

**The Gallipoli Diary
December 1914–September 1915**

———————————————————————————————

Introduction to the Gallipoli diary

This diary opens in December 1914, four months after the outbreak of war with Germany, with George Pirie applying for a commission in the R.A.M.C. After training, Pirie sailed with No.15 General Hospital to the Mediterranean in early March 1915, arriving at Alexandria, Egypt on 14 March. Three weeks later he was transferred to the 89th Field Ambulance, in support of 86th Brigade, 29th Division. The infantry of 29th Division were regulars withdrawn from overseas garrisons across the Empire.[1] However, some of the supporting services, like 89th Field Ambulance, were Territorial units from Britain – the 89th being recruited in North East Scotland. Among the friends Pirie made in the 89th was Lieutenant (later Major) George Davidson, R.A.M.C., who also kept a diary and subsequently wrote *The Incomparable 29th and the 'River Clyde'*. This book mentions Pirie on a number of occasions. Another diarist in the same unit was the Reverend Oswin Creighton, the chaplain, who later wrote *With the Twenty-Ninth Division in Gallipoli*.

29th Division, commanded by Major General A.G. Hunter-Weston, was committed to the landings at Gallipoli, as part of Sir Ian Hamilton's army, initially around 75,000 men strong. This army also included the Australian and New Zealand (ANZAC) Corps; the Royal Naval Division, whose infantrymen were found from Royal Marines and surplus sailors; and a French corps. Compared with the British Expeditionary Force in France, this expeditionary force was seriously short of artillery.

Turkey had joined Germany and Austria Hungary in November 1914 and the aim of the Allied expedition was the enticing prospect of capturing Constantinople and knocking Turkey out of the war. This would enable the Allies to send urgently required supplies to Russia through the Black Sea, remove one of Germany's allies and seriously threaten the position of the Central Powers in the Balkans. Unfortunately, what had originally been seen, in November 1914, as a combined operation requiring substantial troop numbers was, with troops not immediately available, changed to an essentially naval operation, beginning in February 1915, to break through to Constantinople, to give urgent assistance to the Russians. When it failed, after substantial loss of ships, the Turks were alerted to the danger of major landings and had more than five weeks to strengthen their weak defences. On their side, the British, looking at the recent

---

1   See Appendix II.

poor performances of the Turkish Army in the Balkan Wars and late 1914, seriously underestimated its fighting effectiveness.

Whilst a number of senior German officers were very fearful of the consequences of Allied success at the Dardanelles, did the Gallipoli campaign ever have a reasonable chance of success? Brigadier General Aspinall-Oglander, who wrote the official history of the campaign, had been a senior staff officer for the expedition. He argued that the campaign was a great lost opportunity that prolonged the war, as did Winston Churchill, who had pushed for it from the beginning. In their view, the concept was sound, but the execution, at a number of critical points, was bungled. On the other hand, whilst recognising serious mistakes were made, a number of more recent historians have argued that the campaign was fundamentally misconceived and doomed to failure from the beginning. Indeed, E.J. Erickson[2] has gone so far as to suggest that if only the Turks had used some of their extensive reserves early on, the Allied landings could perhaps have been destroyed at the outset. Instead, these reserves were held back from fear of Russian and Greek attacks. Aspinall-Oglander argues that Gallipoli inflicted serious and lasting damage on the Turkish Army[3]. However, Erickson, whilst recognising heavy Turkish casualties, asserts that Turkish victory at Gallipoli was of overall benefit to the Turkish war effort, and prolonged the war.[4]

After arrival at Mudros, Pirie, keen to see action, was, to his disgust, transferred to the *Aragon*, a hospital ship. He witnessed the naval bombardment and landing by 29th Division at Cape Helles on 25 April, whilst the Australians landed a little further to the north. In spite of the bombardment, 29th Division encountered fierce resistance from the Turks and suffered heavy casualties. Pirie was soon busy attending to some of the boatloads of wounded men. The *Aragon* then sailed with its cargo of wounded to Alexandria and Malta, as the nearest bases with adequate hospital facilities. Although the Allies had successfully landed, failure to advance quickly meant they found themselves hemmed in by Turkish reinforcements. It was also now apparent that the capability of the Ottoman Army had been seriously underestimated.

Pirie returned to Gallipoli on 15 May, landing on 'W' Beach. 29th Division held the western sector at Helles. During his absence the Allies had received some reinforcement drafts, but the Turks had substantially augmented their own troops on Gallipoli, launching fierce counterattacks. Both sides had suffered heavy losses, with the Allies making little progress, as they were still bottled up into cramped positions not far from the original landing sites. 'There was scarcely a corner of the ground in Allied occupation that was immune from hostile shelling and every officer and man, from highest to lowest, went day and night in constant and almost equal danger to their lives.'[5]

2   Erickson, *Gallipoli – The Ottoman Campaign*, p.91.
3   *History of the Great War – Military Operations Gallipoli* Vol.II, p.486.
4   Erickson, *op.cit.* pp.182-3.
5   Aspinall-Oglander, *op. cit.* Vol.I, p.viii.

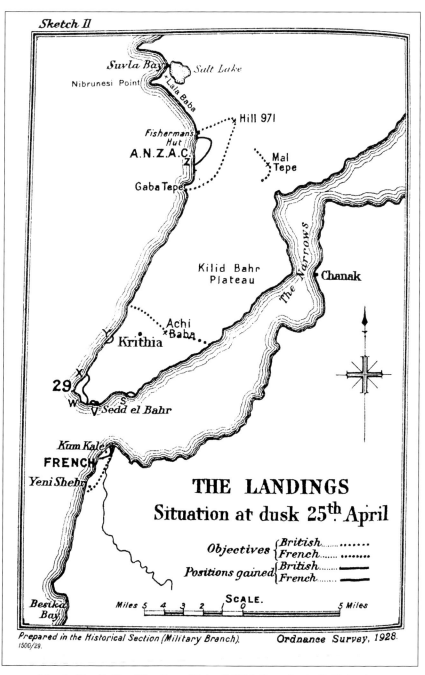

Map 1. The Gallipoli landings 25 April 1915, from Aspinall-Oglander,
History of the Great War Military Operations Gallipoli Vol. I.

The Allies were short of men and artillery ammunition and incapable of major attacks, whilst ship losses led to a reduction in naval gunfire support. But they still managed to make a number of small advances during May into early June. The Turks, however, were constantly being reinforced. Even so, a massive Turkish attack on the Anzac positions was bloodily repulsed on 19 May, with Turkish casualties exceeding 10,000. The next day Pirie joined 2nd Hampshire, in 88th Brigade, as their R.M.O.

The Allies made a major attack at Helles, in spite of inadequate artillery support, on 4 June, the Third Battle of Krithia, but the results were disappointing. 29th Division was now led by Major General H.B. de Lisle, under Hunter-Weston commanding VIII Corps. Although the Turks lost many men, Allied losses were also heavy and where attacks were successful, most of the ground gained had to be given up because of the failure of flanking attacks and lack of reinforcements. Fighting against units of Halil Sami's experienced Turkish 9th Division, 2nd Hampshire captured two lines of trenches, at the cost of heavy casualties and Pirie tended the wounded from this action. Two days later a Turkish counterattack led to a very dangerous situation. Eighteen year old Second Lieutenant G.R.D. Moor, a Hampshire officer, rallied the retreating troops and recaptured a trench. He was awarded the V.C.

Pirie did not stay long with 2nd Hampshire, falling out with the C.O. and his Adjutant. On 14 June he transferred to 2nd Royal Fusiliers in 86th Brigade, and was much happier. It should be noted that there were at this time two Lieutenant Piries, and probably both called George, serving with the R.A.M.C. on Gallipoli as R.M.Os. Pirie mentions assisting his namesake on one occasion. He seems to have been a Scot from Nairn, but they do not seem to have been related. He was R.M.O. to 1st Lancashire Fusiliers. The tribute by Major Farmar to 'Pirie the surgeon' in Creighton's book[6] and quoted in my earlier book, I believe now is to this man, rather than to our Pirie.

Pirie frequently mentions Gully Ravine, which offered some cover, springs for water, a route to the front lines and accommodation in its sides. It was crowded with activity, with dugouts, dressing stations, headquarters and supply dumps, as well as human and animal traffic going to and from the trenches. Nevertheless, the western side was swept with bullets. Aberdeen Gully, which Pirie also mentions, was connected to the main gully and was the location for 89th F.A.'s dressing station. The Reverend Creighton described this in mid-June – "It is about 500 yards from the firing line in a little gully called Aberdeen Gully (as the 89th come from there) which runs off from the big gully. A narrow path about fifty yards long had been cut out of the bed formed by a stream, now dry. The path runs up into a little natural amphitheatre in the cliff, about fifteen yards in diameter. The sides of the gully are almost precipitous, but it has been widened enough at places to make a dressing -station, cook-house, and officers' mess, and the amphitheatre is also used as a dressing station if necessary. It is almost

6   *With the Twenty-Ninth Division in Gallipoli*, p.191.

completely safe, but bullets have a way of dropping anywhere and a man got one in his arm last night, and one was at the foot of my dug-out this morning."[7]

During June and July the heat became unbearable, there were flies everywhere, the stench of decomposing bodies and much sickness, including dysentery. The sheer size of the problem seems to have been overwhelming and it was simply not possible to take adequate preventative measures or to evacuate many of the sick.

Late June and early July also saw prolonged fighting, the Battle of Gully Ravine, as the Allies sought to improve their cramped positions. With 29th Division much weakened, it was reinforced with 29th Indian Brigade and 156th Brigade from the newly arrived 52nd Lowland Division. Artillery support was still meagre compared with the Western Front, but was supplemented by naval gunfire and was more substantial than in any previous British attack at Gallipoli, although not evenly distributed. The attack went in on 28 June against the Turkish 11th Division. At the cost of heavy losses, substantial progress was made on the left. The Turks saw their position as seriously threatened, threw in reinforcements and counterattacked repeatedly, regardless of loss.

After disappointing results for the Turks, they planned a grand counterattack for early morning on 5 July, with three divisions of reinforcements brought up and artillery support carefully organised. So confident was Army commander Liman von Sanders, that he invited the Austro-Hungarian military attaché to view the assault. However, the bombardment was short and relatively ineffective. Some Turkish infantry reached the British first line positions, but at a terrible cost. British counterattacks threw the Ottomans out and demoralised Turks fell back under intense British machine-gun fire. The Turks suffered around 5,000 casualties in this single attack. Unfortunately, lacking reserves of men and ammunition, the Allies were not strong enough to take full advantage of the Turkish repulse. Pirie observed some of this action whilst with 2nd Royal Fusiliers.

The British refused Turkish requests for an armistice to bury the dead, believing the Ottoman soldiers would be reluctant to attack again over the bodies of their comrades. However, both sides were now to suffer from the stench of huge number of decomposing bodies and plagues of flies, so Turkish bodies were buried or burned as fighting conditions allowed. (By 14 July, Pirie writes that the smell was 'indescribable' and 'everything tasted of dead Turks.')

Although the Turks had suffered terrible losses in their great counterattack, an Anglo-French attack on the eastern flank at Helles on 12-13 July failed to make significant progress.

Earlier, the Government had decided to substantially reinforce Hamilton in the hope of achieving a breakthrough at Gallipoli, and thereby supporting the Russians who were under great pressure from the Germans and Austro-Hungarians. But even though the Ottoman attacks in June at Anzac and July at Helles had failed

7   Creighton, *op.cit.*, pp.136-7.

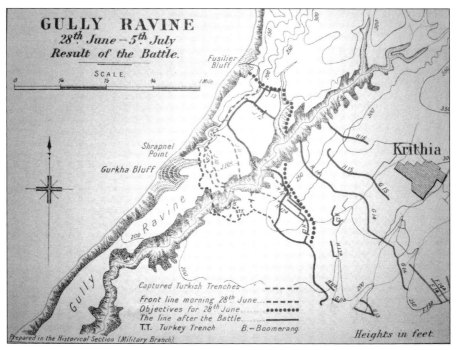

Map 2. Gully Ravine 28 June-5 July 1915 from Aspinall-Oglander,
History of the Great War Military Operations Gallipoli Vol. II.

catastrophically, the Turks were still able to prevent any significant Allied advance and had substantial reserves.

With reinforcements available to him now, Hamilton tried to break the deadlock on the peninsula with further landings at Suvla Bay, a little north of the Anzac positions, on 6/7 August, under Lieutenant General Stopford. The Turks had expected further landings but there was, initially, very little Ottoman opposition. But a complicated plan, inexperienced commanders and raw troops again produced an Allied failure to press ahead from the beachhead, whilst the attempted breakout from Anzac was stalled. Back at Helles, a diversionary attack was launched on 6/7 August. The reinforced 29th Division was in the assault against the Turkish 10th Division, but artillery support was, as so often at Gallipoli, insufficient, and Turkish strength had been seriously underestimated. 88th Brigade was shattered, with nearly two thirds of the 3,000 engaged becoming casualties. An Anglo-French attack the following day was also unsuccessful.

By 10 August, Hamilton's plans were in ruins. The Helles garrison had failed to prevent the Turks moving reinforcements; the Anzacs had been fought to a standstill; and the Turks had held on to the surrounding hills at Suvla. The new landings had simply produced yet another narrow beachhead, dominated by higher ground and at the cost of heavy losses. Hamilton now finally asserted himself and sacked Stopford, replacing him with 29th Division's commander, de Lisle. First one brigade, then the rest of 29th Division, followed their old commander to Suvla.

Pirie arrived at Suvla on 20 August. The next day a major attack was launched to seize the higher ground, including Scimitar Hill; shorten the line to be defended against the Turks; and give some protection to the beaches from shellfire. Again the Turks proved to be in much greater strength than expected, with Mustafa Kemal now having seven divisions to defend the Suvla area. British artillery support proved ineffective and successive attacks led only to heavy British losses. After the failure of 11th Division and the veteran 29th Division, the raw 2nd Mounted Division of Yeomanry, advancing dismounted, simply added to the casualty list. Scimitar Hill proved the most costly, in proportion to its size, and the least successful, of all the Gallipoli battles. The troops at Suvla remained in an overcrowded bridgehead with little or no cover from enemy shelling. Indeed, Pirie, himself, was wounded by a shrapnel ball on 4 September. He was evacuated to Malta and then taken back to the U.K.

After Pirie's departure, there was comparatively little fighting on Gallipoli. The British Government had lost faith in the campaign and Bulgaria's attack on Serbia led to another front demanding resources – Salonika. The Turks on Gallipoli, moreover, were stronger than ever, with more than nineteen divisions committed to the campaign by the end of August. The British Government was worried about the loss of prestige in the Moslem world if Gallipoli was given up, and the dangers around evacuation. Nevertheless, during the winter first Suvla and Anzac, then Helles were abandoned. Ironically, the most successful parts of the campaign were the evacuations.

The Gallipoli diary ends with Pirie's return to Scotland on 29 September. He seems to have given up keeping a diary for the next six months, although he went back to the front line – this time on the Western Front – in December 1915.

1

From Edinburgh to the Dardanelles, December 1914–May 1915

14.12.14.

Received papers from the War Office to fill in for a Commission in R.A.M.C. (R.S.) [Royal Army Medical Corps, Special Reserve]

16.12.14.

Medically examined and sent papers off filled in to War Office.

3.1.15.

Received notice from War Office saying Commission granted as Lieut. [Lieutenant] in R.A.M.C. (R.S.)

16.1.15.

Reported myself at Aldershot for 14 days probationary training.

30.1.15.

Finished training and passed the exam. I enjoyed my course very much. We had four hours a day of drill on the square and one or two lectures. Men in my batch for training were G.M. Scott, J.W. Wood, F. Oppenheimer, W.H. Williams, J. Bradly, Anderton and Sanders.

19.2.15.

Since beginning of the month been route marching with R.A.M.C. men and drilling recruits. Enjoyed it all thoroughly. Received orders 'to proceed overseas with No.15 General Hospital, Col. James, R.A.M.C. in command', Williams and Sanders go with me. Am feeling most excited at getting over but don't yet know where we are to go or when we leave. Rumour hath it either to-morrow or three days hence. No leave granted to go to Edinburgh. Gilbert received a D.S.O. [Distinguished Service Order] and mentioned in dispatches.[1] Been having lots of rain. I was gazetted on 27th Jan., 1915, and my seniority dates from 2nd Jan. and confirmed in rank to-day.

26.2.15.

Been waiting for news when to go overseas, all sorts of rumours of where we are to be sent – France, Servia [Serbia] and even Dardanelles!

27.2.15.

Got news. Leave on 4.3.15. Got leave to go to Edinburgh.

28.2.15.

Travelled overnight to Edinburgh.

3.3.15.

Back to Aldershot. Had a glorious 3 days in Edinburgh. On my return got orders to get a helmet and Khaki drill suits as we are going east. Obtained helmet but not drills. Had a very busy day. I am now ready to leave to-morrow at 5.45 a.m. for Avonmouth where we are to embark. Somewhat disappointed at going east as we may not see fighting. Would have liked France better.

4.3.15.

Up at 4 a.m., Scott and Oppenheimer saw me off with rest of No. 15 General Hospital. Arrived at Avonmouth Docks (Bristol Channel) 12 noon. Got on board transport *Minnewaska*, 14,000 tons, a very fine boat.[2] Sanders and I share a deck cabin. H.M.S. *Cornwall* is in dry dock being repaired after the Falkland Island fight.[3] 36 officers and 280 R.A.M.C. aboard, besides R.[Royal]Engineers, A.S.C.[Army Service Corps] and Army Vet. [Veterinary] Corps and about 600 mules and horses aboard. Sailing to-morrow.

---

1   Major (later Lieutenant Colonel) Gilbert Ormsby, R.A.M.C., was married to Pirie's sister Alice.
2   Built as a liner in 1909, she was taken over a troop ship, was badly damaged by a mine in 1916 and became a total loss.
3   This armoured cruiser of 9,800 tons had, with H.M.S. *Kent*, sunk the German light cruiser S.M.S. *Dresden* during the Battle of the Falklands on 8 December 1914. The eighteen hits she had sustained in return had not caused serious damage. Four out of five German cruisers were sunk, and the earlier British defeat at Coronel was avenged.

5.3.15.

I am medical orderly officer for the boat so can't get ashore. Sailed at 9 p.m. Sad at leaving old England. Picked up a convoy [escort] of two torpedo destroyers.

6.3.15.

An Army Chaplain held a very impressive service on board before we sailed. Our convoy left us at 7 a.m. A swell on, not been sick!!! Great scare this afternoon at 3.30 – what appeared to be a periscope was sighted 500 yards off so at once the steamer was swung round stern on but no torpedo was fired. It may have been a French submarine as we were then opposite Brest. Have been put in charge of 20 men and one N.C.O. [Non Commissioned Officer] and an iron pontoon which we must launch in case of fire.

7.3.15.

Feeling A1. The Captain of the boat held a nice service and Brigadier General Stanton read the lessons. Had fire drill.

9.3.15.

Sighted the North African coast at 7 a.m. and saw Tangier about 9 p.m. [sic.], after breakfast we saw the Spanish Coast and soon after Gibraltar which looked lovely with the sun on it. As we got opposite Gib. a torpedo boat came along-side and told us to go in closer for orders which we did and an Inspection Ship came near by and signalled orders but not near enough to give off our mails. We unfortunately didn't get ashore. We got orders to go straight to Alexandria and not stop at Malta, much to our disgust. We were an hour off Gib. and then went on. Has been a glorious day, warm with a cool breeze – just what I have always imagined the Mediterranean Sea to be! In the afternoon we passed the *Glengorm Castle*, formerly called the *German*, fitted up as a hospital ship going east like ourselves. We are due at Alexandria on 15th March.

10.3.15.

Sighted North African Coast all day and saw fine snow capped Mts. [Mountains]. Also saw Algiers which is quite a big town. After lunch, passed a French 3rd class cruiser quite close and exchanged cheers. Had a concert in the smoking room in the evening. Cold and a heavy swell on, some fellows sick again.

12.3.15.

Passed Malta last night, saw the light house and search lights at 11 p.m. Vaccinated against smallpox to-day. Weather warmer. Boxing Contest amongst the men to-day had to be postponed owing to a shower which made the deck too slippery.

13.3.15.

Boxing contest held this afternoon, was quite good. Been a lovely day.

14.3.15.

Arrived off Alexandria at 7 a.m. An Arab pilot took us into the harbour which is very big and full of transports. City looks very eastern with its white flat topped houses and palm trees. We got alongside the Quay at mid-day and received orders to disembark next day and go into a 'rest camp' which is reputed to be full of fleas! Therefore don't fancy it. Officers allowed ashore after lunch. Went ashore with Lieuts. Bates and Birch and walked through the slum quarter which was very picturesque with the veiled women and maze of colours, but very dirty. Then got into the high class quarter which was cleaner and fine houses of French type. Rather hot walking. Had tea in a lovely hotel – the Savoy. Got back for dinner. Lovely and cool.

15.3.15.

Orders are to disembark and not to go to the rest camp, but to Moustapha Pasha Camp three miles out of the town in one of the suburbs. Disembarked at 3.30 p.m. and proceeded by tramcar to the camp which is beautifully situated alongside the sea and the tramline. 8th Lancashire Fusiliers[4] are in the regular barracks and we in fine square tents. Sanders and I share a tent. Our servants got our camp beds etc. out. We are very comfortable except for the sand. We messed at the Carlton Hotel near by. This place reminds me very much of the Cape with its sparrows, wagtails, tamarisk trees, and the sun with the glare on the sandy soil.

16.3.15.

Slept last night like a top in spite of a thunder storm. Col. James went to Cairo and returned to-day with the news we may have to set up hospital here for a short time and then be sent up to the Dardanelles, in the meantime we do nothing. We are now messing in a hut in the barracks. Went into Alexandria by tram and made some purchases.

17.3.15.

Went into Alexandria with Lieuts. Wilson, Delmege, Bates and Birch and saw Pompey's Column[5] which is over 2,000 years old. Then went and saw the Catacombs[6] which were very interesting. My vaccination against smallpox has been giving me beans!!!

---

4   42nd Division.
5   A column 25 metres high, also known as 'Pompey's Pillar', although erected by Emperor Diocletian.
6   A somewhat spooky tourist attraction.

Figure 5.
The French Navy and the
Dardanelles – 'Look the sea calls
us to conquer at the Dardanelles'.
(Author's collection)

20.3.15.

The last two days had lovely bathing in a cove five minutes from Moustapha Pasha Camp called the Jesuit's Pool. This afternoon we went to see the Arab quarter called Ras-el-tin which was very quaint. We saw the exterior of the Khedives IV [?] Palace and the Ras-el-tin English Barracks and on the next point stands an old fort which Beresford shelled.[7] This Fort stands on the first site of a light-house in the world.[8] Rumour hath it we are to be here for 2 months and a temporary hospital of 500 beds opened in a school in Alexandria, then when the operations in the Dardanelles begin we shall be moved up to Lebnos[9] which is to be the Base. We also hear that the 29th Division is on its way out and 60,000[10] French white and native troops land at Alexandria to-day.

7   Lord Charles Beresford had distinguished himself here in 1882 in command of a gunboat, in the British bombardment of Alexandria during the nationalist Arabi uprising.
8   The Pharos was one of the Seven Wonders of the Ancient World.
9   The Greek island Lemnos.
10   A possibly misheard number – the French initially deployed around 16,000.

21.3.16.

Had a service in the Garrison Church and I was Church orderly officer. In the afternoon we drove to San Stefano to see the Indian Hospital which is full of wounded Indians from France.[11]

22.3.15.

We started a course of semaphore signalling to-day. We are definitely to open a Hospital of 200 beds in a school in Alexandria. Rumour says the French troops won't land here but go straight to the Dardanelles. The 29th Division and a Naval Division[12] are on the way to the Dardanelles via Egypt. Our Hospital is to accommodate their sick.

26.3.15.

Semaphoring going strong. The Naval Division arrived here yesterday from Lemnos. They had gone straight out there and were to be landed at the Dardanelles but the sinking of the three battleships[13] and weather changed the plans and they were sent down here. Then this afternoon they got orders to go to Port Said. We heard from the R.[Royal] N. [Naval] Division that a lot of French troops were also up at Lemnos. Now these French troops are due to arrive here on Sunday, 28th March. Ten officers have been chosen to run the hospital, but I am not amongst them so I still have hopes of seeing fighting and not be stuck here. An English mail arrived here last Wednesday, but I got none – worst luck, most annoying!

28.3.15.

French troops have been arriving all to-day.

30.3.15.

British and French troops have been arriving. British are the 29th Division and with it comes No.17 General Hospital, Bradley and Oppenheimer are in it. British troops are camped at Mex and Chatby Les Bains. Went out to see the French camp at Victoria. It was a wonderful sight as they are encamped on the beach and desert and with their uniforms of various colours, with small bivouac tents and palm trees it would make a fine picture.

11   Substantial numbers of Indian troops served in France 1914-15, but later most were transferred to the more appropriate climate of the Middle East.
12   The Royal Naval Division was formed initially from Royal Marines and surplus sailors and was first deployed at Antwerp in 1914.
13   Three old pre-Dreadnought battleships, the French *Bouvet*, and the British *Ocean* and *Irresistible*, were lost to Turkish mines on 18 March whilst Allied naval forces attempted to force the Dardanelles.

1.4.15.

Orderly officer to-day. Got orders that the whole hospital shifts from Moustapha Pasha Camp to the Abassia School in Alexandria where we are to set up hospital so I am afraid we are fixed here and No.17 will go up to the Dardanelles. However, I yet hope to get away with a regiment. I am sorry we are leaving Moustapha as we shall miss the bathing. We have received no mail yet!

5.4.15.

Got mail to-day at last! Been attached to the Surgical side of the hospital till I am sent to the Front. To-day is a public holiday 'Shem-el-Nessem', the last day of the cool north breezes.

6.4.15.

Got orders to-night to report myself to the D.A.D.M.S.[Deputy Assistant Director Medical Services] at Head Quarters in the Excelsior Hotel, Alexandria to-morrow. Sanders and Griffiths have to do likewise.

7.4.15.

I reported myself to Col. Yarr[14] and have been attached to the 89th Field Ambulance, 86th Infantry Brigade, 29th Division. It is the old 1st Highland Field Ambulance (Territorials). I am very pleased with the move. I left No.15 General Hospital to-day and drove out to Mex and joined my ambulance. Griffiths and Saunders are attached to the 87th and 88th Field Ambulance of this same Division. Williams is now M.O. [Medical Officer] to a Howitzer Battery.

10.4.15.

The Bearer Division of the Ambulance sailed on the 8th and we (Tent Division) are supposed to sail to-day and are just waiting orders. I have been jolly lucky in joining this Ambulance as the officers in it are awfully nice, Col. Fraser in command, Capts. Kellas, Fiddes, Agassiz, and Stephen (latter of Banff).[15] Lieuts. Whyte,

---

14   Later Major General Sir (Michael) Thomas Yarr. Born in Ireland in 1862 he had a long
       and distinguished career in Army medicine. He was commissioned in 1886 and served in
       the Boer War. Yarr retired in 1921.
15   Arthur Kellas, born 1883, studied medicine at Aberdeen and then for a diploma
       at Edinburgh University when Pirie was there .He had been commissioned in the
       R.A.M.C.(T.F.) in 1909. He was killed in action at Gallipoli 6.8.1915. James Fiddes,
       later Major and M.C., survived the war. Cuthbert Agassiz, M.C., born in Canada in
       1887, worked as a doctor in London .He survived the war. John Stephen, (Later Lt. Col.)
       D.S.O., was a lieutenant in the local Artillery Volunteers, 1904. He also survived the war.
       The Piries originated from Banff and Pirie's grandmother was a Stephen.

Davidson[16], Thomson, Morris, Dickie. All men and officers are North Country.[17] Our brigade is the Fusilier Brigade and consists of the Munsters, Dublins, Royals and Lancashire Fusiliers and all are regulars.[18] They have all left Mex Camp, and embarked and are away. We expect a stiff resistance to our landing. It has been a great sight to see these regiments marching out – I wonder how many will come back!! This Mex Camp is very hot and sandy. Got another lovely mail!

11.4.15.

Received orders to-day to embark to-morrow on Transport *Marquette B 13*.[19]

12.4.15.

Struck camp to-day and it was very hot work. We arrived at the docks at 2.30 p.m. and went aboard. Our transport led, we officers rode in with full kit on and men marched. We have mostly the transport of various regiments aboard, – 5th Royal Scots (T.F.) [Territorial Force], Munsters and Royal Fusiliers, Highland Mountain Battery, R.E.s and our own. This boat is not nearly so nice as the *Minnewaska*.

13.4.15.

Been fearfully hot all day with a wind off the desert, laden with sand. Been loading all day long and I finished the wagons at 7 p.m. Loading been very slow from want of cranes. Transports have been moving out all day with troops and still lots more to go. Another mail.

15.4.15.

Awfully fed up as I have been taken off the Transport *Marquette*, and put on as Medical Officer to the *Melville*, an awful tub! However, I am to rejoin the 89th Ambulance at our destination. The *Marquette* left to-day and I did envy them getting away. We are to sail to-morrow. The *Melville* is carrying transport and ammunition for two ammunition columns. We also have horses and mules and men of the 5th Royal Scots, Surreys,[20] Hants and R.F.A. [Royal Field Artillery]. A fellow, Leys Geddes, in the R.T. [Regimental Transport?] funnily knows lots of Edinburgh people I know.

---

16   George Davidson served at Gallipoli from the first landing almost entirely with the 89th F.A. until he left sick in November, rather than much of his time as an R.M.O. like Pirie. Pirie was a friend and is mentioned a number of times in his *The Incomparable 29th Division and the 'River Clyde'*.

17   I.e. from the north of Scotland.

18   See Appendix II.

19   Built as a liner 1897. Torpedoed and sunk October 1915, off Salonika.

20   There was no regiment from Surrey in 29th Division.

16.4.15.

Were to have sailed to-night but at the last moment had to take on beef so are going to-morrow morning.

18.4.15.

Sailed yesterday morning at 6 a.m. and am very glad to be off. Haven't been sick but have a lot of men every morning at sick parade but nothing serious. Passed Rhodes and a lot of other small islands to-day but they look rather bare and very little habitation on them.

19.4.15.

Early this morning a torpedo destroyer picked us up and brought us safely into Mudros Bay on Lemnos Island.[21] She told us a Turkish Destroyer was about. We arrived at Mudros Bay at 5.30 p.m., it is a wonderful bay about 4 miles long and well sheltered. There are a few villages round the bay and vineyards. When we cast anchor we got word that 61 men had been drowned on the *Manitou* owing to a rope breaking when the boat was being lowered. The Turkish destroyer fired three torpedoes but missed each time and the transport arrived here safely.[22] This bay contains crowds of transports and battleships. Shortly after our transport S.S. *Melville* came in, Capt. Fiddes came over for me from the *Marquette* which was quite close by and took me back to her and I got orders to return to-morrow to my unit, the 89th Field Ambulance on the *Marquette*. I shall be jolly glad to get back.

21.4.15.

Only managed to get to the *Marquette* to-day and that with a deuce of a stiff row and wetting as the bay has been rough the last 2 days. I had no sooner changed into my dry drill clothes than I got orders to go with Lieut. Thomson (in place of Capt. Stephen who was ill) and a squad of men as a tent sub-division for the 86th Brigade which was on the *Caledonia*.[23] Our job as a tent sub-division shall be to act as a clearing hospital into which the bearer division will carry their wounded and then we shall attend to them, and send them on to base hospitals. We shall be immediately behind the firing line. The 86th Brigade is to be landed first so we shall have a hot reception but of course the Naval Guns are to clear the way for our landing and we shall land under cover of them. After having changed into wet [sic.] clothes in a great rush, here we are

---

21   About 60 miles from the tip of Gallipoli.
22   The *Manitou* transport, built 1897, 6,800 tons, had been attacked as Pirie heard. Chased by British destroyers, the Turkish torpedo boat *Demir Hissar* ran aground. *Manitou* survived the war.
23   S.S. *Caledonia*, 9,200 tons, built as a liner 1905. Torpedoed and sunk en-route to Salonika December 1916.

not away to the *Caledonia* yet and it is evening and the *Caledonia* is supposed to sail to-morrow evening and the landing effected at 5 a.m. (daybreak) on Friday. The 29th Division is to land at the point of Gallipoli, the Australasian Army Corps further up on the Gulf of Saros and the Naval Division is to make a feint attack further up the Gulf of Saros while the French are to land on Asia Minor on the opposite side of the Dardanelles from us. My Brigade, 86th, is selected to effect the landing for the 29th Division. We now hear the Turkish destroyer was rounded up by our destroyers and she ran herself ashore to escape on to a Greek island, but another Greek [sic.] destroyer is still supposed to be on the loose. These destroyers sneak out of the Dardanelles with ours one night and are commanded by Germans.

22.4.15.

Here I am on the S.S. *Aragon*[24] – much to my disgust!!! I got orders to come here so I was taken off the tent sub-division and Capt. Agassiz took my place. I was very fed up because I have missed seeing some wonderful fighting. I was sent to this boat and I found Saunders here also. We two, with a Lt. McLauchlan are to run this ship for a few days as a hospital ship – she is supposed to be able to hold over 2000 wounded so if she is full we shall be mighty busy!!! However we are only to bring the wounded from the Dardanelles to Lemnos and then the wounded are transferred to Hospital Ships and Hospitals. As soon as she ceases to be a hospital ship I return to the 89th Ambulance and I hope that will come quickly because I am very keen to be in the field. However, I shall, no doubt, be there sooner than I reckon on!! The *Aragon* is a big and very fine boat.

23.4.15.

The transports began to move out to-day, including both British and Australian. I saw the *Caledonia* go out and was most envious. We are to go to-morrow and operations to begin on Sunday. It will no doubt be a very wonderful bombardment, and fill a page in our history!!

24.4.15.

It is evening and we are steaming very slowly with ten other transports to the scene of the action. The battleships and transports have been moving out all day long and as each ship goes out there are loud cheers, the men are full of enthusiasm. It was a great sight to see the *Queen Elizabeth* go – a veritable floating fort![25] Lemnos is only 50 odd miles from the Dardanelles and as we sailed at 4 p.m. and are followed by the other transports we are not to be at the Gallipoli Peninsula until 5 a.m., we must go

---

24   9,600 tons, torpedoed December 1917, off Alexandria.
25   H.M.S. *Queen Elizabeth*, a recently completed 'super dreadnought' of 31,000 tons, armed with eight 15" guns, served in and survived both World Wars.

slowly, we are to have breakfast at 5.30 a.m and land when after that I don't know! In spite of the fact there is to be a great battle to-morrow I don't feel in the very least different from any other day and can scarcely believe that many of these men on board the boat may never return. I feel I could have a good night's sleep and have no fear of anything or of to-morrow – I suppose it is simply because I don't know what it will be like. I have one great regret, I didn't get mail before leaving Lemnos. I was unlucky as we sailed out past the *Marquette,* Fiddes and Dickie signalled 'Letters' and held them up but I could not get them!! We have the 4th Worcester and 2nd Hants of the 88th Brigade on the *Aragon* and General Napier (the 88th Brigade General).

25.4.17.

This has been the most wonderful day, I should say, I have ever spent!! I got up at 4.30 and got on deck about 5.30 a.m. I was told the Naval bombardment of the Gallipoli Peninsula had begun at 9 min. to 5. The morning was lovely with a thick mist over the land and as the sun rose it was like a ball of fire. You could see the flashes of the Naval guns but not the effects of the shells owing to the mist. Behind, the warships and transports were all drawn up and busy getting troops into landing barges and rugs [sic.] in order to effect the landing. As the sun rose the mist lifted and as our transport, the *Aragon*, went right up the Dardanelles we could see the landing being effected. The rifle fire began at 10 to 7 and between that and the naval guns it was a terrible noise. We had got orders we needn't expect any wounded for 48 hours after landing, so we weren't worrying ourselves, when suddenly a steam pinnace with three boat-loads of wounded came along-side. By jove they were a ghastly sight and I was quite unnerved at first, but I pulled myself to-gether and we got them on board, and very soon after a minesweeper brought more. It was extraordinary – the Worcesters were to go ashore on the mine-sweeper and in spite of seeing these wounded they went off with loud cheers. These wounded were mostly Naval and they had been raked with bullets as they were landing the troops, one poor middy [midshipman] was badly wounded and a Lt. Commander died on board. Well, we were jolly busy till lunch time and for the rest of the day we could watch the operations. The H.M.S. *Cornwallis*[26] was lying between us and the shore and the *Queen Elizabeth* in front of our bows, so you can imagine the noise but, by jove, their firing was accurate. We could see the troops being landed all day long and advancing on to the top of the cliff and lying in captured trenches and men cutting the barbed wire. We could also see the stretcher-bearers at work. It was all a wonderful sight. On the other side of the Dardanelles we could see the French landing and fight-ing.[27] They were being assisted by Naval Guns also. Well, this <u>has</u> been a wonderful day!

26   A 13,000 ton pre-dreadnought battleship, with four 12" guns, sunk by a U-Boat in the Mediterranean, 1917.
27   At Kum Kale on the Asiatic shore.

26.4.15.

To-day has been a quiet day. We transferred our 50 wounded to a hospital ship but last night, heavy fighting went on and we heard to-day the Turks counter attacked last night and drove us back a bit. We heard General Napier was killed on landing,[28] and that the casualties were heavy while landing so perhaps I have escaped with my life by being taken off, the tent subdivision. I should like to know how my ambulance fares. We hear from the wounded that the Turks are bayoneting our wounded – ghastly!!

27.4.15.

Been a busy day again. We took 400 odd wounded from the hospital ship *Soudan*,[29] amongst them was General Hare.[30] We went down to the Island of Tenedos to get these wounded. It is only 6 or 7 miles from the Dardanelles. Then we went back to the Dardanelles for orders and were told we are to take wounded from other ships. Fighting has been going on all day, we heard we had taken Sedd el Bahr last night.

29.4.15.

Been very very busy and am nearly done up as we have only 4 doctors including the ship's doctor and 20 R.A.M.C. orderlies and we have 1,086 wounded including 3 Turks and 94 French. We sailed for Alexandria to-day at 4p.m, and I am so glad as I want to see these poor men safely in hospital, as we can't do them justice, so under-staffed. When we left to-day the fighting was all on a ridge just beyond Krithia and below Achi Baba.

30.4.15.

Had a most fearful day of work – never worked so hard in all my days. I did my first big operation to-day – amputation of a leg and managed it all right. We are due in Alexandria to-morrow and I am very glad as I hope to get letters which I am longing for.

1.5.15.

Arrived at Alexandria this afternoon at 4 p.m. but we only were allowed to load off three serious cases, I had hoped they would load off the wounded all night. I am very anxious about some.

---

28   The confusion arising with the heavy loss of senior officers was a factor in the failure to make early progress.
29   Built 1901, 6,700 tons, it survived the war.
30   Brigadier-General S.W. Hare commanding the Covering Force.

2.5.15.

Been very busy all day unloading. We had to off load 486 including the French and the remainder we had to take to Malta. We have got off all our serious cases and a lot of the walking ones and I was glad to see them go off because after what they went through they deserve good treatment. It took us all day to off load and after dinner in the evening I went up to No.15 General Hospital to see Wilson. All the Hospitals in Cairo and Alexandria are packed, hence our going to Malta.

3.5.15.

Sailed from [sic.] Malta early this morning where we load off the remaining 600, take in coal and food and then we are to return to the Dardanelles where I hope I shall be able to rejoin my field ambulance because I want to see fighting and get my mail.

5.5.15.

Here we are, lying in a bay on the Island of Malta called Marsasirocco.[31] We arrived here at 6 p.m. and went through our inspection by the naval authorities and got orders to anchor here for the night and proceed to-morrow morning for Valetta to off load the wounded, then we return to Mudros Bay at Lemnos Island. We expect to be at Valetta for a few days coaling. We haven't been so busy since we left Alexandria, but I amputated a finger yesterday.

6.6.15.

We left Marsasirocco at 8.30 a.m., and got into Valetta harbour at 9.30. It is a most wonderful harbour with a series of small bays and it bristles with French men-of-war coaling. We also saw one of the famous monitors[32] with which they bombard the Belgian Coast. This is quite the quaintest place I have ever seen. The town rises sheer from the harbour and the houses are rather eastern, and the harbour swarms with small boats selling their wares. We started off loading at one o'clock and were kept busy till 7 p.m., we off loaded 641 officers and men. We are to coal and do some repairs then return to Lemnos on Monday or Tuesday so I mean to go ashore to have a look around.

7.5.15.

Been ashore to-day with Lieuts. Sanders and McLaughlan for the first time since we left Alexandria – 18 days ago. We saw the Chapel of Bones of Maltese soldiers killed by the Turks in 1561[33] during the great siege of Malta. Then we saw the hospital with

---

31   Now Marsaxlokk.
32   Relatively small, shallow draft vessels with a heavy armament.
33   Actually 1565.

the longest ward in the world – 305 feet[34], next the guard room which is famous for its paintings on the walls done by officers at various times, next the Armoury in the Governor's Place and the Cathedral with its ceiling beautifully decorated with paintings. Then we went into the bastions and got a most wonderful view of both harbours and the city, and lastly I bought 3 lovely water colours. Valetta is a very quaint city with steep narrow streets. In the docks at sunset a gun is fired and each warship fires a rifle and the National flag is pulled down and bugles are blown.

8.5.15.

We took the little train inland to see the ancient capital Alta Veccha [CittaVecchia -now Mdina] which was a very dead place. The country is all terraced up and is very rocky and uninteresting.

9.5.15.

We sailed from Malta to-day at 7a.m and we are bound for Lemnos but instead of taking 2 days we are to take 3 and go round Crete because we hear some Austrian submarines are about. Weather has been rough but I have not been ill.

12.5.15.

Arrived at Lemnos this morning early but no news of a move. The Naval and Military transport authorities have taken our transport the *Aragon* as a sort of office. We have taken on board some survivors of the H.M.S. *Goliath* which was torpedoed three times by a Turkish destroyer disguised as one of ours. Two survivors are middies of which six survived out of nine.[35]

15.5.15.

Sanders and I have been ordered to rejoin our unit and we leave to-day by a fleet [mine] sweeper to go to the Dardanelles. Had a topping mail yesterday – 17 letters!

34   The Knight's Hospital or Sacra Infermeria built 1574.
35   H.M.S. *Goliath*, a 13,000 pre-dreadnought battleship, was sunk by a Turkish torpedo boat which was mistaken in the dark for a British vessel.

2

At Gallipoli, May–September 1915

16.5.15.

Last night we arrived at W. Beach and disembarked at 9.30 p.m. in the dark. No one knew where my unit [89th Field Ambulance] was so we just slept on the beach. To-day Sanders and I were sent up to Gully Beach as our ambulances were supposed to be there. We went round by Steam Pinnace and found Sanders' unit was there but mine was not. We had breakfast, and then found out by wireless that my unit was at W Beach so I returned there partly on foot and partly on wagons, it being about 2 miles. Just as I reached W. Beach the Turks shelled it with 6 inch Howitzers and dropped about 8 shells and I had one near me and fragments whistled over my head. It is a mighty nasty experience!! After it was over I walked across the valley to our camp and found all well and only a sheep had been killed. I was feeling tired but the shells didn't worry me much. Firing went on all last night and all to-day. It is a most wonderful sight to see the aeroplanes being shelled in the air and puffs of smoke of the shells remain in the air.

17.5.15.

To-day has been absolute hell. I have found it very trying. All morning Capt. Stephen and I made a dug-out to protect us against shrapnel and splinters. We had it half finished at 12.15, when those shells began and we all ran for cover under the cliffs. They gave us about 6-8 inch shells and then stopped. We had lunch in peace and in the afternoon we lived under the cliffs as we had two more bouts of shelling and they killed four men. Oh God, how mangled they were! It was ghastly. The shelling ceased about 6 p.m., and then we returned and completed our dug-out, unfortunately our naval guns can't get at these two howitzers as they are dug into a gully and only howitzers will get them out which we hear are to land very soon and I hope they finish them. Our ambulance operating tent was absolutely torn to bits by one and a big lot of horses and mules have been killed.

18.5.15.

This morning at 6 we had a rude awakening by being shelled so I slipped on my breeches and boots, grabbed my shirt and tunic and off to the cliff, but we had breakfast in peace. White, Fiddes, Dickie and I spent the morning under the cliff on the west side of W. Beach and while sitting there three shells fell into the sea near us. We finished our dug-out by sunset but about 6 p.m. we had some shrapnel just above the camp on the aviation ground and one burst so near Lt. Davidson that it blew him over but he only hurt his wrist and did a good sprint. About sunset there was a terrific shelling of a gully on our left flank where these Turkish guns are supposed to be, so we hope they are silenced.

19.5.15.

We heard one fierce fight last night at 10 on the French side[1] and to-day some prisoners were brought in. To-day has been peaceful, no shelling so we hope the "Coal Box" guns[2] are done for!! I got orders to relieve Lt. Morris at the Hants [2nd Hampshire Regiment] Regimental Aid Post and go up to-morrow so it will be a new experience.

20.5.15.

This morning Agassiz, Davidson, Dickie, Thomson and I went round to V. Beach and went over the famous S.S. *River Clyde*,[3] which was most interesting with its shell holes in it and as Davidson had been on her at the landing he told us all about it. We got back to lunch and after, V. Beach got a good dose of Jack Johnsons.[4] At 7.30 p.m. a guide arrived to show me the way out to the Hants Aid Post, so I shouldered my soldier's pack and we set out. The sun soon set and after ¾ hour's walk we arrived at the White House in the dark and found Morris so he walked back. This house is an old farm house with three rooms and a closed – in yard and a bake house with a quaint old well inside the sort of square, and it has fig, quince and nectarine trees around it. It is more or less in ruins and I sleep in the corner of the yard on a stretcher with a water-proof sheet stretched over me to keep off the dew. The bullets whizz like a bee over our heads and strike the far side wall of the yard, but I am quite safe. We can also hear the Turkish shells whistling past over us and our batteries around us likewise make a nasty noise.

---

1   The substantial French contingent held the eastern side of the Helles front.
2   Named for the black smoke of their shell explosions.
3   The ship had been used to bring men in for the initial landing on 25 April. Unfortunately, there were sufficient Turkish defenders to inflict devastating casualties on the British soldiers attempting to get ashore from the ship and accompanying small boats. Davidson gives a detailed account in his book.
4   Shells named after the celebrated black boxer.

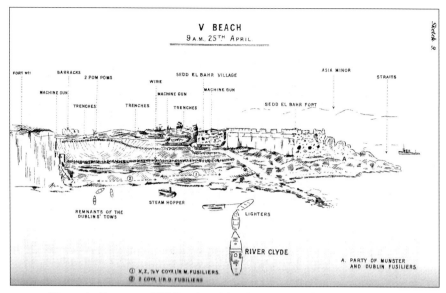

V BEACH
9 A.M. 25TH APRIL

FORT Nº1   BARRACKS   2 POM POMS   SEDD EL BAHR VILLAGE   ASIA MINOR   STRAITS
WIRE
MACHINE GUN   MACHINE GUN   MACHINE GUN
SEDD EL BAHR FORT
TRENCHES   TRENCHES   TRENCHES

STEAM HOPPER
REMNANTS OF THE   LIGHTERS
DUBLINS' TOWS

RIVER CLYDE
A. PARTY OF MUNSTER
AND DUBLIN FUSILIERS
① X,Z, ½ Y COYS I/R M. FUSILIERS.
② Z COYS I/R D. FUSILIERS

Figure 6. Drawing of 'V' Beach, 25 April 1915, from Aspinall-Oglander, *History of the Great War Military Operations Gallipoli Vol. I.*

21.5.15.

Last night it was beautiful moonlight and all night the rifle fire went on and I found it difficult to sleep with such noise. The bullets <u>did</u> whizz past! We are just behind the reserve trenches and about 16,000 yards [sic.] from the first line of trenches. I marvel they haven't shelled us. The stretcher-bearers go up to the trenches for 24 hours and then off for 24 hours, five are on and five off and each morning early, just before daylight, they fetch in the wounded and we redress them and send them down to the 88th Field Ambulance who cart them to the beach. To-day has been quiet except for a swine of a sniper who snipes you if you go outside the walls. He did kill one man.

22.5.15.

Got orders to move from the White House last night after dark, so I borrowed a pack horse and set out with my stretcher-bearers. We daren't go direct to the gully as the snipers were too active so we came back by the west Krithia Road, past the Pink House Farm, and then turned right and there we lost ourselves but by asking we eventually found the gully. But oh! the bullets did whizz about as a fight was on in front of us. When we were walking up the gully, bullets were dropping all round, however on we went and as we couldn't find the place we slept in some old dug-outs with Scotch R.Es. [Royal Engineers] It was beastly hard but I slept well till rain woke me up. We set off early up the gully and found the place and it is just 450 yards from the trenches.

This afternoon, after I had made my dug-out, there was a deuce of a fight above us and what a noise it did make in this gully, it was deafening!!! We get lots of bullets and shrapnel shells shifting by overhead.[5]

23.5.15.

There was a big fight on above us and we had 50 Royal Fusiliers wounded last night and yet I slept through some of it. To-day has been quiet.

24.5.15.

Lt. Davidson came up to-day and brought a glorious mail for me. It was topping to get amidst all this noise.[6]

We had another noisy night but only had one Hants man wounded. I just grub with my men and I am getting tired of bully beef, biscuits, jam and tea, however, it keeps one going and have nix to grumble about. These Tommies <u>are</u> fine fellows and the way they rescue wounded, it's worthy of a V.C. every time, and yet they are full of beans and ready for anything. We are having gorgeous weather and lovely moonlight nights. I prefer this to the cold and wet of France. The Turks have been using hand grenades and what ghastly wounds they make!!![7] It was a lovely sight to see one of our aeroplanes up and the puffs of Turkish shrapnel bursting round it. We could count as many as a hundred puffs round it and yet it still flew on.

25.5.15.

I heard yesterday that Clive[8] was wounded and a prisoner, I am glad he is safe. To-day I got a parcel with sweets, etc., which are most welcome out here. This afternoon I was asked to go and see a Hants man in the first line of trenches. I didn't like the idea, and then it is against orders for us to go into the trenches, so I went to the Hants' Head Quarters and saw the Adjutant, he seemed nasty about it so I decided to go and risk

---

5   The Turks attacked and seized KOSB Trench and a T-Sap, but a counterattack by the Gurkhas recaptured the trench.

6   Davidson later recalled that visit: 'Beside us is the grave of a Turk who smells as all Turks do. Our men, I fancy, think they do not deserve much burial. This reminds me of a Turk on the top of whose grave I lunched with Pirie up in the firing line last Sunday. A man the day before was digging a funk hole, and coming on something soft he plunged his spade into it. The smell was so terrific that he threw his spade and bolted, and the Turk had to be covered up by sand thrown from a distance of several yards.' Davidson *The Incomparable 29th*, p.39.

7   The Turks seem to have been well provided with these, whilst the British often had to improvise. 88th Brigade's war diary (WO95/4312) records on 26 May 'All units told to send in empty jam tins and to send 1 N.C.O. and 6 men for instruction in making jam tin bombs.'

8   Not identified.

it. A man guided me and we climbed up the side of the gully and got into the second line of trenches and had to keep low all the time as a few bullets were flying overhead. We first passed Sikhs and then Worcesters and then came on our line of trenches, one place was awful mud so we got on top of the trench to pass it and mighty quick we had to be!! When I got to the communication trench I found it didn't link up with the first line of trench completely by about 15 yards, so I thought I would risk it and run the gauntlet and by gum, I did sprint across and simply dived into the first line of trenches. I found the man but it was hopeless – shot through the brain – so I bandaged him up, and had a rest before going back. I did a sprint across the open but couldn't say if any bullets followed me – all I know was I was quite glad to get back to the second line and waded through the mud which was above my boots and I eventually got back all right. It looks like rain to-night.

Our guns have just been dropping some 'Jack Johnsons' into the Turks' trenches and what a noise they make!! I have just heard they made an awful mess of the Turks' trenches.

26.5.15.

This has been a very exciting day for me!! At 6.30 a.m. I was wakened and asked to come and see a Hants in the first line of trenches so I went and ran the gauntlet but it was slightly less than yesterday. The man was Sergt. Jackson of the Machine Gun [section], and a very valuable man. He was also shot through the head by a bullet glancing off a rifle. His case was hopeless, I bandaged him up and got a fine big chap, Pte. Yeates, to carry him in. I again ran back and a sniper had a shot but missed me. Lucky! Yeates gave me a French bayonet and a Turkish pocket knife. I had something to eat and went back. He hadn't been away long when he walked in wounded through the left breast and left upper arm, not badly though. He was a very fine fellow and that was the third time he was wounded in this campaign. In the morning Capts. Kellas and Agassiz and Lts. Davidson and Thomson of my ambulance came to see me and while they were with me a man rushed in for a doctor to come to the Lancashire Fusilier trenches so I went at once but he was dead – sniped through the neck! As I rushed out of the trench to return I was sniped at, and the sniper just missed me – I got a nasty fright and felt a bit shaken after it. We had a terrible rain shower this evening but managed to keep my dugout and blankets dry. The Hants have moved out of the trenches to-night after 10 days in, their men are about done out, they have gone back to rest just beyond the Pink House Farm so we shall leave the Gully Ravine to-morrow.

27.5.15.

Left our Aid Post in the Gully Ravine this morning and trekked down to the regiment. One place we had to come down in the open, between two of our batteries and every minute we expected a dose of Turkish shrapnel, but escaped. This is a rotten place, we are in just now, we seem to get shrapnel on us all day, being so I have had to dig again, I am in an old trench and have dug in under the bank so am fairly safe, I would much rather be back in the gully, am feeling tired and badly need a bath – haven't had my clothes off for a week!!!

28.5.15.

Here I am back at the base. I managed to get away as the 89th Field Ambulance agreed to do my Hants sick, they being together near the Pink House. I walked back in time for lunch and after had a shave, sea bathe, and clean clothes. It was ripping!

31.5.15

Here I am back in Gurkha Bluff, (formerly Gully Ravine) as the Hants have gone into the reserve trenches. I had a lovely rest at the base except for a bomb from an aeroplane one morning and some shrapnel from the Asiatic side, but no damage was done. I had a spiffing parcel and letters. Yesterday Pte. Pink came in with an order to return and have a medical inspection of the Battalion at 2 p.m., so I rode out and inspected them. It was mostly for fleas and I found the men bad with them. We trekked across the open, past Pink House, through the gully after dusk, but very few bullets were flying. We are now encamped further down the Gully than before as the regiment is in the reserve trenches. I have been awfully busy as 200 odd 10th Manchesters (Terr.) [Territorials] have been attached to the regiment and these chaps are rotten with 'crawlers' [lice] as they have been so long in the trenches without a change of clothes, so we boiled about 120 shirts in a cresol preparation. Been very hot to-day.

1.6.15.

Boiled more shirts yesterday. Got an order in the afternoon to go with my stretcher-bearers down the reserve trench to a gully on the right flank and form an aid post in it, as the Hants were to dig a trench in the open, so they expected a lot of casualties. Well, we set off at 6 p.m., and went down the trench to the gully and at a place where the trench crosses the Gully called the Death Trap or Clapham Junction we entered the Gully, Corp. Carlie and I went up the right wing of the Gully to find an aid post but every good place was occupied and it was a shallow gully and afforded poor cover, so on advice we were guided up to the left wing of the gully to the Manchesters' old Head Quarters and by this time it was dark. We just reached the place over some open [ground] when a hail of bullets came over but we were safe. After some time Corp. Carlie and the guide went to look for the trenches which were just beyond us but they came back as it was an impossible place for getting wounded into, so we had to trek back to Clapham Junction amidst many bullets and we made the Aid Post there. I told the Hants Sergt. where we were and how to bring the wounded down – as no word of wounded came – we trekked back to the gully in the early morning. When we got back the C.O.[9] and the Adjutant of the Hants insulted me grossly because we hadn't got away three wounded men. It was really the Adjutant's fault that we didn't get the wounded away because the Adjutant didn't point out where the trench was to be dug and he arranged more or less where the aid post was to be, which was really my duty – if he had shown me the spot for the digging I would have made the post near it. I felt furious and spoke straight to the Adjutant but got no reasoning out of him so what can one do with one who hedges like that. I have written [to] my O.C., 89th Field Ambulance, asking to be taken off the Hants Regt. The Regt. is moving up to-night so we are shifting over to Clapham Junc[tion] Gully, and an unsafe place it is too!!! It was fearfully hot to-day.

2.6.15.

We moved yesterday from Ravine Gully about 5.50 p.m. and walked down the reserve trench to Clapham Junction Gully, and then went up to the right hand Gully and chose a spot for our dressing station. We were all feeling tired and thirsty and I was lucky to find a Manchester Infantry Officer who had just come out of the trenches having tea, and he invited me to join him so you bet I did! Then I began to dig my dugout on the left bank of the Gully and had just completed [it] after dark when my messenger came back with mail but I couldn't read it as the lamps wouldn't work. Just then Lieut. Morris came to relieve me so I set out for the base with stray bullets all around. One man was hit along the road, but not badly. I got down to camp about 10.30 and brought a Hants Officer to hospital whose nerves had gone.

3.6.15.

I have made my statement about the whole affair[10] but I hope no trouble is caused as I am all for peace. I return to the Hants to-morrow early. Been an awful day of wind, dust and heat.

5.6.15.

Yesterday was a day I shall never forget. I was up at 5 a.m. and on the trek by 5.15 a.m. back to join the Hants in Clapham Junc. Gully but on account of taking wrong advice I went too much to my right and found myself in the Naval Brigade Gully and so had to retrace my steps and only reached the Hants aid post at 7 a.m. I relieved Morris, had breakfast which was most welcome, and was asked by the O.C. Hants, Colonel Williams to come up to the trenches and see him. He told me they were to have a big fight and asked if I thought that the aid post was in the best place. I thought it

9   Lieutenant Colonel Weir de Lancey Williams, born 1872, was the son of a Lieutenant General and served on the North-West Frontier, West Africa and in the Boer War, before becoming a staff officer. He commanded a division from 1917.
10   The dispute with the Hants. officers on 1 June.

was. Well, the fight began with a fierce bombardment of Turkish trenches at 11 a.m. and lasted thirty minutes. Then our men rushed the trenches and at 11.40 another bombardment took place. Oh, what a noise and dust our Jack Johnsons made. We, being only 300 yards behind our trenches, so had lots of bullets about us and then the Turks shrapnelled us, and we had a lot all round us and a shell-nose fell into our dugout, it being quite hot. The second bombardment lasted over an hour and it was a dreadful noise – something like Neuve Chapelle,[11] I should think.

Heavy fighting went on all day and at one o'clock Hants wounded began to walk in and we were dressing and sending them to base as quickly as possible, and all under a fusillade of rifle [bullets] and shrapnel. In the meantime the regimental stretcher-bearers were in the firing line dressing and getting the wounded out and doing magnificent work. We were dressing all day until after dark with short intervals when we would snatch a cup of tea and a biscuit. We were pretty done up after wounded stopped coming down so we snatched a few hours sleep and were up before sunrise to-day and at it again and were quite busy up till mid-day when almost all the Hants wounded had been brought in. Our men did very well, capturing three rows of Turkish trenches, and we would have captured Achi Baba (Tree Hill) if the French hadn't retreated and got our right flank enfiladed and if we had only got reinforcements up.[12] I hear to-day the Hants have only 105 men left out of the original battalion of over 1000, but in this fight they went in over 200 strong (fortunately most are wounded). It was an awful day and night and I hope never to see such again. All day yesterday crowds of prisoners passed down the Gully and I was struck with the Turks being such big men and all seemed well clad. They had surrendered in crowds, I had one of my bearers hit in the shoulder to-day, Colonel Williams is badly hit, and so is Rosser the Adjutant.

6.6.15.

Not been so busy to-day but last night was very exciting as some troops on the right flank retreated[13] and left the Hants exposed, however they stuck to their positions and were congratulated but they are done to-day! We have a few wounded in the front trench but can't get them out as the communication trench is not complete but we shall get them out to-morrow, when it will be completed.

This afternoon I had another bearer wounded in the leg, T. Franklin, and this afternoon we got real iron rations – we were heavily shrapnelled, and we had shrapnel dropping all around, and a lot of men were wounded and killed along the Gully,

---

11   The first British attack on the Western Front of 1915, in March, which relied on a short but intensive bombardment and was initially successful.
12   In fact, in this Third Battle of Krithia the British attacks on the left had also been unsuccessful. With failure on both flanks, as well as lack of support, most of the captured ground in the centre had to be evacuated.
13   Other sources say the left.

especially the Marines who were coming up to reinforce us, who had thirty odd casualties. The R.A.M.C. stretcher-bearers have suffered too. Only one officer of Hants is left, and before this battle (which lasted Friday, Saturday and Sunday) we had five of the original battalion and we got fourteen to replace others from home. The Hants hope to be relieved to-night. We had an awful dose of common shell about 6 p.m. from the right side of the Gully, it drove us out of our dugouts, when I returned I found a chunk of casing in my dugout.

9.6.15.

Last night the Regiment shifted from the right flank to their old position on the left, so I shifted my aid post back to Gurkha Gully this morning, I ran across Lieut. A.R.C. McKerrow, R.F.A. and Darkie Sievwright of a Marine F. Amb. so we had a great Edinburgh talk.

10.6.15.

The Regiment (Hants) came out of the trenches at sunrise and we trekked down Gurkha Gully to Gully Beach where we are to rest. I saw Lieut. Sanders to-day and he hadn't been off that Beach since we landed.

12.6.15.

Went down to 'W' Beach yesterday and had a good bath and clean clothes. I got a huge mail, which I answered to my ability. Then last night just after I had gone to bed in a tent the Turks began to shell us with Jack Johnsons so I shifted into my dug out and next morning early returned to Gully Beach. I have been prostrate with dysentery all day and to add insult to injury have to walk to the top of the Gully as the Hants go back to the trenches to-night.

13.6.15.

Got up to the top of the Gully absolutely exhausted and slept like a top. This afternoon I got orders to leave the Hants and be medical officer to the Royal Fusiliers as another M.O. is to replace me. I expect it will be Panton who was wounded. He was their former M.O.

14.6.15.

Left the Hants this afternoon and was replaced by Capt. Cromie, a regular from West Africa. The Royals I found half way down the Gully in the reserve trenches.

16.6.15.

On Monday night after dark had a disturbed night as the Inniskilling Fusiliers (commonly known as 'the Skins'!!) were digging trenches in front of us and their wounded came to my aid post. We heard to-day that we are to move to Gully Beach at daybreak to-morrow early and then when we go back after the rest the Regt. will no doubt go into the trenches. Been having awful days of wind and dust.

18.6.15.

Moved down with the regiment yesterday morning early and after breakfast I had an inspection for 'Crawlers' and found them fairly clean. I have been having a lot of men bad with dysentery which I think is due to the sand and dust. I went down to W. Beach, got my mail written and a change of clothes and fortunately escaped being shelled as W. Beach has been shelled daily by 'Asiatic Anna' from the Asiatic side. I had the good fortune to see one of our Cruisers (which was well guarded with 9 destroyers and 6 minesweepers as we have had 3 ships torpedoed lately) shelling 2 ridges on the Asiatic side – by jove she did break up those ridges!!! I returned in time for dinner.

19.6.15.

The Regiment got sudden orders at breakfast to move up to the reserve trenches so we all trekked up and got my aid post fixed half way up to the Gully. Then as the expected Turkish attack didn't come off, all but one Coy. [company] went back to the beach, then when myself and stretcher-bearers began to return we got a terrible shelling for over an hour with Jack Johnsons (one just sailed over my dugout and landed on the road which it <u>did</u> tear up!!) and shrapnel which fell all around us but luckily no one was hurt. Then when we did come down the Gully shell burst all along it but, thank goodness, I am O.K.

20.6.15.

It is exactly 8 weeks to-day since the wonderful landing took place.

24.6.15.

The regiment moved up to the firing line this morning early and took over the trenches occupied by the K.O.S.Bs. [1/King's Own Scottish Borderers] I went round with the O.C., Major Fisher[14] to inspect the trenches which were anything but sanitary so had them put right. We hold a most wonderful position. We have 2 Coys. to the right of Ravine Gully and one to the left, linking up with the Gurkhas and on the right, Munster Fus. We share a trench with the Turks, only a barricade of sand bags separate us and we bomb each other. This trench called 'The Turkey Trot' leads off from our firing line in a crescent thus [see reproduction of sketch on next page] and in the angle 'X' are crowds of dead Turks, which are easily seen with a periscope and oh, what an

14   Julian Fisher, born 1877, was commissioned in the Royal Fusiliers in 1897, winning a D.S.O. for service in Tibet.

Diagram based on version appearing in Pirie typescript (see previous page).

awful smell!! Then the Turks are only a short distance off and they hold a wonderful trench called the 'Boomerang' which is on the other side of the gully and absolutely commands us, it is like this V and so if you take it you are enfiladed right and left. I feel very sorry for the men in those trenches as it is boiling hot and then the awful smell.

27.6.15.

I have been inspecting the trenches each morning and it is a beastly hot job as the sun has been terrific. It has been fairly quiet since the Regiment has been in the trenches and except for Lieut. Sartoris being killed, which was a sad business, only a few men have been wounded. The whole regiment came out of the trenches this afternoon and are to have a good night's rest as they are to take part in a big fight to-morrow. I hate to think of to-morrow because it means loss of life again. After dinner to-night the O.C., Major Fisher, held a long conference with his officers and as I sat afar, I looked at those fine fellows and wondered at each one's fate, their chances are small in these attacks as I hear five rows of trenches are to be taken. I do wish this war would cease as it is absolute murder. I am to have my aid post in Gurkha Bluff on the extreme left as we can get the wounded in so much better to that place so I trek over there after breakfast with my bearers and orderlies, 19 in all.

29.6.16.

Yesterday was another of those horrible days. It was a terrible battle.[15]

My bearers and self moved to Gurkha Bluff at 8 a.m. from Ravine Gully and had just about reached our post and got it fixed up when the battle began. It began by our bombarding the Turkish trenches for 2 solid hours. I have never seen such a rain of shell fall into the trenches and it was deafening! All sorts of artillery were used, howitzers, field guns and mountain guns and these shells sailed over our heads in the bluff into the Turkish trenches and by jove, they sent clouds and clouds of dust and smoke up. I can't imagine anyone on earth standing such a shelling. It was extraordinary, we could actually see the big howitzer shells just before they fell into the trench and they looked like small stones. During all this shelling the Turks shelled us in the bluff with shrapnel as they knew troops had to come up the bluff to get at them. Then Turkish trenches are just beyond ours on top of the bluff and a lot of splinters from our

15   The Battle of Gully Ravine – first day.

Figure 7. A 60 pounder battery in action at Gallipoli. (© Imperial War Museum, ref. Q 13340)

own shelling threw back on us so it was a mighty hot spot and we had to creep away into dugouts for those two hours. I shall never forget that shelling as shrapnel bases, fuses and bullets were whizzing about like a heavy shower of rain. As soon as the bombardment stopped at 11 a.m. our men charged and captured five rows of trenches all right, but then our work began and we were kept pretty busy as first walking cases came in and then the bearers brought in the stretcher cases. This went on all day long and it was interspersed with being shelled by the Turks but our worst shelling during the day (except the first 2 hours) was just after dark when I was having something to eat and the worst of it was we couldn't see where it was falling. Practically all the wounded had been fetched in by dark so we had a quiet night and had some sleep. Early this morning the battalion was relieved and they were absolutely done so rested on Y Beach at the bottom of Gurkha Bluff. It was a sad sight to see these men reduced in numbers, weary and dirty. On enquiry I found only 3 officers left, the O.C., the Adjutant, Captain Wilson and Lt. Payne, all the 3 captains killed, 2 Lts. Missing and 3 Lts. Wounded, 2 of which I dressed. It makes one too sad for words. The 3 officers were absolute wrecks, so done up for want of sleep and anxiety. We moved from Gurkha Bluff to Ravine Gully in the afternoon and are to sleep there and they need it badly. The regiment's casualties are calculated to 250 killed, wounded and missing.[16]

16   The battalion's War Diary (TNA WO95/4310) records for 28-29 June, 3 officers and 29 O.Rs. killed; 3 officers and 175 O.Rs. wounded; and 3 officers and 57 O.Rs. missing; and 3 officers and 412 O.Rs. as the remaining effective strength. 'The men were for the most part in a terribly exhausted condition having had 24 hours fighting under the most trying conditions with very little water. The heat was very trying.'

30.6.15.

Last night was a very disturbed one. I think the Turks must have attacked us as there was a fearful noise of machine gun and rifle fire from our men and the mountain guns near us were going at it all night. We could see the shells in the dark flying over our heads just like a tiny red coal. Then the Turks shelled us which kept us awake.[17] To-day has been a sad day for me as one of my bearers, L/Corp. Johnston was badly hit in the head with shrapnel and I am afraid he is done for. It is such a sad affair as he has been through it since the landing and then to be done for while resting! We have been shelled a lot to-day again. I think the reason for that is because the Mountain Battery is just on the other side of the gully from us and they are trying to get at them but their shells fall short so we get it in the gully. We moved down to Gully Beach this afternoon and it is most peaceful.

4.7.15.

The Regiment (Royal Fus.) got orders to move up to the trenches in the centre so I came up yesterday afternoon to select my aid post because the Regiment was to come up in the dark. I settled on the Brigade dump as we were taking over from the [1/] Essex. The Regt. had a good rest on the beach but had 3 men wounded with spent bullets on the cliff side. We had no casualties coming up last night. We are about 2 miles [sic.] in front of the Pink Farm.

7.7.15.

We have had it very hot these last few days and when the wind blows from the Turks it brings down a horrible odour. It has been very quiet in our lines.[18]

12.7.15.

To-day the Dublins [1/Royal Dublin Fusiliers] had a feint attack at 4 a.m., preceded by a bombardment. This was in the centre next our regiment. This was to draw the Turkish reinforcements from the French. Then all the artillery turned to the Turks in front of the French on the right and by jove it was a terrific bombardment for about 2 hours and I watched it with my glasses from the aid post at the Brigade dump. It was a wonderful sight to see the 'Jack Johnsons' shells throw up the earth hundreds of feet into the air and I thought I saw one Turk pitched into the air. The way our shrapnel raked the ground was fine too and I am sure jolly few Turks escaped from those trenches. The wind was blowing from the Turks to us so it blew all the smoke and dust away and you could see the effect of each shell. The Turkish shrapnel was

---

17   The Turks had attempted a counterattack, which was repulsed with heavy losses to them.
18   A massive Turkish attack early on 5 July had been thrown back with enormous Ottoman losses.

very poor as it burst too high. After the bombardment we could see the French advancing amidst many shells and then reach a trench and dig for all they were worth, and all the time rifle and machine gun fire were going on hard and probably Turkish! In the afternoon I went to the 89th F. Amb. in Aberdeen Gully and while I was there a fierce shelling began again by us and I had to wait until it stopped a bit because the Turks were shelling us. Then I started back and when I got to the trench I was to return by, it was being shelled so my orderly, Kimber, and I had to make a run for it. When I got back I found one of my bearers had been wounded at the aid post. I then took my glasses and watched the end of the battle which was an advance by the [52nd] Lowland Division. You could see the Highlanders [of 157th Brigade] running through the barbed wire and trenches and others digging themselves in. It was really wonderful!!

13.7.15.

Last night I had two escapes from bullets within a few minutes. One bullet hit the parapet in front of my dugout and I had just moved, otherwise I would have had it in the head. Then as I went round the corner of the trench to see a sick man I again nearly had my head blown off. The bullets seemed to be flying in all directions as the Turks seemed to be counter attacking the French and the Lowland Division. Needless to say I got into my dugout after that! This afternoon the French again had another bombardment and an attack which all proved unsuccessful, I have been messing in the trenches with the O.C., second in command and Adjutant, i.e. Major Fisher, Captain Wilson and Captain Cripps, and on my way up to the trenches to mess, a shrapnel shell burst in front of Kimber and me and how we were missed I don't know. We could only lean up against the mule trench wall as we were in a straight part of this wide mule trench up which the ammunition and rations come to the trenches. One shrapnel bullet passed between our legs and the trench wall and it only had a space of about 2 ins. to go between so I have had another escape!

14.7.15.

We came out of the trenches this evening and Oh! I was glad. We have done eleven solid days and they were long and trying as it has been very hot and the flies an awful plague and the smell of dead Turks was indescribable and latterly everything tasted of dead Turks and I got that I couldn't eat and was quite done up and badly needed a change. Then I have had to instruct the new Regimental Medical Officers of K's army [Kitchener's New Army] in trench sanitation. These men have just come out with Regiments. This instruction is a result of the Brigade staff hearing of a system I have evolved for the trenches. However, it shows they approve of it. We are sleeping in Gully Ravine to-night and are to go down to Gully Beach to-morrow morning.

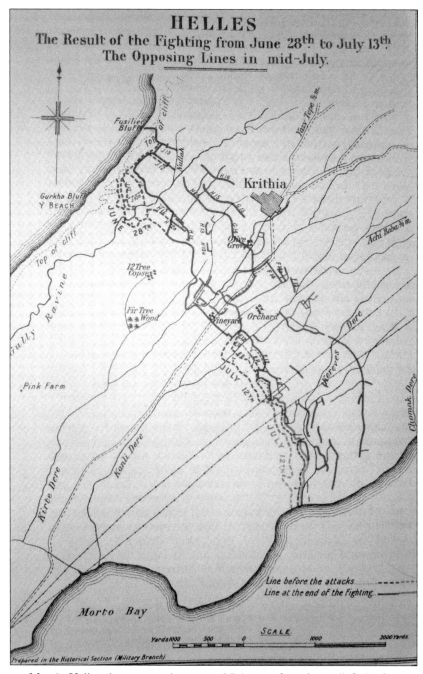

Map 3. Helles: the opposing lines in mid-July 1915 from Aspinall-Oglander,
History of the Great War Military Operations Gallipoli Vol. II.

15.7.15.

The Regiment moved down to Gully Beach this morning and as we are to embark for Lemnos to-night from V. Beach I rode down to W. Beach and had my valise sent to Gully Beach by the 89th Field Ambulance. I had two fine bathes to-day and it is gorgeous down here after those trenches.

16.7.15.

Here we are on Lemnos Island and it is fine to be away from the noise and smell and to feel you can walk about in the open with absolute freedom. We marched from Gully Beach last night to V. Beach and when we got to V. Beach we were all dead beat so we just lay down on the grass with our packs as pillows till it was time to embark. I hadn't been asleep long when I heard the whistle of a big shell and then a crash just behind us. These were followed by more and some went over us to W. Beach so we all sought refuge behind a pile of French biscuit boxes and both V. and W. Beaches got a good dose. Then we moved on to the pier alongside the S.S. *River Clyde* and again I slept soundly and finally embarked on a minesweeper about 2 a.m. and arrived at Lemnos this afternoon and came ashore. We were camping in open fields and I have my bed on a stretcher under a big tree as we have no tents.

21.7.15.

I am enjoying the rest immensely and feeling quite fit again. It is simply great to be free to walk anywhere without being fired at. Everything seems so peaceful seeing the peasants (Greek) going to market, also seeing the fowls, cows and such like. Last Saturday I went on to the *Aragon* which is lying in the harbour and had iced drinks and lunch with the ship's officers. I was on the *Aragon* again yesterday for lunch and tea and it was fine, to see again what luxury and comfort was like after one's experience on the Gallipoli Peninsula.

22.7.15.

We got a sudden order yesterday at 11 a.m. to return to the Peninsula, much to my disgust, as we were all so comfortable and feeling so much better of the rest and I had it arranged to have my birthday (24th July) on the *Aragon* with the ship's officers and also I was to have inoculated the whole Battalion (750) against Cholera and so everything was knocked on the head. Rumour hath it we were hurried back because the Turks were massing in huge numbers for a big attack. Well, the Battalion fell in at 1.30 a.m. and we marched to the Australian pier amidst clouds of dust. On our way to the pier we halted opposite N.15 Stationary Hospital so I went and said good-bye to Dr. McLaughlan and had a beer with him. He, Sanders and I ran the *Aragon* as a Hospital Ship. We embarked on a destroyer, the *Beagle*[19] at 2.30 p.m. The officers

---

19   Built 1909, around 900 tons, it survived the war.

aboard were awfully decent to us and gave us grub. We left Lemnos at 6 p.m. and went like a hare reaching V. Beach at 9 p.m. and disembarked, fortunately without being shelled. Then we marched to Gully Beach via W. and arrived at our destination about 12 midnight, feeling very tired. Our short rest of 5 days was grand but all too short. The 89th Field Ambulance arrived at Lemnos on Tuesday evening and encamped near us. I was awfully sorry to leave as I had visions of exploring the island with them. We have got Major Guyon back. He was hit in the head and he is now O.C.[20] and Major Fisher second in command with Captain Cripps as Adjutant. Capt. P.N. Wilson is in hospital at present. We have an awfully nice mess with these fellows, they rag the life out of Harding the Quarter Master and they call me 'The Pill'!!!

25.7.15.

We have been having horrible weather these last few days, wind and dust galore and we get the benefit of it being on Gully Beach, then to add insult to injury I have developed an ulcer on the under aspect of my eyelid and sand irritates it badly so I have had to wear a bandage over it for the last four days but it is getting better now. We have been 'standing to' each morning at 4.30 because information says that the Turks are massing troops and we must be ready to move at a moment's notice, however, except for a feeble attack by them nothing has happened and we are to move up to the trenches on the 28th. Yesterday was my birthday and it was very quiet and uneventful. To-day I gave Lt. Pirie of the Lanc.[ashire] Fus.[iliers] a hand to inoculate his batt. [battalion] against Cholera and he is to help me to do my Battalion to-morrow.

26.7.15

Pirie and I did my Battalion for Cholera to-day and it was a tedious job. We are supposed to give the next dose 10 days hence but I expect it will be later as we shall be in the trenches on the 10th day. A German aeroplane, a *Taube* flew over us this morning and dropped a bomb but it landed in the sea and did no damage. My eye is O.K. again and I am jolly glad as it looks bad a medical officer going sick!

27.7.15.

After the 4.30 a.m. 'stand to' Captain Cripps the adjutant and some of the newly arrived officers and I went up to the trenches we are to take over to-morrow and I found we were to hold our old trenches and a part where the Munsters [1/Royal Munster Fusiliers] were in last time on our right. The Cheshires [8/Cheshire] and Wilts [5/Wiltshire] of K's Army are in them and I can foresee a busy time cleaning them up as K's Army seems to have a jolly poor idea of sanitation!!! We got back to

---

20   George Guyon was killed as a Lieutenant Colonel on the First Day of the Somme, 1 July 1916.

Gully Beach at 10 a.m. feeling jolly hungry as we had a 3 miles walk each way and then dodging about the trenches. Wilson is back again but he isn't very fit. Capt. Agassiz of the 89th Field Ambulance came up to-day with mail and said they were returning from Lemnos. I was very glad as I look upon them as my home and I enjoy going to Aberdeen Gully to tea, which is their advanced dressing station in Ravine Gully. I am glad we are going up to the trenches to get away from the dust and sand but I shall miss the bathing very much.

28.7.15.

The Regiment came up to the trenches[21] this afternoon and our Division, the 29th, have taken over from the 13th Division and rumour hath it the 13th with two other K's Army Divisions are to effect a new landing about the Australians at Gaba Tepe and push across the Sea of Marmora and cut off the Turks and we are to remain here and make a slight attack and so get this campaign over by September because by that time the seas are so big they absolutely can't land anything as the piers we have built are too weak. I sincerely hope it is true and we manage to cut the Turks off as then the Fleet will force the Narrows. Soon after the Regt. went into the trenches one of our own shells burst in our trench and wounded a Sergt. of ours and five R.E. sappers.

29.7.15.

Had 3 casualties last night, 1 killed (head) 1 wounded (head severe) and one in the hand, self inflicted so he will be court martialled when better and may be shot for it. Had a busy day getting the trenches cleaned up which had been left in a filthy state.[22] The previous M.Os. who have occupied my dugout in the old trench at the Brigade Dump at the end of the Mule Track, during my absence have turned it into a regular palace by putting on a sandbag roof in place of my old waterproof sheets and now it is lovely and cool and to add to the household comforts I have put up a gauze curtain over the door which (having whisked the flies out) makes life worth living. I go to Head Quarters mess in the trenches to feed as of old. I am about 800 yards from Hd.Qr. The Hd.Qr. mess consists of Major Guyon O.C., Fisher, Capt. Cripps Adjutant and self. The mess is in the support trench just behind the firing line.

30.7.15.

Been very hot to-day, am burnt brown as a berry. We heard to-day of the great victory over the Turks on the Euphrates at the Persian Gulf so to celebrate it the whole line

---

21   From Essex Knoll to Worcester Flat.
22   The battalion war diary on 28 July agreed that 'The trenches had not been kept up to the standard of the Royal Fusiliers either in sanitation or safety. Consequently a good deal of work will have to be done. The men worked well throughout the night in making the parapets safe, filling in old latrines, etc.'

from one side of the Peninsula to the other fired a *Feu de Joie* beginning on the right with the French, right through us in the centre to the left. I was in the firing line and we cheered at the same time and as soon as the Turks heard the firing and cheering they began a furious rifle fire because I suppose they expected a charge. However we only disturbed their afternoon sleep as this occurred at 5 p.m.[23]

2.8.15.

Yesterday and to-day our artillery have been ranging on the Turks' trenches in front of us so I suppose there must be a battle coming off soon, but from what I hear we are only in reserve and I am glad for our men's sakes. I watched our shells bursting in the Turkish trenches from our ones with a periscope and it was a sight. Looking back in my diary I see I had fears I wouldn't see any fighting – I laugh when I think of these days now!! We have had no casualties the last two days.

3.8.15.

Had an extra busy day walking about inspecting trenches and such like. Then I had to go up B. Communication trench to the old Turkish redoubt to see a wounded man who turned out to be Wheatley one of our ammunition carriers. He had been getting in some Turkish barbed wire and he had got his upper arm badly fractured with a ricochet bullet. On my rounds of the trenches to-day I had the luck to see Corp. Everest fire his Garland Trench Mortar. The wee shell has a tail just like a kite and with a periscope I saw it drop bang into the Turkish trench and explode. I was jolly nearly a casualty this afternoon. My orderly, Kimber, (who is a splendid youngster and always accompanies me on my rounds in case one is hit, otherwise one might lie for hours in one of those lonely communication trenches) and I were going up to the trenches about 4 p.m. and we were in Communication trench A. and had just passed a Lanc. Fusilier when one of our 6" howitzer shells burst in a Turkish trench about 150-200 yards ahead of us. Having just passed this man we were on the right side of this narrow trench when all of a sudden next my leg I heard a huge thud, and dust flew up and I jumped and looked round and behind us we picked up a nasty piece of this shell about an inch square all jagged and boiling hot which had flown back. I was glad it didn't hit us.

5.8.15.

Yesterday we had to take over the line the Lanc. Fus. were in, which includes the Northern and Southern Barricades, so I had to go round the new line to see it was clean. In the afternoon Capt. Agassiz and Kellas came to see me and I went back

---

23   According to the battalion war diary, this victory was 'near Nasiriyah on the Euphrates' and 'The road to Baghdad is now open.' Sadly, that campaign was to lead to disaster in April 1916, with the capitulation of Townshend at Kut.

with them and had tea at Aberdeen Gully. Last night before dinner I inoculated our officers and Head Quarters Coy., for the 2nd dose of Cholera, in the trenches. Then I went down to the 86th Brigade Head Quarters and inoculated General Wolley-Dod (an awfully nice old fellow 5'4" in height)[24] and his staff. I just got back to my dugout when I got a chit from Capt. Cripps asking me to come up to the trenches to see Capt. Lang so I went up and at the time a bit of a fight was on and lots of bullets flying, flares going up, lighting up the whole country and the Turks fired their trench mortar which looked exactly like a falling star with a stream of sparks behind it. Capt. Lang had sun stroke so I had to send him to hospital. I got back to my dugout safely after 11 p.m., very tired and slept solidly. Yesterday Lt. Dann had his face nastily cut with fragments of a periscope, as he was looking through it a sniper riddled it. Major Guyon also had his periscope smashed by a sniper, but he escaped except for a scratch. We have our Hd. Qrts. mess next the Marble Arch (made of sand bags and wood!!) in a support trench. We are to have a big battle to-morrow but, thank God, my regiment is not to be in it. The 88th Brigade consisting of Hants, Essex, Worcesters and 5th Royal Scots are to be the actors. My Regiment is to leave the firing line at 5.30 a.m. to-morrow and go into the reserve trenches while the Essex, Hants and Worcesters are to attack from the firing line, we and the Munster Fus. hold and in the order as above, from left and right and the Royal Scots are in support. The bombardment is to begin at 2.30 p.m. as the three regiments above must be properly organised for the attack which begins when the bombardment ceases at 3.50. Then when the three Regts. above advance my regiment goes back to our firing line and holds it. My Regiment won't be in this battle but I shall help with the wounded and I am looking forward to the work but am awfully sorry for the men who will be in the battle. War nowadays is such awful slaughter. Yesterday I got four parcels of eatables, they were most welcome in this isolated spot.

7.8.15.

Yesterday was the saddest day I have spent on this Peninsula. At 5.30 a.m. the regiment moved back into the reserve trenches and the 88th Brigade took over. I had breakfast with Major Fisher in our old Headquarters in the support trench then I went to each company to see that they had their stretcher-bearers and found they hadn't in spite of orders so got them fixed up. On my way back to the aid post I met Capt. Kellas and Lt. Thompson of the 89th F. Ambulance getting their bearers posted for carrying wounded from the regimental aid post to the Field Ambulance. Lieut. De Boer, the

---

24   Owen Wolley-Dod, D.S.O., born 1863, was commissioned in the Lancashire Fusiliers in 1883. He was the senior staff officer with 29th Division in April 1915. With the heavy loss of senior officers during the landings at Helles on 25 April, he was sent ashore by his divisional commander with authority to issue orders on his behalf. As Hunter-Weston, offshore, continued to issue orders, there was some confusion. Wolley-Dod commanded 86th Brigade from June as Brigadier General. He was placed on the sick list 13 August 1915.

Dublins' M.O. was with them and I had Lieut. Hunter (Dr.) of the Essex with me. We were standing talking over arrangements in a trench when I heard a bullet strike and to my horror I saw Capt. Kellas fall like a log, shot through the left eye right along side of me and he died in a few minutes. Oh God! it was a ghastly affair and we four doctors could do nothing to save him. Our heads must have been above the parapet and a sniper picked him off. It was all so sudden and it completely unnerved me for some hours. He was such a nice fellow and such a loss to the profession.[25] I had lunch with Major Fisher in the old Headquarters mess and then returned to the aid post before the bombardment began at 2.30 p.m. The bombardment was something terrific and the monitors with their 14" howitzers[26] also took part. All the time we shelled them they gave us likewise and we had it hot at the aid post. The noise was terrific and it was made worse with our machine guns firing from behind us. Their continual crack, crack is more deafening than a big gun I find. I got a fair quantity of other regiments' wounded into my aid post and dressed them. Then about 6 p.m. I went up to our firing line after the advance and found the attack had been more or less a failure. The Essex on the left and the Worcesters on the right had captured a part of their trench but the Hants in the centre were simply mowed by machine guns and had to come back in spite of that terrific bombardment. Really, I don't know how a single Turk was left after it. I found a good number of wounded and dead in the Northern and Southern Barricades, so I dressed them and got the bearers to carry them away. Then I went down the firing line, Sergt. Pridham helped me, and we dressed a lot all along, mostly stretcher cases that had crawled in over the parapet after dark. I saw two men go out with a ladder and fetch in a wounded comrade in spite of bullets flying. Really, the Tommy Atkins is a wonder – he does not seem to know what fear is!! All the time we were dressing these men in the trenches a regular fusillade of bullets and shrapnel from the Turks was going on. It was difficult dressing wounded in the dark, we had to resort to matches, and besides that, the trenches are narrow and were packed with fighting men. After I had done the line more or less I came back to my Regiment Head Quarters feeling done and famished, so I managed to raise some grub and tea and felt much better after it. Then I was kept more or less on the go all night with wounded in the trenches but I snatched a little sleep about 3 p.m. by sleeping under our rough and ready mess table in the trenches – I really think that this is the first occasion I have ever slept under the table!!! At about 3.15 a.m. the O.C., Major Guyon, said they had orders to shift back to the Eski Lines and advised me to go down to the aid post and have a sleep which I did. Getting back to the aid post very sleepy at twenty to 4 and I slept soundly till twenty-five to 8 when a Hants officer came in and told me their Dr., Capt. Levi had been killed by a shell. I knew him also, he was an Australian. He had his aid post just at the end of B. communication trench,

---

25 Davidson *The Incomparable 29th* p.67 wrote 'I never respected a man I met more than Kellas, he was most gentle and brave, and in every way a good sort.'
26 Presumably Abercrombie class – main armament two 14" guns.

behind the firing line and I had spoken to him the evening before. This morning there was another battle on our right, the East Lancashire Division had to make the advance. I went down an old trench near my aid post and watched part of the battle. The bombardment of the Turks' trenches was terrific, smoke and dust galore. Then I saw the men advance over the open amidst a rain of Turkish shrapnel and although they were charging they seemed to go forward very slowly and in spite of all the shrapnel, machine gun and rifle fire I didn't see a man fall. As they advanced, our guns fired over their heads to cover the advance. They captured three rows of trenches then I saw them retreat in small lots and again they would at times be absolutely obliterated with the dust of the bursting shrapnel but presently emerge safely. They retreated to the first line of captured trenches and seemed to hold it but I can't say I saw a single Turk, but I heard their rifle and machine gun fire as their bullets were flying over our heads. A battle like that is too wonderful for words and baffles all description and I am glad I have seen it. There is some rumour that our brigade have a battle on to-morrow which will involve my regiment but I hope it isn't true, as it means loss of men. We heard the good news this morning that a new landing had been effected further up the Peninsula and 500 prisoners had been taken. I sincerely hope they can push across the Peninsula and cut off the Turks down in the front of us. Major Fisher, D.S.O. I have had to send away to hospital as he is suffering from concussion of the brain and spine caused by a huge shell bursting on the parapet which blew him against the opposite side of the trench and really, he is lucky to be alive.[27] In this battle we had 43 wounded and about 10 killed in the Southern barricade.[28]

9.8.15.

The regiment is all in the reserve and our battle is not to take place. I am very glad as these battles are horrible. I hear we are to take over the Munsters' line of trenches in a few days so I shall have to give up my lovely dugout at the dump and go further forward to just behind the front line. The days are shortening fast and the weather looks very like rain these last few days.

11.8.15.

Yesterday afternoon after O.C.'s daily conference at Brigade Headquarters Major Guyon told me there was to be a demonstration against the Turks in the way of bombing the Turks from the Northern and Southern Barricades and our regimental bomb throwers were to take part in it, also the Dublin Fus. as the Dublins were holding that part of the trench. It was to take place at 2 a.m. and begin with bombing

---

27   Fisher later moved to Intelligence work, was promoted Lieutenant Colonel and lived to 1953.
28   The Allied attacks at Helles on 6/7 August were intended to divert the Turks from moving reinforcements against the offensives at Anzac and Suvla. They failed in this objective and at the cost of heavy casualties.

Figure 8. Stretcher-bearers with cases on their way back through a communication trench at Gallipoli. (© Imperial War Museum, ref. Q 13325)

the Turkish trenches from the inside of the barricades for 15 minutes, then at 2.30 they were to go out and bomb the Turks close to their trenches, the barricades being only 30 yards from the Turkish trench. So I took Sergt. Pridham and Sewell, my 2 medical orderlies and 13 stretcher-bearers as we expected some casualties and I went up about 9 p.m. and took up my position in the firing line at a place called Marble Arch and had a short sleep, before the demonstration began, at 2 a.m., on a bit of ledge in the trench. The bombing was a great success and they gave the Turks a good shaking and much to our joy we had no casualties so we came back to the aid post at 3.30 a.m. and to my sorrow, found Snow, one of my stretcher-bearers had been wounded in the abdomen by a stray bullet while asleep in his dugout and I have great fears he won't recover. I did my best for him and went to sleep. Soon after I was called to see a man hit in the head but he died. Then I went to sleep again but hadn't been asleep long when I was called to see another man hit in the abdomen and he likewise was in a bad way so it wasn't a very cheery night at all, so I had a bath in a waterproof sheet sunk in the ground, after seeing the last man at 6 a.m. Jove, it was great because it's the first for over a week!!!

13.8.15.

I had quite a busy day yesterday as I inoculated W. Coy in the Eski lines and X Coy. at the Dump, against cholera, mostly for the second time. To-day I did X. Coy. in the reserve trenches and in the afternoon went down to Aberdeen Gully to have tea with Capt. Stephen and Lt. Thompson. This morning we had bad luck, a shell burst in Z. Coy's trench and killed Sergt. Cross and Corp. Jackson, both excellent men, and wounded 7 others. To-night I feel very sad and depressed as I got news of the pater being so ill[29] and on top of that the news of the new landing at Suvla Bay doesn't seem to be such a success as at first rumoured.

17.8.15. [16.8.15?]

Yesterday afternoon, at tea-time, we suddenly got orders to move at 12 mid-night on to the extreme left of the line which runs down on to the sea, and the Naval Brig. were to take over the line from us. Then soon after, it was changed to 8 a.m. for the move, which was more sensible. I was sorry to leave that part of the line because I knew it so well and it meant giving up my palace of a dugout at the old Dump in front of Fir Tree Copse. It seems foolish to move us as we know the line so well and the Naval Brigade know nothing about it, and we again, have to learn the new line. We shifted at 8 a.m. to the new line and I have my aid post with Batt. Headquarters in a steep ravine running down to the sea which is called Border Ravine. It is quite a nice place and we get a lovely view of the sea and Imbros and Samothrace in the background and the sunsets are gorgeous over Imbros. The disadvantages are it is very sandy and hot especially in the afternoons as the sun strikes full into the Ravine, worse luck we daren't go down and bathe as the Turks' snipers are always about – part of the line we hold is only 25 yards from the Turks and so there are great bomb throwing contests with the result that I have some horrible wounds to dress. We relieved the 87th Brigade which is the Border Brigade and we took over the line held by the Border Regiment, Border Brigade – Border Regiment, K.O.S.Bs., S. Wales Borderers and Inniskilling Fusiliers.

---

29   His father had in fact died at Cape Town on 5 July, aged 77, but Pirie was not to receive this news until 24 August.

17.8.15

I went round our lines of trenches to-day and they run right down to the sea, down the cliff face and up on the flat. It is simply a maze of trenches and saps.[30] After I came back I had two awful cases to dress. Both were bomb throwers, and evidently the one had held on to the bomb too long after it was lit, with the result that he was minus his right hand and badly wounded and the other bomber was wounded all over, it was an awful sight. To my disgust I sent Kimber, my orderly, down to the 89th F.A. at Aberdeen Gully for drugs and he returned to tell me that the 89th have gone up the Anzac where the Australians are with the 87th Brigade which we relieved, so now I shall have an awful job to get my mail again, and besides I shall miss them very much. We are to be relieved to-morrow by the Lancashire Fus. and we go to Gully Beach for 3 days' rest, it isn't much of a rest considering we have done 22 days in the trenches. We were in the firing line from the 28th July till the 6th Aug. (day after the battle) – 10 days, from the 6th till the 16th in the reserve trenches – 10 days, from the 16th till to-morrow in the firing line – 22 days in all so it is longer than they do in France where the usual is 48 hours in and 48 hours out. After our three days we shall return to some part of the line on the left. I am hoping to be promoted to Captain soon as I saw in the London *Times* that all Special Reserve R.A.M.C. Lts. with six months mobilised service are to be made Captains so as I have 8 months which includes 6 months on actual active service I hope to receive the promotion. Just heard from the O.C., Major Guyon we are not to be relieved till 20th!

18.8.15.

Had four casualties last night, one killed and three wounded. The Turkish sniper seems extra good on this part of the line as we daren't show a periscope, much less a head or it is shot down, so instead of periscopes we use a piece of glass on a long stick placed lying on the back wall of the trench. We hold a barricade in our line of trenches which only separates us from the Turks by 25 yards and there are great bombing contests. As protection to our men in the barricades we have overhead screens made of netting wire so when the bomb strikes the screen it just bounces off and bursts outside the barricade. Major Guyon is very amusing about the barricade. He calls it the rabbit hutch. Our line is very close to the Turks, ranging from 25 yards to 180 so

---

30   According to the battalion war diary for 16 August, a new front line was being sapped forward 'and in some places the Turks are within fifteen yards or less. When we took over it was found that the Turkish snipers had the upper hand, the loopholes were being shot way & periscopes could not be put up for more than two or three seconds, also bombs were being thrown into our trench. The steel loopholes are useless at such a close range & were being blown to splinters by the Turks.' It confidently continued 'Steps are being taken to deal with this & to make the Turks understand that we will not allow it to continue. We are in communication [with] H.M.S. *Wolverine* (T.B. Destroyer) who fires or turns her searchlight on when required.'

we are making free use of the new rifle grenade which is a sort of cylinder (which on striking ground breaks into 70 odd pieces) on a steel rod which is pushed down the barrel of the rifle and then an ordinary cartridge minus the bullet is fired and it drives the grenade vertically into the air. We are also using trench mortars. At this stage I must record the fact that two torpedo destroyers, the *Wolverine* and *Scorpion*[31] in turn patrol just off the end of our line and pelt the Turks every now and again and lately they have been joined by two ancient cruisers, the *Edgar* and *Endymion*, which have been made torpedo proof by having three rows of tanks with air and water in them. They are funny old-looking craft but do good shooting.[32] This afternoon the *Wolverine* and *Edgar* were patrolling as usual off our line and a seaplane had been up for about two hours when it began to volplane down and landed near the *Edgar* but didn't move towards the ship. Then the destroyer came along-side her and towed her away to Imbros so she may have been hit or perhaps it was engine troubles. Our Regiment was to have rushed the Turks' trench and hold it after the old gun 'Wandering Kate' had destroyed the barricade at almost point blank range. This was to have taken place to-morrow morning at 5.30 a.m., but now it is put off for 24 hours.

19.8.15.

This part of the diary is written on 25th Aug. as I have been unable to keep a daily record lately due to moving. All was arranged for the stunt to-morrow when at one o'clock we got a sudden order to pack up and be ready to move at 2 p.m. as the East Lanc. Division (what was left of it) were to relieve us and we proceed to Gully Beach and embark the same night to either Anzac or Suvla Bay at W. Beach. Well, we packed up everything, all our mess amongst other stuff and got it away with fatigue parties. To our disgust we waited and waited and no regiment arrived and eventually, after dark, they began to leisurely roll up, we were famished and it was bitterly cold! Then we thought all was right and we were just going to move off when it was found their machine guns hadn't come up so our gunners couldn't get away as machine guns were imperative on that part of the line. This was about 8 p.m. and eventually these Lancashire gunners were found asleep in a side trench at 12. We were furious over all this wait. Then we moved off and were blocked every now and again in the mule track by mules with loads. The mule track only permits of one loaded mule to go along. We trekked down the Ravine Gully and by the time we reached Gully Beach we were all dead beat as we were hungry, we had done 23 days in the trenches and then this 4 mile walk finished us so we just lay down anywhere on the beach and slept like logs. It was bitterly cold but luckily I had my Burberry [coat] in my pack so I slept with it on. That was the coldest night we have had for months.

31   Both destroyers were of the same *'G'* or *Basilisk* class as the *Beagle*. *Wolverine* was sunk in a collision in 1917.
32   These were *Edgar* class protected cruisers of 1894 vintage and around 8,000 tons, armed with 2-9.2" and 10-6" guns.

20.8.15.

We rested all day on the beach to-day as we had been relieved too late to embark last night. Had a nice bathe in the sea and got orders we were to march to W. Beach at 7 p.m., which was about sundown, and embark at 8 p.m. when it would be dark, which we did. We sailed by the Fleet Sweeper *Clacton*,[33] which held the whole regiment and found we were bound for Suvla where the whole 29th Division were going. It was 1 p.m. before we reached 'C' Beach in Suvla Bay and were landed in huge barges which were run ashore as far as possible and then we had to jump ashore. I had a good sleep on the deck. The Regiment had orders to dump all their packs on the beach but I hung on to mine as I had all my valuables in it. We were guided by a soldier to the hill 'Chocolate Hill' and that march seemed endless. At last we reached it just before dawn, after about 6 miles' walk and we were glad as we were told you were shelled if you were found out on the flat. We were all very tired, we slept on the side of the hill to wake up being shelled!!

21.8.15.

We had breakfast under 'Chocolate Hill' and then got orders to be in reserve in a battle that afternoon so I went out to reconnoitre the ground for an aid post and settled on a low hill where a communication [trench?] began and it ran back over Chocolate Hill to where we had slept and where the Field Ambulance Dressing Station was to be. We also had lunch under Chocolate Hill and then my bearers and I moved over to the aid post and the regiment (Royal Fus.) was to be at the same spot at 3.30 p.m., when I got there I found the Munster Fus. lying in the lee of this low hill at my aid post, ready to go out and attack and I did feel sorry for them as no one knew who would come back. Our bombardment began and then we got it hot with shrapnel and as the hill was low it afforded very little shelter and men were hit all round one, and amongst others, Munson, one of my medical orderlies was hit with a shell case on his back but luckily wasn't killed. He is a big loss to me. The result was I was mighty busy even before the action began. About 3.5 p.m. the Munsters and then the Lancashire Fus. went out to attack and it was grand to see them go out as if there was nothing to fear and yet a hail of bullets was flying everywhere and I don't know how one is alive to tell the tale. Then the Turkish shrapnel set fire to the scrub round the aid post and it was so fierce and hot we had to shift out of the aid post, and what between fire and bullets it was absolute hell.[34] However, wounded began to pour in and we were at it all day and night of Saturday except for about two hours when I snatched some sleep and I was jolly

33   Of around 800 tons, she was sunk by a U-Boat in 1916.
34   As part of the disastrous Scimitar Hill action, 86th Brigade on 29th Division's right was to capture 112 Metre Hill. 1/R.Munsters led the attack, followed by the 1/Lancashire Fusiliers. Taking heavy losses, they were unable to get within five hundred yards of the Turkish front line. 2/Royal Fusiliers, in reserve, were not committed.

glad of it as I was dead done. I was up again just at daybreak and was at it all day until the Regiment got orders to move back at 4 p.m. Saturday. At night I had a big row of Munsters on stretchers and was desperate to get them moved when Capt. Cripps gave me a big fatigue party and they got them to the Field Ambulance. He also gave me a camel tank of water which was a blessing for the wounded as water was awfully scarce. Then on Sunday morning early a sniper somehow got the outskirts of the aid post in line and he was picking off men with horrible results so he was an extra plague.

22.8.15.

As I have said above we had wounded in all day Sunday and my bearers worked very well. The Regt. was luckily not in the attack as the attack failed so the regiment wasn't sent out and jove, I was glad as I should hate if any of the officers were killed as I know them so well. We got orders to move back to Chocolate Hill at 4 p.m. where we had come from and just before we moved away the sniper who had worried us early in the morning must have moved round and then fired blank into the regiment and did ghastly damage, so we were all very glad to get to Chocolate Hill. We had dinner at Chocolate Hill and at 8 p.m. when it was dark we marched across to take over trenches on the left. The Brigade Major Sinclair Thompson guided us and as we were so tired we marched for 15 mins. and rested for 5 and I can truly say I slept as we marched. We marched over the open for about 4 miles and reached point 28 where I decided to sleep the night and reconnoitre the ground in the morning for my aid post. Oh! I was glad to get a sleep as I was dead done, I slept for 5 hours and was up after sunrise.

23.8.15.

Jackson, one of the Brigade orderlies, said he would guide me up to our trenches and of course he took the left instead of the right-hand footpath and we walked right into range of the snipers, and my jove, my poor tired legs did yeoman service!! I ran like a hare and eventually got into the trench and found my Headquarters. Had breakfast and found I would have to have my aid post in the firing line so went back (but by the right way) and got my men and things up. I was astounded to see the equipment and dead men of ours who had fallen the day of landing, 6th Aug. This country is very pretty. It is quite flat with any quantity of oak and fruit trees – pears, mulberry, figs, etc. – and many fields which have been harvested, in some cases and all stacked barley it seems to be. Then this flat slopes up to the high hills all round us and it is formidable country to fight in. Our trenches are beautifully shady with trees, shrubs and creepers growing on the parapets and we have some farm houses along the line and luckily splendid wells.

24.8.15.

Got mail to-day and to my sorrow heard that father had passed away on the 5th July. I am most downhearted, I had 3 stretcher-bearers wounded in the last battle.

25.8.15.

Major Guyon told me he had sent in my name for recommendation to Brigade Headquarters for my work during the last battle so I am keen to know what happens. A Turkish soldier came into our trenches this morning early and surrendered. He proved to be a Greek and came in with no arms.

31.8.15.

Been very quiet in the trenches since the 25th, only a few casualties. The weather was very wet for a few days but it is fine again. The nights are very clear but cold. Another Turk walked in and surrendered this morning. He was a real Turk and seemed very hungry so was given food and cigarettes and seemed very pleased. We have now done 34 days in the trenches and had 2 fights in that time (6th Aug. and 21st Aug.) so that is about a record. However, we are to go back to a shallow Gully to-night where the Munsters are and have our rest. I am very sorry to have to go back because we are very comfortable in the firing line in decent dugouts under decent shade whereas the Gully is shelled daily, which I don't like and has no shade. Each M.O. of my Brigade was asked for a report on the physical and mental condition of each regiment so I sent in a 'Home Truth' one about my regiment, so now I hear we are to get 8 days 'rest' such as it is (the men having to dig trenches each night) then we go to Lemnos for one week's rest which I call scandalous and yet I (of the Officers) have been here the longest with the Regiment now, the others being casualties or gone sick. There is not one here who took part in the battle of Gully Ravine on the 28th June, so I must be lucky to be alive!!!!! I saw Lieut. Bert Mitten on the 21st Aug. (the morning of the battle), he had just landed two weeks before with a Field Ambulance of the 13th Division .The Lancashire Fusiliers relieve us to-night. I have received official intimation to-day that I am to be mentioned in dispatches 'For devotion to duty on every occasion in action, he has been indefatigable and is the most useful and hard-working medical officer one could possibly have.' I am jolly pleased about it but I don't think I have done any more than other M.Os. I received congratulations from Major Bell the Assistant Director of Medical Services out here.[35]

1.9.15.

Came out of the trenches last night at 8 p.m. with Headquarter Company and it was a weird feeling all marching in single file in the dark and bullets flying about, one wondered every minute if one would be hit and we had a sense of security and peace of mind when we got to our rest Gully.[36] We had only one man hit out of a batt. of 1,015 strong which was very lucky. This morning early we had some rain and it was beastly

---

35   Davidson *The Incomparable 29th*, p.75 remarks 'We have all admired, and often spoken about, the good work and earnest devotion of Pirie, and are delighted these are to be recognised, even in this small way.'
36   Behind Hill 28.

cold so this afternoon I set to and made a nice dugout between two rocks and sand bagged it up and put my black waterproof sheet on as a roof so now feel secure from the rain. This morning I went down to the 89th F. Ambulance dressing station to visit Agassiz and Davidson, while there Lt. Wisely, the Lanc. Fus. M.O. was brought in hit through the head. He had taken over from me in the trenches and I had a chat with him yesterday morning, a sniper had got him while he was dressing a wounded man.

2.9.15.

While we were having dinner last night after dark, all of a sudden the Turks shelled the top of the Gully we were in and then a terrific rifle fire began and as bullets were flying in all directions we had to cease dinner and seek cover under the low sand bag walls of the mess and there we were pinned for over an hour, when the fire calmed down we went on with our dinner. We have not been able to find out if the Turks attacked us or what the cause of all the noise was. I heard to-day that Wisely had died, poor fellow.

13.9.15.

Here I am in hospital at Malta! On Saturday 4th September I was hit with shrapnel on the back. I was doing my morning sick when the Turks began to shell a ridge between us and the Brigade Headquarters with a new gun they had brought up in the night. The Turks had evidently seen the Dublins crossing this ridge in large fatigue parties on their way to work on a communication trench in the day time and it was they who drew the fire. The Turks had fired about 20 shrapnels at a party of Dublin Fusiliers and then all of sudden I found myself doubled up and a pain in my back and I knew I was hit. I don't recollect hearing the shell come or feeling being hit, the shell had burst right over us in the dressing station (my own one) and it only hit myself and a sick man who got it in the arm. The remaining four orderlies were not touched although Sergt. Pridham had a shrapnel bullet through the sick reports which he had in his hand. Sergt. Pridham at first thought I was hit in the abdomen and how I wasn't I don't know because I was facing in the direction in which the shell came. Major Guyon, O.C., and Capt. Cripps, the Adj., and Harding the Qrt. Master and Coy. Officers came down when they heard I was hit and said they were sorry to lose me and hoped I would come back to them. I was dressed and walked down to the 89th F. Ambulance Advance dressing station, feeling like an old man as my back was sore and stiff. I found Capt. Fiddes there, had some dinner with him as I had been hit about 10 a.m.[37] Then he walked down to the beach with me (my servant Jackson and Draper an orderly carried my kit) and I had to

---

37   Davidson, *The Incomparable 29th* p.77: 'My friend Pirie, M.O. to the Royals, passed through this in the afternoon, having been wounded in the back while he was holding his Sick Parade – only a "couchy wound," such as the Irish pray to the Virgin Mary to send them at the beginning of a fight, so that they might escape something worse. Pirie walked in with his usual smile, and pleaded with us, before we knew there was anything wrong, "not to make him laugh as it was sore". (To everyone's sorrow, Pirie was afterwards killed in France.)'

rest every now and again as it was rough going. I went in and saw the rest of the officers of the 89th and then had to walk to another beach as their pier of boats had been washed away as the result of a high wind. At the other beach their boats had also been washed away and we were eventually only taken off in stretchers on a barge about 12 midnight and four men stripped carried us out and the water was up to their waists. Then the barge with 9 stretcher cases was towed out to the hospital ship *Valdivia*.[38] It took an hour to reach her as it was rough. I was kept in bed and we lay off Suvla Bay till Monday afternoon, 5th September then we went to Lemnos and took in water. We arrived at Lemnos the same day after a few hours sailing and left there again on the 8th arriving at Malta on Saturday afternoon, 10th, and we were unloaded next day, first into a barge then by motor lorries to hospital. I am in Tigné Military Hospital which in peace time is an Artillery Barracks. We officers are in the officers' mess quarters and are awfully comfortable. Funnily enough I ran across C.P. Joubert who was a doctor on the hospital ship, and then in hospital here I found McCall Smith also an Edinburgh Graduate and to-day Professor Gulland of Edinburgh[39] came in and saw me. We are having great feeds of grapes, peaches, and pears here. Last night I was in great spirits as I was told I was to be sent home next day on a hospital ship but this morning my spirits fell as I was then told the boat was full so I couldn't go but I hope to get off by the next one. I was wounded exactly six months to the day that I embarked. I am in a two bed ward with a Lieut. O'Brien of the Buffs who has a shrapnel bullet in his knee. He is an awfully decent fellow and has spent many years in Rhodesia. I was up yesterday and to-day am going on nicely.

15.9.15.

Yesterday morning after breakfast I was told I was getting home on the *Dover Castle* which is now a hospital ship.[40] Lieut. Russell, A.S.C., Captain Delmege, 21st Lancers and I were taken in a motor ambulance down to the docks and put aboard and we sailed about 2.30 p.m. I was about mad with excitement at the idea of getting home. I got into my clothes to-day for the first time and am going strong. I made a voyage in this boat in April 1909 from the Cape to come home to start medicine and little did I think I would make another voyage on her in my present condition. There are just over 600 cases aboard but most are convalescents. We are to be off loaded at Southampton and are due there to-day week. I found Dr. Donald Watson, a fellow I knew, on the staff aboard.

38   Built as a 7,000 ton passenger ship by the French, she survived the war.
39   Professor G.L. Gulland was an haematologist and would have taught Pirie at Edinburgh.
40   She was sunk by a U-Boat en-route from Malta in May 1917.

18.9.15.

This morning before breakfast Gibraltar loomed in sight and by 8.30 p.m. we were under the shelter of it. It was rather misty which spoiled the view. We off loaded some R.A.M.C. orderlies and then proceeded on our way at 10.30 p.m. There was crowds of shipping at Gib. being inspected by the naval authorities and amongst others a huge steamer full of Italians evidently reservists being taken back. Then as we were going through the Straits we saw another boat full of them.[41] Weather has been very good.

22.9.15.

I am feeling much better and now got my back straight but I find I can't do much with it and I get tired easily. We ran into a fog this morning and had to stop for a bit. We get to Southampton to-morrow and jove, I am most excited about it. Delmege Russell and I have had great fun teasing a fellow Gore of the A.S.C., we pull his leg badly!!!

23.9.15.

When we arrived at Southampton this morning at 11 a.m. the embarkation officer came round and put Russell and me down to go to Osborne, Isle of Wight. It used to be Queen Victoria's but King Edward VII gave it for a Convalescent Home for officers, and it is now called King Edward VII's Home for Convalescent Officers. We were sent over from Southampton by a paddle steamer at 2.5, and took an hour to Cowes and then we were motored up here which stands high above Cowes and we get a lovely view of Hampshire and the Solent. I don't know how long I am to be here but I expect till next week.

26.9.15.

Russell and I walked down to Cowes yesterday, it's a quaint old village with narrow streets. I am to go before the Medical Board to-morrow so I hope they let me away.[42] I have quite enjoyed being here, it is so peaceful and we have lots of croquet and billiards. This a beautiful place with lovely grounds.[43]

29.9.15.

Arrived in Edinburgh at 7.15 a.m.

---

41   Italy had entered the war on the side of the Allies in May 1915.
42   The Medical Board's findings on 27 September, in Pirie's War Office file, were 'That a shrapnel bullet inflicted a small flesh wound about three inches to right of 10th Dorsal Vertebra which is nearly healed.' It expected him to need seven weeks recovery from the date of his wounding. A further Medical Board on 21 October judged him still unfit. He was pronounced fully recovered by a Board on 13 November. (T.N.A. WO339/ 16259).
43   Robert Graves was here in 1917 – see his *Goodbye to All That* pp.306-309.

Part II

**The Western Front Diary
March 1916–July 1917**

Introduction to the Western Front Diary

George Pirie was to see almost all of his service on the Western Front, from December 1915 to his death in July 1917, as Medical Officer to 9th Battalion East Surrey Regiment in 72nd Brigade, 24th Division. He developed a deep affection for the unit and its officers and men.

9th East Surrey had been raised as a 'Kitchener' or 'New Army' battalion in September 1914. Most of the men of the original battalion seem to have been residents of what is now Greater London, and were predominantly working class, from a very wide range of occupations. The first officers were overwhelmingly volunteers of very little military experience – largely upper middle class men who had attended public school and been members of their school or university Officer Training Corps (O.T.C.). By the time the battalion first saw action, perhaps only two of its officers had served as regulars, and both very briefly. Both the C.O. and his second in command, were elderly former militia officers who had seen no active service.

24th Division, only recently arrived from England, was put into an attack on only its second day at the Front, in the Battle of Loos on 26 September 1915.Its losses were catastrophic, with battalions like 9th East Surrey, which started out more than 900 strong, suffering fifty per cent casualties, including more than 160 killed or mortally wounded. To add insult to this terrible injury, the division was accused of 'bolting' and was treated as a failed unit. Ironically, the enemy was more generous: 9th East Surrey's nickname, 'The Gallants', is believed to have arisen from remarks made by German officers after the attack. The divisional commander, a retired Indian Army officer, resigned, to be replaced by Major General J.E. Capper. The division was also corseted with four regular battalions, in exchange for four of its original battalions. 72nd Brigade's commander, Brigadier General B.R. Mitford, kept his place, but he had the C.O. of 9th East Surrey removed and a regular officer of much experience, Lieutenant Colonel H.V.M. de la Fontaine, replaced him.

By the time Pirie arrived with the battalion on 13 December, at Tournehem, near St. Omer it was still traumatised by its experiences at Loos. It was also relatively inexperienced in trench warfare, having served some weeks, only, at St. Eloi, near Ypres, before being withdrawn for a month's rest and training. In early January 1916, 9th East Surrey returned to the Ypres Salient at Hooge. This was a particularly unpleasant spot, full of human remains from intense fighting the previous year and with much of the front line waterlogged. Fortunately casualties were relatively light.

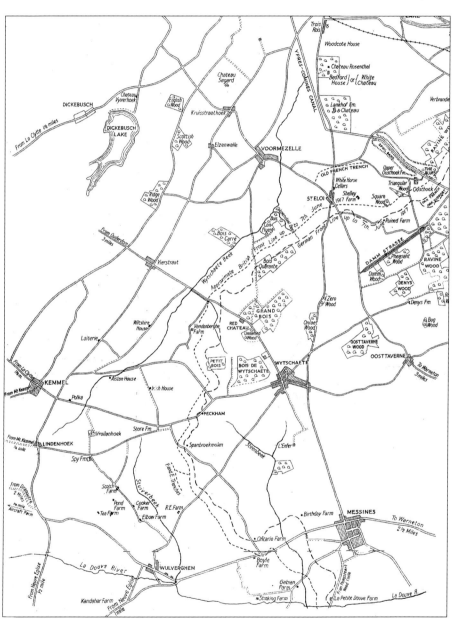

Map 4. Map of south and east of Ypres from Pearse and Sloman,
History of the East Surrey Regiment Vol.II.

Pirie recommenced keeping a diary on 18 March, just as the battalion was moving a little to the south. This was to Wulverghem, in rolling countryside between the British held Kemmel Hill and the German held Messines Ridge. Unlike Hooge much of the sector was not under German observation and it had the reputation of being a quiet one. Moreover, the trenches were a great improvement on those at Hooge, being good and dry. Unfortunately, things at Wulverghem soon went downhill. The aggressive Pomeranian 45th Reserve Division had moved opposite and increasing activity by the British artillery was followed by German retaliation in kind. From their trenches the Germans were firing mortars and rifle grenades – to which the British sought to respond with interest – and by night their snipers and machine guns were very active. Pirie personally experienced the attentions of a sniper during the day. The first six-day tour cost 9th East Surrey five dead and ten wounded. Later, on 24 April, there was an intense German bombardment, to which the British replied the following day. Unfortunately, Second Lieutenant Howell, 9th East Surrey, was killed by 'friendly fire', a piece of British shell falling short. Pirie records his funeral as a particularly sad occasion.

The Germans, meanwhile, were preparing a poison gas attack to accompany a large-scale raid to disrupt British tunnelling. This took place at night on 30 April. 1st North Staffordshire was holding 72nd Brigade's front line, but a working party from 9th East Surrey helped repulse the raiders. The Germans had some success, but their casualties were not light.

The Germans tried gas once more on 17 June and again there was a working party of 9th East Surrey present. Although there were a number of British casualties, including from gas, the Germans were unable to advance, as the gas blew back towards them and the British were on the alert. This was followed by a heavy German bombardment, reckoned the heaviest yet suffered by the battalion, on 23 June. A number of men were buried and had to be dug out, with Lieutenant Youngman being shot dead whilst on such a rescue mission.

The division was relieved on 30 June. The battalion had sustained nearly two hundred killed and wounded in three months at Wulverghem, although the trenches were much preferred to those of St. Eloi and Hooge. After a week's rest, the division moved to take over the line near Ploegsteert, a little way south. This was a quiet sector, as both sides considered they had nothing to gain from belligerence there. However, the division was soon to be moved on. It had a brief rest and training from 19 July, soon to be followed by a move to the Somme.

The great Anglo-French offensive on the Somme had commenced on 1 July. Kitchener had wished to avoid committing the British Army to major operations until his new divisions were all fully trained and equipped. Yet he had been forced to recognise with operations during 1915, including Loos, and again now with the Somme, that Britain had to become heavily engaged in order to prop up its Allies. Moreover, with much of their country, and particularly its industrial base in enemy hands, there was no way that the French were prepared to accept a purely defensive strategy. 1 July, however, had seen catastrophic losses for little gain over much of the British Somme

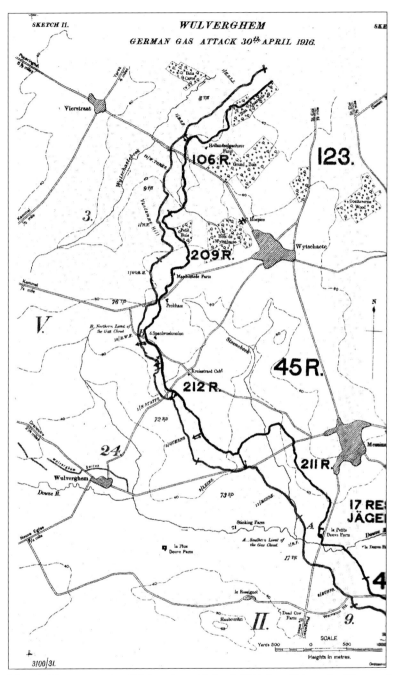

Map 5. The gas attack at Wulverghem 30 April 1916 from Edmonds, *History of the Great War Military Operations France and Belgium 1916 Vol.I*

front. But the attacks were continued, with the need to put as much pressure as possible on the Germans to reduce their assaults on the French at Verdun. On 14 July, with concentrated artillery support on a narrow front, the British infantry was able to seize much of the German Second Position. The Germans, however, responded with heavy shelling and counterattacks almost regardless of cost.

Pirie decided he was quite looking forward to the Somme on 22 July, but added 'I just hope the Regt. does well but I hate to think of the casualties' and 'I just hope I manage to do my part properly and not be a funk.'

Figure 9. The 'Prussian hyena' at St. Quentin - a French cartoon of the German occupation of northeast France. (Author's collection)

9th East Surrey arrived at the Sandpits near Albert, immediately behind the Somme Front, on 1 August. The next few weeks saw a series of piecemeal British attacks, intended to secure better positions for a large-scale attack. The losses, however, were heavy.

By this time, Pirie felt very much one of the family as far as the battalion was concerned and a good number of the officers were his friends. Since Loos casualties had been relatively light (during the first seven months of 1916 the battalion had less than ninety fatalities.) Those officers who had survived that disaster were now better trained and experienced and had been joined by new officers, many of whom had frontline experience in the ranks. The officers seem to have been a properly coherent and professional group, who also enjoyed each other's company. Lieutenant Colonel de la Fontaine was a highly respected and popular commander with all ranks, and relations between officers and men appear to have been good.

Sadly, the battalion was to be torn apart on the Somme. On 10 August it took over reserve trenches at Maricourt. Three days later two companies took over front line trenches near Arrow Head Copse, facing the village of Guillemont. This stood, in ruins, on high ground and the Germans had turned it into a fortress with underground shelters and tunnels. Guillemont was held by a most determined garrison – the Württemberg 27th Division. It had already been repeatedly attacked, without success. On 16 August, two companies of 9th East Surrey were to attack in conjunction with 3rd Division on the right. The Surreys were to seize a strongpoint and a section of sunken road in front of the village.

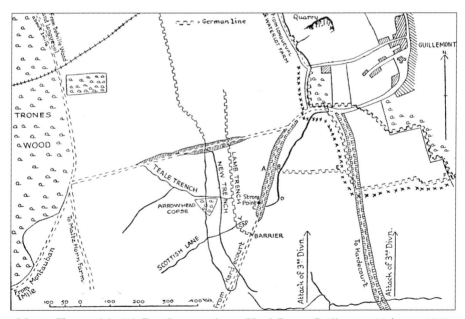

Map 6. The attack by 9th East Surrey at Arrow Head Copse, Guillemont, 16 August 1916 from Pearse and Sloman, *History of the East Surrey Regiment Vol.II.*

Unfortunately, the artillery support proved quite inadequate and 3rd Division's attack on the right failed. Pirie's friend, Captain Vaughan, led the Surreys into a hurricane of fire. Only two officers and one or two N.C.Os. managed to reach the enemy trench and were never seen again. Vaughan and five more of the nine officers in the attack died and one was wounded and nearly three-quarters of their 240 men were casualties. Pirie found that day 'Worse than Hell.' He was devastated by the loss of so many friends and comrades, and was reduced to tears when his corporal was mortally wounded whilst evacuating the last stretcher cases.

The battalion was in support two days later when two of 24th Division's brigade made an all-out attack on Guillemont. Unfortunately the attack met with only very partial success, capturing the western outskirts of the village only, at heavy cost. The defenders were now relieved by 111th Division, in which was serving Ernst Jünger, future author of *The Storm of Steel*, probably the most famous German account from the war. Guillemont only finally fell in early September.

24th Division was pleased to be relieved, commencing 22 August. However, it soon found that it was to be sent back to the line: this time to Delville Wood.

Delville Wood, after weeks of fighting, more resembled a wrecked abattoir than a wood, with the trees no longer providing any cover, whilst the ground was littered with decomposing bodies. By the time 9th East Surrey arrived to take over trenches at the eastern edge of the wood on 1 September, its fighting strength was reduced to around 325 all ranks. The Germans having failed to retake the wood with infantry on 31 August, and with two brigades of 24th Division counterattacking on 1 September, now determined to make it untenable for the British with intense artillery fire. Nevertheless, 9th East Surrey, in spite of its weakness, was ordered to support an attack by 7th Division, on its right on 3 September. However, with artillery support ineffective and the brigade attack on the right unsuccessful, the Surrey attacks failed. Lieutenant Colonel de la Fontaine was very badly wounded leading an attack. The battalion also took very heavy casualties in the German bombardment. Soon there were only nine officers and 100 to 150 men left.

Brigadier General Mitford appreciated the desperate situation, and had no confidence in the division on the right. He had sent reinforcements from 1st North Staffordshire, but by 4 September he realised they and 9th East Surrey were both exhausted. Unfortunately, orders came early in the morning cancelling the relief for that night .The four remaining 9th East Surrey officers in the front line sought immediate relief in view of the exhausted state of the men. (As did the Germans of IR 88 opposite, the following day.) Lieutenant Clark, the Adjutant and now the senior surviving officer, urged them to hold on until relief was due. They answered they would hold on to the last for the sake of the regiment and the remains of the battalion held on, under continued heavy fire and taking further casualties, until relieved on 5 September. Pirie left graphic accounts of the terrible conditions in Delville Wood and the arrangements to evacuate the wounded, not only in his diary, but also in his only surviving letter (see Appendix III.) The battalion had lost more than one hundred and sixty men killed in action or died of wounds, on the Somme, with many more wounded.

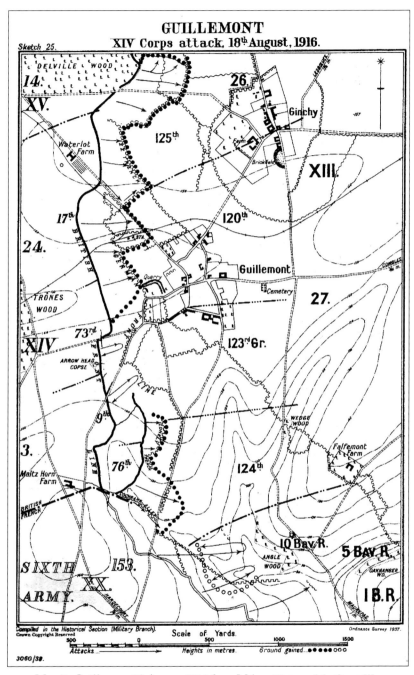

Map 7. Guillemont 18 August 1916 from Miles, *History of the Great War Military Operations France and Belgium 1916 Vol.II.*

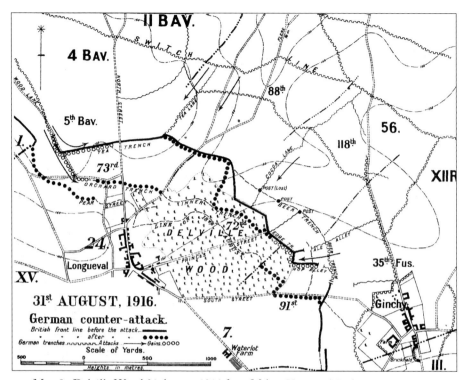

Map 8. Delville Wood 31 August 1916 from Miles, *History of the Great War Military Operations France and Belgium 1916 Vol.II.*

In the following weeks, the survivors were given some rest and recreation, with Pirie getting to Paris, and the battalion was gradually rebuilt with drafts and returned wounded. Lieutenant Colonel H.S. Tew, another regular East Surrey officer, took over command. Pirie, who had enjoyed excellent relations with de la Fontaine, found him 'very quiet and dry, but nice'. Among those now arriving was Second Lieutenant R.C. Sherriff, later to win celebrity as the author of the most famous play set in the war, *Journey's End.*

After training and integrating its new officers and men, 24th Division was sent to Vimy Ridge. This had seen heavy fighting previously between the French and Germans and was to be captured finally by the Canadians in spring 1917. Here the Division faced the Saxon 23rd Reserve Division, also engaged in recovering from fighting on the Somme. Initially things were quiet, but aggression from 24th Division's combative 2nd Leinster led to a matching response from the Germans.[1] After being in

---

1   For the 'Live and Let Live' system, graduated retaliation, etc. see Ashworth, *Trench Warfare 1914-18.*

reserve and furnishing working parties, 9th East Surrey went into the front line on 10 October, by which time things were quite lively.

However, 9th East Surrey's tour on Vimy Ridge was to be a short one, with a move in late October to the Hulluch-Loos sector. Pirie was sorry to leave Vimy Ridge, referring on 17 October to it as 'a nice piece of the line, good dugouts and such like'.

At Hulluch, where it had come to grief the year before, 24th Division was facing 8th Division from Prussian Saxony and Thuringia, again attempting to recover from the Somme.

Shortly before the move, Tew had a serious accident and was succeeded in command by T.H.S. Swanton as C.O. Swanton was another East Surrey regular officer, although at 28 much younger and less experienced than his predecessors. Unfortunately he proved to be a martinet who soon made himself widely unpopular within his battalion.

The Loos-Hulluch sector was a mining area, with the front line running through villages and across slagheaps. Pirie was not impressed, referring to it on 25 October as 'a wretched looking country, flat and nothing but dirty coal mining villages with crowds of huge slag heaps and chimney stacks'. The opposing trenches were often too close together to be attacked by hostile artillery, but the area was notorious for trench mortars. The condition of the trenches was often bad and the men were heavily occupied, when in reserve, with working parties and there was mutual aggression with the Germans. However, the battalion spent an enjoyable Christmas out of the line, with good food, drink and entertainment. The Germans opened the New Year with a heavy bombardment. The weather was now to turn extremely cold for many weeks, which was, at least some relief from mud.

Pirie's relationship with Swanton by now had deteriorated to the point where Pirie, who was very fond of the battalion, saw no alternative to a transfer out of it. In early January, he left for 74th Field Ambulance, one of three with the Division. Here his role was undemanding as, with little fighting taking place, the unit was running what was effectively a convalescent home. However, Pirie kept in touch with 9th East Surrey, which he was soon missing. During these first months of 1917 24th Division and the Germans of 8th Division repeatedly raided each other, with mixed success. 9th East Surrey launched a successful raid on 25 January, for which Pirie's successor, Lieutenant Hartley, gained an M.C. Pirie, always happy to tend the wounded in the front line and have some excitement, led the retrieval of casualties from another, unsuccessful, raid in mid-February by another battalion.

Pirie was by now wanting to go back to 9th East Surrey, even at the cost of putting up with Swanton, who agreed to support his return. Brigadier General Mitford also agreed to give his support when Pirie approached him. In early March, Lieutenant Colonel de la Fontaine, recovered from his Somme wounds, resumed command of 9th East Surrey, which, after a period of rest, had been transferred to the Cité Calonne sector, a little south of Loos, facing Liévin. Pirie now lobbied Mitford and de la Fontaine, who both thought highly of him, to be transferred back to the battalion, and was successful. The hard winter weather continued with snow into April.

The Battle of Arras commenced on 9 April with a great success as the Canadians captured Vimy Ridge. This forced the Germans to give up much of the Lens salient and on 13 April patrols from 24th Division found the Germans had abandoned their front line. 9th East Surrey followed up the German withdrawal, nearly to Liévin, but within a few days it was back to static trench warfare. 24th Division was relieved on 19 April and the battalion moved to Coyecques, near St. Omer for rest and training. It had a relatively quiet time since the bloodletting on the Somme, with fatalities from October to April amounting to just sixty.

Following the catastrophic failure of General Nivelle's grand French offensive in April on the Chemin des Dames, and with Russia tottering and the Americans only just entering the war, the British Army would have to take the full burden of engaging the Germans on the Western Front. 24th Division returned to Ypres in mid-May. On 14 May, 9th East Surrey was back in the Hooge trenches. Final preparations were underway for a grand assault on the Messines Ridge as the first stage of a great offensive in Flanders. This, it was hoped, would clear the Ypres Salient and the Belgian coast, with its bases for U-boats, which threatened to starve out Britain. On 7 June the Battle of Messines commenced with the explosion of nineteen huge mines and a crushing artillery bombardment. So successful was the attack that 72nd Brigade, in reserve, was not required. However, the battalion now took heavy losses from shellfire during the rest of June, in holding the captured ground, thirty nine of them when a tunnel collapsed. The battalion was then given rest at Coulomby for the first half of July.

By this time, Pirie was planning to leave the battalion again. Major Swanton was making life unpleasant for him and he applied for a medical administrative post. He then left for his last leave from 5 July. He was not keen to return. This may have been because of Swanton, or a strong premonition of his own death. Letters written to his family by friends after his death refer to him having been deeply affected by the breaking off of his engagement, although it is not clear when this was, and also that when he said goodbye to a Dr. Jardine, he said that he would never come back again. (see Appendix IV).

9th East Surrey returned to the front line at Ypres on 21/22 July near Klein Zillebeke, as preparations continued for a resumption of the offensive at the end of the month. Pirie wrote the last entry in his diary on 21 July, including 'I am not looking forward to going into the line to-morrow night. It's a beast of an area'. Typically, his last words were concern for a comrade 'I hear Lt. Royal has been invalided out of the army with consumption. Jolly rotten luck.'

On 22 July, Battalion H.Q. and two companies, going via Hill 60, took over positions around the village of Zwarteleen, whilst the other two companies occupied a front line trench, Image Crescent, a little to the north of Klein Zillebeke. The German artillery was very active and, during the course of three days, three officers (Pirie, Lieutenant Picton and Second Lieutenant Bogue) and three O.Rs. died, with others wounded. Pirie was killed by a shell that hit his dugout on 24 July 1917, his 29th birthday. The regimental history later paid tribute to him – 'In the death of Captain

Pirie the Battalion sustained a severe loss. He had been attached to it almost continuously as Medical Officer since its early days and had done gallant service with it in the Battles of the Somme, 1916.'[2]

Following Pirie's death 9th East Surrey took heavy losses in August, fighting in terrible conditions at the start of the Third Ypres campaign. Lieutenant Colonel de la Fontaine was killed, whilst Sherriff was sent home wounded. After a quiet autumn and winter the battalion was caught by the great German offensive of March 1918. The battalion's remnants, led by Pirie's friend Clark, made a famous last stand on 26 March. The unit was then reconstituted and two more of Pirie's friends, Hilton and Whiteman, were still serving with it in the final advance to victory and the Armistice. The battalion had sustained losses of more than 800 killed in action or died of wounds in a little over three years of active service.

With respect to illustrations, a number have been used from German sources. By the time that Pirie arrived in France, ownership of a private camera was a court martial offence in the B.E.F. Photographs were taken by official photographers, but none of those at I.W.M. are identified as of 9th East Surrey before Armistice Day. The Germans, however, took a more relaxed attitude and many of their soldiers took cameras into the front line. Rather than generic images from the British side, I have chosen to use more specific, and unfamiliar, German ones. Most are unofficial and a number feature the men and the kinds of weapons opposing 9th East Surrey.

2   Pearse and Sloman, *History of the East Surrey Regiment* Vol.II, p.75.

1

Facing Messines Ridge, March–July 1916

18.3.16

It's to be good-bye to Wipers [Ypres] to-morrow and we shall all be glad to see the last of the Menin Gate, Lille Gate, the cellars, etc. We are to be released by the Canadian Mounted Rifles to-morrow and we go down South to Wulverghem, Belgium. We are at present in the Zillebeke Dugouts and the N. Staffs. are in Hooge. Things have been extraordinarily quiet, can't understand it. I hope it's quiet for us moving out to-morrow night.

20.3.16

Yesterday was another quiet day. I rode back to B Camp with Whiteman[1], our R.T.O. [Regimental Transport Officer] It was a most beautiful night, moonlight, to come through Wipers and not a shot was fired, although the Bn. had five crumps just over their heads as they got on to the train at the Asylum; these were our parting gifts from Fritz. We are to rest all to-day and then march off to-morrow afternoon southwards for about ten miles, so it isn't far. Lt. Spofforth had a most violent attack of neuralgia to-day and it was a job to stop it. To-day I ran across Segt. [Sergeant] Petit, 2nd Royal Fus. He used to be our M.[achine] Gun Segt.[2] and is now with the 1st Bn. He gave me a lot of news of the 2nd Bn. Segt. White, my bearer segt. is now bombing segt. Pte. Hayes, a bearer, was drowned in the Blizzard in Gallipoli.

---

1   Lieutenant, later Captain Eric Whiteman, was a friend of Pirie's. Born in 1893, a clerk educated at St. Paul's School, he served in the ranks of the Surrey Yeomanry before being commissioned and joining 9th East Surrey as Transport Officer in 1915. In the desperate fighting of March 1918, he won an M.C., was wounded and took command of the remains of the battalion. Thereafter he gave up Transport for a rifle company. He was still serving with the battalion in November 1918, when wounded again.
2   At Gallipoli.

TRANSPORT

Lieut. E.L.Whiteman.

Figure 10. A caricature of Lieutenant (later Captain) E.L. Whiteman by Private Edward Cole, early 1917. (© Surrey History Centre)

22.3.16

We left B Camp at 3.30 p.m. yesterday and marched via Reninghelst, Westoutre, crossing the border into France just outside W. We rested on the frontier and then continued through Berthen, a very pretty village and reached our billeting area, just outside Flêtre, about 10 p.m. in the dark. We are in France now and it's wonderful to see how much more prosperous it is in comparison with Belgium. The farm buildings are better and the people much more hospitable. I don't like or trust the Belgians. The Regt. is billeted in a number of farms which makes them rather spread out, but we are very comfortable and the peace of the place is too wonderful for words as we are well back in Corps Reserve. We are to be here 5 days and then move up to the trenches.

24.3.16

Been into Bailleul to-day or Boolool, as the men call it. It's a fine town with decent shops and a good Exped.[itionary] Force Canteen. We have been having poor weather, much rain, and to-day it's been snowing.

25.3.16

To-day the O.C. [Lieutenant Colonel H.V.M. de la Fontaine] and all the Coy. O.Cs. and M.G.Os. [Machine Gun Officers] etc. went up to see the trenches we are to take over and have just brought back good accounts of very good trenches and a quiet area which will be a paradise after Hooge and Y. Wood.

26.3.16

I went with Sergt. Ericson[3] of the signallers and Corp. Adams of the snipers to see our area to-day. I rode into Berthen and there picked up a motor lorry and we went via Westoutre, Locre to Dranoutre, and from there walked up to the Bn. H.Q. It is most interesting to see the civilians farming up to within a mile from the firing line. They don't seem to mind the shells. As we left Dranoutre we walked along the road and passed Antiaircraft Farm[4] and then swung round to our right through the hamlet of Lindenhoek and over the Hog's Back which is a ridge and from it you look right over to Messines, the scene of the London Scottish charge in Dec.1914. It is all in ruins now and stands on a high ridge which overlooks the Hog's Back so we were only allowed to go over it in 3's in case of drawing shell fire. We went down the other side and left the pavé road and went across a field to Tea Farm down in the hollow and in it were billeted a lot of Canadians. We had to go to Cooker Farm which was to be our future Bn. H.Q., so after being shown the way we cut across the open fields as it is only about 800 yds. from Tea Farm. Just as we reached Cooker Farm a sniper had a jolly good shot at us but missed us so we went in behind a hedge and walked along it, and reached Cooker safely. I wanted to go up and have a look at the trenches but the Doctor, Capt. Hayward, M.C. of the Canadian Army Medical Corps said 'he didn't hold with going up to the trenches'. Anyhow I got all the information I wanted and we three trekked back at 3.30 p.m., and caught our lorry back. To-morrow we are to be up at 5.30 a.m. to march off at 7.30 so I'm off to bed as I'm tired.

27.3.16

Here we are at Tea Farm. We were sad to leave our comfy billets this morning especially as it was raining buckets, but when duty calls you can but go and look cheerful! We were supposed to be inspected by Sir Douglas Haig, our Commander in Chief, en-route, but the weather was too bad so he didn't turn out. We marched via St. Jans, Capelle, then up an appalling hill and then on to Dranoutre, in pouring rain and thence to Antiaircraft Farm, and not a man fell out which is good for wet weather and full marching. The March was about 10 miles and we reached Aircraft Farm at

---

3   Sergeant, later Second Lieutenant Eric Ericson, Military Medal (M.M.) (for Wulverghem) was commissioned in 1918 and killed serving with 7th Royal Sussex.

4   I believe this was very likely the same farm as that usually called Aircraft Farm, due south of Mount Kemmel.

11 a.m. and relieved the Canadians there. The D.Coy. (Lt. Vaughan O.C.)[5] went on to Kandahar Farm, which is on the Neuve Eglise-Wulverghem Road, and the remainder stayed at Aircraft Farm till it was dark because you daren't cross the Hog's Back in large nos. by day to Tea Farm. After dark C. & B. Coy's (O.C.s Lieut. Yalden and Captain Anslow[6] respectively) remained at Aircraft Farm while we, H. Quarters and A. Coy. (Capt. O'Connor, M.C.[7] as O.C.) moved to Tea Farm, which for a marvel has never been shelled and yet is very close to the lines.

Figure 11.
Captain J.L. Vaughan.
(© Surrey History Centre,
ref. ESR/25/LYNDH)

5   John Lyndhurst Vaughan, later Captain, was another friend of Pirie's. Born in 1896, he was commissioned immediately from Harrow and its O.T.C. and won an M.C. at Hooge. He was killed in August 1916, leading the attack on Guillemont.
6   Lieutenant, later Captain Thomas Yalden, unusually, was a former regular N.C.O., having been a Squadron Sergeant Major in the 6th Dragoons in 1914. He had joined 9th East Surrey in November 1915 and left through wounds in April 1916. Robert Anslow, born 1876, was an accountant. Enlisting in September 1914, he was commissioned two months later and served with 9th East Surrey at Loos.
7   D. Patrick O'Connor, born 1891, the son of a doctor, served briefly as a regular officer in the East Surrey Regiment after Sandhurst, before resigning for financial reasons in 1912. He then worked as a tea planter and in the Fiji Police. Commissioned again in October 1914, he was wounded and won an M.C. at Loos with 9th East Surrey.

28.3.16

The Regt. moved into the trenches last night and I have my dressing station in a small house about 80 yds. from Cooker Farm, and as it stands on a bend of the road it's called Elbow Farm. I can't say I liked Tea Farm. It was too confined and each time our guns fired the windows rattled and made an awful noise, so I wasn't sorry to leave it. L. Cpl. Allam[8] and I came over after tea in daylight (and took care to avoid the sniper!!) to take over and let Hayward away in daylight as these open fields at night are rotten for stray bullets as we are only about 1000 yds. from the firing line, in a valley with the trenches on the Wulverghem Ridge above us.

This is a wonderful dressing station. It has a kitchen and two living rooms (the cellar has fallen in) and it has two attached outside rooms, one we use as a drying room and the other as a store room. The walls of my room are covered with pictures of all descriptions. *La Vie Parisienne* cuttings predominate and they are very *Parisienne*!!!![9] I sleep in the room in which we do all our dressings so I'm easily wakened up if any wounded come in. The only thing I don't like about this place is if a shell lands on it and we [are] inside we shall all go up in the air as we have no sandbags etc. for protection. Then we have a swine of a sniper who shoots at us along the road between here and H.Q., and he is some shot as he has picked off ten Canadians at 1200 yds. He shoots down our valley from a place on the ridge called Span Broukmoulen [Spanbroekmolen], hence he is called Mr. S.B. Moulen, and don't we hate him! Corp. Halliday, my bearer Corp.[10] and I went up to have a look at the trenches this morning, and they are extraordinarily good with fine dugouts and you don't need to creep about like Y. Wood.[11] You get a fine view of Messines and Wytschaete from our line. They stand on a ridge about 1000 yds.from us, and there is a valley between.

3.4.16

We came out of the trenches last night but I must say it isn't just as quiet a piece of the line as it's made out to be as we had over thirty casualties including Lt. Yalden, O.C. C. Coy., wounded in the toe and Lt. Schooling died of an abdominal wound received while building up the parapet. He had just joined up and had done two days in the trenches.[12] We are back in Dranoutre village at present and are very comfortable; two Coys. are in tents and the others are billeted in farms. I am to get my leave soon. Jove, I will be glad, as I'm sick of the sight of wounded and sick, and I need a change badly. I have been out here four months now. I landed in France on the 1st. Dec., 1915.

8   Bertram Allam, later Corporal, was awarded an M.M. for the Somme and survived the war.
9   The magazine was famous for its risqué illustrations.
10   Francis Halliday was to win an M.M. at Wulverghem. Pirie was to be particularly distressed by his death in August 1916.
11   Near Hooge.
12   Schooling had been repeatedly warned of the danger by an N.C.O.

5.4.16

I'm off on leave to-night. How excited I am! It's a most wonderful feeling at getting away from all the noise and strafe and to feel you won't see any poor fellows wounded and in agony. Oh! it makes one long for peace at almost any cost, but on thinking, we must thrash the Hun very severely first. The weather has been wonderful lately, real springlike. My leave is from the 6th to the 15th Ap[ril]. I get a day extra travelling allowance for going to Scotland.

7.4.16

Here I am in Auld Reekie [Edinburgh] and it is fine and peaceful. I left on Thurs. night late and rode in with Baker, my groom, who brought my horse out again. I was in a dickens of a funk as my relief didn't turn up and it was from the 72nd F. Amb. so I got Lt. Rudke in the 73rd F. Amb. at Dranoutre to do my morning sick till someone came. I decided to get away before I was stopped. When I got to the 72nd in Bailleul I found the A.D.M.S. had forgotten about sending the message to them and they had only received word twenty minutes before and it was then twelve midnight. I slept at the 72nd that night and was up at 4.30 a.m. to catch my train at 5.30. We got to Boulogne at 10.30 and we sailed at 12.30; reached Folkestone at 2 p.m. and we were in London by 4.30 p.m. By luck I met Lt. Stump, K.O.S.Bs. and Capt. Anderson R.A.M.C., so we three went and had a good dinner at the Piccadilly and then I caught my train at 11.30 to Edinburgh and arrived at Waverley at 8 a.m. this morning.

16.4.16

Here I am back again with the Regt. and oh so fed up at having to come back to all this strafe and noise!! When we got to Victoria station next morning [I met?] Jack Fenton and he told me the 3rd and 4th Armies had been recalled from leave and all leave was stopped so I thanked my stars I had got mine in safety! We hadn't such a good crossing as when we came over; however I wasn't sick!! I met Cherry Monro, Capt. R.A.M.C. and M.O. to the 3rd Rifle Brigade on his way back from leave so we travelled up together last night as far as Bailleul and there I got off and had an awful strafe for a bed and it ended in getting passes from the Town Major before I got one. To-day I got a lift out on a motor ambulance to the Transport field; had lunch with Whiteman and then came up so far as behind the Hog's Back by cart and walked the rest to Kandahar [Farm] as the H.Q. was there, owing to Tea Farm being shelled to pieces during my leave. The [8th] West Kents lost twenty-four men in it due to being shelled. I walked along the light railway and then across the fields to Kandahar and found C. and D. Coys and H.Q. there. Goodness, how fed up I am at coming back to this life; how I hate the Boche!! The other two Coys. A. & B. are at Aircraft Farm so I'll have to walk over there daily to see the sick.

Thursday, 20.4.16

The Regt. came into the trenches to-night and I am back in Elbow Farm. Allam, Rand and I used to walk over to see A. & B. Coys. sick daily but I hated it as we invariably got shelled which was 'No Bon' at all!!! I don't want to be 'Napooed'!!! We had to change our course along the light railway and over the Hog's Back via Sapper Farm as both routes were peppered. We also got shelled at Kandahar but no damage was done.

Easter Sunday 23.4.16

I was up round the trenches on Friday morning; all was quiet except for a Woolly bear,[13] Shrapnel and a turnip grenade[14] which burst outside Vaughan's dugout while I was having a cup of tea with him. The last two afternoons have been very noisy, Fritz threw over *Minenwerfers*, trench mortars, whizz bangs, rifle grenades and H.E.,[15] but we had very, very few casualties and when he had finished we lambasted him badly and shut him up. The last three days I have had an awful throat, raw and beastly sore, and my voice had gone to a whisper. It's rotten being ill here. I hear leave opens again on the 25th so Tetley and O'Connor, who were about to go on leave to be invested with their M.Cs. will go now. O'Connor got his at Loos and Tetley at Hooge quite recently.[16] This afternoon we had a little fun over-head about tea-time. A Hun aeroplane was flying over our lines and our guns were very busy firing at it when suddenly it began to descend and we thought it was coming down in our area when we noticed it was after a captive [i.e. tethered] observation balloon we had up; however it turned just as it about reached it and was flying rather low when, to our delight, we noticed it was being hotly pursued by two of our planes and they were machine-gunning it, and we expected to see it come down any moment as it was wobbling a bit, but it got away safely, much to our disgust. It was afterwards reported that it had been damaged about the tail. Early this morning the Huns began to shell Tea Farm and set it alight so now it is out of action for good. We landed in Gallipoli to-day a year ago.

13 A type of shell, producing a lot of smoke.
14 A small mortar bomb.
15 A Minenwerfer was a rifled mortar, although here Pirie means its missile; whizz bangs were high velocity field gun shells; and H.E. were high explosive shells.
16 Lieutenant later Captain Gerald Tetley, born 1887, was a barrister. He enlisted in September 1914, was commissioned and joined 9th East Surrey in October 1915. He won his M.C. for rescuing wounded and buried men when a trench was blown in. R.C. Sherriff was impressed by his courage and energy, but amused by his eccentricities and colourful language.

Figure 12. A Gothic style tribute to the *Minenwerfer* troops by Lothar Blankenburg.
(A.R. Lucas collection)

Figure 13.
A caricature of Captain G.S.
Tetley, by Private Edward
Cole, early 1917.
(© Surrey History Centre)

Easter Monday, 24.4.16

Still have an awful throat, voice a whisper; had to give up smoking so I am very fed up.[17] All was quiet to-day till about tea time when Fritz became very active and began to shell heavily especially at R.E. Farm behind our line where B. Coy. is. One fine incident happened during the shelling. The wire was cut between H.Q. & B. Coy. so Signaller Joe Gibbs went out in lee of his dug-out and began to signal the message by flags. He was blown down once by a shell but got up again and began again when he was wounded by a shell bursting in front of him.[18] In spite of all that shelling we only had five wounded and none bad. Lieuts. Amies and O'Brien joined us yesterday from home.

MEDICAL

Capt.   Perry
R.A.M.C. attached.

Figure 14.
A caricature of Captain
G.S. Perry (sic.), by Private
Edward Cole, early 1917.
(© Surrey History Centre)

17   Cole's caricature indicates he was a heavy smoker!
18   Private R.J. Gibbs was subsequently awarded an M.M. for this action.

Tues.25.4.16

I was up earlier to-day as I was to have gone up to R.E. Farm to inspect a draft at 9.30 a.m. but Fritz got busy on the dugouts below the farm so I couldn't get up. They were shelling with heavy H.E.s and all the men had to clear from the dugouts as four of them were knocked in and one of the huge trees alongside the dugouts was felled like a match. We only had one casualty and that was L/Cpl. Ogden, B.Coy. He was a jolly good fellow. He was B. Coy's. sick corporal. This afternoon we gave the Hun trenches an awful shelling but during it a most sad incident occurred. Lieut. W.S. Howell, our bombing officer was killed, sad to say by a piece of our own shell which must have blown back. We are all most cut up about it. To think that poor old Gladys, as we used to call him, has crossed the bar; this is a sad war! Well, he was a hot tempered, but brave man, always looked after his men well and did his work well, and a great loss to us as a friend. It's been a gorgeous spring day, birds singing, heard the cuckoo to-day for the first time this spring. Oh, it sounded so peaceful! The trees are coming into leaf rapidly too and soon the country will be smiling but it's been a sad day with Howell being called away.[19]

Wed.26.4.16

To-day has been very quiet. We gave Fritz such a hammering yesterday that he seems tamed for once. This afternoon at 6.30 p.m., in broad day-light two Huns were seen to dash through a gap in their wire across no-man's land and through our wire into the Bull Ring trench on our immediate left, occupied by the Yorks. We soon found out that they were deserters and were very dejected and had had enough of the war. We first heard that they said 'that the Germans were to make a gas attack on us to-morrow morning at 3-5 a.m.' We knew of course that they had gas cylinders in their trenches because we broke one the other afternoon while shelling them and saw four Huns bolt over the parados to get away from it.[20] Needless to say we were in great excitement as we are to be relieved to-night by the [1st] N. Staffs. and I don't fancy a gas attack, but being warned we would give them a hot reception. However, later we got news to say 'it was a mistake', the Huns were to have attacked this morning at 3.5 a.m. if the wind had been favourable but, thank goodness, it wasn't. I wish they had deserted to us because our C.O. talks German very well. We go back to Dranoutre village for six days. It's been a glorious day.

Thurs. 28.4.16 [27.4.16.]

Here we are back in Dranoutre and thoroughly enjoying it too. It's a wonderful relief to get away from the constant strain and noise. I don't know how mankind can adapt himself to it so wonderfully. Capt. Waugh was very late in relieving me. He only came

---

19   Second Lieutenant Wilfred Howell, born 1890, served pre-war in the ranks of the prestigious territorial unit the Honourable Artillery Company. He had been with 9th East Surrey at Loos.

20   German sources confirm five men were lightly gassed in such an incident on 20 April.

up at 11.15 p.m. I was fed up as it's so nonsensical not to relieve in daylight when you can. Allam walked back with me and at first there were a good few stray bullets about so we stepped out till we got on to the Hog's Back road beyond Tea Farm. We then crossed the H. Back and through the tiny village of Lindenhoek to Antiaircraft Farm where Baker, my groom, was waiting with my horse. Allam and I shared the ride home and it was a beautiful night. We got to our billets about 12.15 a.m., very tired and tumbled into bed and didn't I sleep! A spring bed and sheets; oh, what luxury after not having had your clothes off for about ten days!!!

To-day I have been getting the camp cleaned up as the Staffs left it filthy. It's been very hot to-day but I like it. This afternoon at 5.45 we all fell in for Howell's funeral. He was given full military honours. It was most sad. I had a lump in my throat .The saddest part of all was when the firing party filed away and his bombers who had acted as the choir had marched off. Watmore,[21] Howell's servant walked up to the grave, paused and saluted and I thought I saw tears in his eyes. What a ghastly waste of life this war is and what sadness it brings to thousands.[22]

Friday, 29.4.16 [28.4.16.]

Been a glorious day, very warm. Had quite a busy morning. A man, Budgeon, who had an old wound, I had up before the A.D.M.S. to get him off trench warfare and managed to get him marked 'permanent base'. Then I inspected a draft of twenty-four N.C.Os. They were a good draft. This afternoon Vaughan and I rode into Bailleul and had tea at the tea place in the Rue du Collège and found the South Africans had just arrived on this front. A lot they are too. Then we did some shopping and Vaughan was in great form teasing the French girls. He speaks good French.

Monday, 1st May, 1916

Two nights ago I had dinner with Lt. Whiteman, our Transport Officer and then we two walked over to Vaughan's billet and had a sing song. Jove, there was some noise on! I went off to bed at 11 o'clock quite peacefully when all of a sudden I was wakened up at 12.45 a.m. with all our guns going, also the Hun's so I at once suspected an attack and no sooner had I lit my candle than a message came saying 'Stand to'. The Huns were making an attack with gas on the Staffs. and Queen's. I hadn't heard that two Huns had given themselves up at the Bull Ring on the 29th afternoon and warned us of the attack. We were all up in no time and Allam got his things packed and we moved up to the Hog's Back [spread out] in Artillery formation along the road in case we were shelled. We started off about 2 a.m. and just before they had been trying to shell the road quite near the village but missed and luckily stopped when we came along. It was just grey day-light when we moved up and lined the hedges and trenches

21   Private Albert Watmore.
22   Howell is buried in Dranoutre Military Cemetery.

along the Hog's Back and there we stayed till 7.30 a.m. in case we were needed but luckily were not. The Huns, it appeared, had loosened off two lots of gas and attacked the Staffs. in trench D. Four got in but were bombed out at once. They also let off gas right and left of our line and a lot of casualties occurred from gas, due, I suppose, to slowness in getting the [gas] helmets on. We got back about 8.30 to the village, very tired and sleepy, but I had a clean up and offered to give a hand at the F. Amb. as they were very busy. It was ghastly to see the men gassed. The distress is awful! They didn't need me as they could manage, so I went and had a sleep. Last night I had dinner with D. Coy., Vaughan's Coy., the other officers there were Charles Cuthbert, O'Brien and Denny,[23] all very nice fellows. I came home early as I wanted an early bed. I just had my boots, puttees and socks off at 10.30 when I had the order to 'Stand to' as the Huns were supposed to be gassing the Staffs and Queen's again. Oh! I was fed up as I had visions of a second night with no sleep, so I warned Allam and lay down till we got the order to move, and fell asleep, when the Adj., Clark,[24] came in about 12 and said 'Stand Down and go to bed', but I was too sleepy to undress so just slept as I was till two and then got out of my clothes and slept heartily till 7 when I got up for sick parade at 7.30 a.m., and it was a job to get up!! Been a beautiful day to-day. We go up to the trenches to-morrow night, but where I am to have my dressing station I don't know as poor Elbow Farm was severely shelled and burnt to the ground during the attack. Luckily Capt. Waugh and his staff got out in time, but lost all his own kit and medical panniers. I'm glad I missed that titbit!!!! I am going to have dinner with C. Coy. to-night, Hilton's Coy.,[25] his officers are Amies, Rivington and Jamieson. I had to send Capt. Anslow, A. Coy. to Hosp. to-day. He was knocked down by a motor cycle and got a severe shaking. I sent away Wills the other day with nerves. He and Anslow are survivors of Loos.[26]

23 These three were all Second Lieutenants who had joined since Loos. Cuthbert, born 1892, was educated in Edinburgh. He had served four years as a Territorial in the Royal Scots and re-enlisted in August 1914, in the London Scottish. Francis O'Brien, born 1894 and a business student, enlisted in September 1914. Cuthbert and O'Brien both died in August 1916, whilst J.L.B. Denny was wounded then. Pirie soon after wrote a letter to Denny – see Appendix III.

24 Lieutenant later Lieutenant Colonel Charles Clark, born 1879, was a regular soldier who had enlisted in the ranks of the East Surrey Regiment in 1896 and fought in the Boer War. Company Sergeant Major (C.S.M.) in 1914, he was commissioned in January 1916. He served with 9th East Surrey until March 1918, when he was wounded and captured, leading the battalion's last stand, for which he added a D.S.O. to his M.C. for the Somme. He was greatly respected by, and popular with, all ranks of the battalion, including Pirie and Sherriff.

25 Captain, later Major Charles 'Baby' Hilton was one of Pirie's closest friends in the battalion. Born 1890, he was a produce broker who had enlisted pre-war in the middle class Territorial Civil Service Rifles. He was commissioned in December 1915 and joined 9th East Surrey immediately. His nickname derived from his youthful appearance. Sherriff greatly respected Hilton as a soldier, but objected to his relentless sarcasm towards people he disliked.

26 Anslow also developed neurasthenia following his accident, but returned in November 1916.

Figure 15.
A caricature of Lieutenant (later Lieutenant Colonel) C.A. Clark by Private Edward Cole, early 1917. (© Surrey History Centre)

ADJUTANT

Capt. C.A.Clark. M.C.

C. COMPANY

Capt. C.H.Hilton.

Figure 16.
A caricature of Captain (later Major) C. Hilton by Private Edward Cole, early 1917. (© Surrey History Centre)

Wed.3.5.16

Here we are back in the trenches again. Corp. Halliday and I walked up, leaving Dranoutre at 6.45 p.m., and got up to Elbow Farm just an hour after in just good enough light to be able to see and not be molested by the sniper at S.B. Moulen!! The poor old dressing station is quite changed. The three rooms where self and staff used to live are absolutely burnt out but the drying-room and store-room are untouched. There are crowds of crump holes (shell holes) all round the dressing station, and the trees on the edge of the pond alongside the D.S. [Dressing Station] are knocked down. The young shoots and leaves on the trees are all shrivelled up with the gas. One of the barns at Cooker Farm has had a direct hit too and many holes all round the H.Q. dug-outs. The cat we used to have at the D.R. [D.S.?] died of gas-poisoning. Allam, Rand and I are now living in the dug-out at the end of the D.R. [D.S.?], and the R.A.M.C. bearers in the drying room, and Corp. Halliday and bearers in the store room. On my way up last night I ran across W.H.D. Smith who qualified with me. He is with 7th F. Amb. The night before we came up I had dinner with Hilton's Coy. and had a great time. At 7 a.m. this morning Corp. Halliday and I went up to the trenches on our tour of inspection and all was very quiet and in spite of the raid on the trenches they are very little touched. We had a thunder storm yesterday which cooled the air a lot. On our way back from the trenches this morning the sniper had two very close shots at us just outside the dressing-station. He has been very active of late and this fellow, like the original S.B. Moulen, the Jäger,[27] is a wonderful shot. I am sitting writing outside the dug-out and it's a beautiful day. There is a weird mixture of sounds in the air just now – some denote war and others spring and peace, all jumbled up together! The guns are booming away in the distance, down the line a sniper's shot occasionally rings out and the zip of bullet as it flies past overhead, then overhead an aeroplane is humming, and the Hun shells bursting round it (making puffs of smoke round it), the frogs are croaking away in the pond alongside us and with that the birds are singing beautifully and most peaceful of all the cuckoo joins in every now and again. What a world we live in!!!

Thurs. 4.5.16

Last night the wind veered round to the East-a gas wind, so the 'gas alert' was ordered. Sentries [were] doubled in the trenches and everyone had to wear his gas helmet rolled up, ready to pull down at a moment's notice.[28] I don't suppose anyone ever worried to study the wind till this war, except sailors and airmen. Now we watch it most carefully!! On account of the 'gas alert' we had to have sentries on all night at the dressing-station so as to waken the others in case of gas. I took the first watch from 10 to 12 and it was most weird to watch the Star Shells go up and light up the whole country

---

27 A German rifleman.
28 At this time British troops were still reliant on hoods for gas protection – the box respirator came later.

around, the trees and ruined houses being silhouetted so clearly. Corp. Halliday and Rand took the next two watches 12-2, 2-4. Fortunately no gas attack came off. To-day has been sultry and hot but luckily quiet. We had four bombers wounded this afternoon.

Friday 5.5.16.

Corp. Halliday and I went round the trenches early this morning and got back at 8.30. All was quiet up there. It has been a quiet day except that the Huns shelled our H.Q. at Cooker's Farm and chased everyone out but no damage to dugouts or house was done. They also shelled Dranoutre and knocked down two houses and now the inhabitants are all packing up and clearing out so I'm wondering if we will go back there for our next rest.

Saturday 6.5.16

Yesterday started very peacefully but after lunch it suddenly changed for very much the worse. The Germans began by shelling Battle Axe Farm in front of Cooker Farm, and set it alight. It didn't take long to be burnt down as it was thatched with straw. While it was burning they changed on to Cooker's Farm and the H.Q. Dugouts, chased every one out of them and then just missed the Adjutant's dug-out three times and had a direct hit on Cooker's Farm. Then they turned on to Elbow Farm which is our dressing station and badly wounded Corp. Kelly in the face while he was in the trench between the D.S. and H.Q. It then became so hot for us that we had to run for our lives. That run I shall never forget, Allam and I left the dugout last and ran across the field behind the D.S. like demons and just as I got to the other side of it I heard three big shells coming so I dived under a hedge with my steel helmet on and fully expected to be done in but they luckily burst to the left and behind me. I was going to run on towards the Hog's Back but Halliday called us to the left and as I was running towards him three more came along so down I flopped then up again I got and we all ran to Ring Redoubt. When I got there I was absolutely done, no breath left, and legs aching. I have never run like that before. It was lucky we didn't run straight on as that area was all shelled. After a bit they stopped so we began to go back but they began again so we had to return to the Ring Redoubt. Then they shelled Wytschaete Rd. and Burnt Farm and we got the benefit of the splinters in the redoubt. We eventually got back about 6.30 and found no direct hits, but shells had dropped all round. I hope we don't have any more affairs like that, they are 'no bon'!!!

Sunday 7.5.16

Just at lunch time they began to drop some whizz-bang shells very close to the D. Station and as we thought this was the prelude to the heavies coming I made all clear out, except Allam and self, but luckily they turned to Burnt Farm and R.E. Farm and then all was quiet, which we were thankful for.

Figure 17. A German howitzer - a 10.5 cm ('4.2 inch') *leichte Feldhaubitze* of an unidentified unit. (© Andrew Lucas)

Tuesday 9.5.16

Monday was a very quiet day but no doubt due to the wet and windy weather. We came out last night and were lucky to have very few stray bullets about as we crossed the fields, although just before we left they turned a machine gun on to the field just behind the D. Station. We are back on a farm above Antiaircraft Farm on Mount Kemmel. It is extremely pretty up here, might be in the Highlands, all the trees are out and looking beautiful. The only thing is we are rather crushed as the O.C., Lt. Col. de la Fontaine,[29] Major Shirvell, 2nd in command, self and Lt. Clark, the Adjutant, all sleep in the same room; still we can't grumble.

Wed. 10.5.16.

This afternoon Lt. Rivington and I rode into Bailleul for the afternoon, did some shopping, had tea at the Rue du Collège and came out just before sunset.

29   Henry de la Fontaine had been born in India in 1872, the son of a colonel. Commissioned in 1893 he served two years in the Boer war, being wounded. He graduated from the Staff College in 1909 and initially served as a staff officer in 1914, before taking command of 9th East Surrey after Loos. He was popular with, and respected by, all ranks.

Monday 15.5.16

Here we are back again at Elbow Farm. The dressing station is in the same place and hasn't been shelled while the N. Staffs. occupied it. The last couple of days at Wood Farm were very wet, rain galore. We had one gas alert while back but it lasted only about half-a-day, and the wind veered round to our way again.[30] Last night Major Shirvell and I left Wood Farm at 7.30 p.m. and picked up Allam at Antiaircraft Farm which is at the bottom of the hill and walked up together via the Hog's Back and Tea Farm (now in hopeless ruins) to Elbow Farm in the dusk, just in time to escape the stray bullets. We weren't any too late in getting up before they played a machine gun on the sand bags outside my dug-out and on the field behind the dressing station. That gun must be at Spanbroekmolen. This morning Corp. Halliday and I were up at 6.15 a.m. and round the trenches and it did rain too. We went all around and I had some tea with Vaughan and Cuthbert in their dug-out. That was all I had for breakfast as I was feeling very livery.

Wed. 17.5.16.

Yesterday was a quiet day except for a few whizz-bangs round Cooker Farm about 8. a.m. This morning Corp. and I were up at 6 o'clock. Croxford made us some tea before we went off and we went round the trenches. All was peaceful up there till we were on our way back to R.E. Farm, but whilst we were coming back across an open field from the supports to the farm we heard a big shell coming and got down, lucky for us it was an H.E. shrapnel and burst about seventy yards from us so we made a run for the farm and three more came bursting on Shell Farm which is just up the road from R.E. Farm. After the fourth they stopped and carried on with whizz-bangs down towards Cooker Farm so then I managed to get the draft of twenty men inspected and got back to my breakfast of grape nuts and bacon at 8.30. It's been a beautiful day and we have had it peaceful. The shelling was all behind the supports and R.E. Farm.

Thurs. 18.5.16.

The sick are coming down at dusk now as the sniper was a nuisance and as the days are lengthening fast it's eight, as a rule, before they get down to the dressing-station. Last night the wind swung round to the N.E. which is a favourable direction for the Huns' gas so 'Gas Alert' was ordered and all sentries doubled and gas helmets worn rolled on the forehead. At the dressing station L/Cpl. Allam took the first watch from 10-12, and then the four R.A.M.C. bearers the remaining times. Just after, Allam came off, the sentry came in to warn us 'the gas hooters were going down the line', and we could hear them quite plainly. However, it didn't come our way so we went to sleep again. We were up early this morning to inspect a draft at R.E. Farm and got

---

30   I.e. it was now blowing towards the German lines, which would prevent German use of gas.

back without being molested. It's been a glorious day again. Yesterday and this after-noon we got busy on filling sand bags and put up a good buttress at the end wall of the dug-out. Jove, but it was 'some' work. The night before last, it being a very bright moonlight night, the Huns had planes up and dropped three bombs on Dranoutre but no damage was done. We go back to-morrow night, a day earlier than usual, to Dranoutre this time.

Friday 19.5.16.

This morning Halliday and I were up at 6 a.m., and went round the trenches, all was peaceful. After breakfast I had a sleep as I have not been sleeping well up here. Just as I was nicely asleep a few shells began to drop near us and woke me up but we didn't move out. Then they put one at the very gable of the dressing station so we all cleared up the trench to Cooker Farm and while we were in it a few more fell near the dressing station so we followed the trench past Cooker's and got away back towards Pond Farm and then Cooker's got shelled and everyone had to flee but not in time for the sentry to [avoid] be[ing] killed, the shell falling practically on top of him. He was horribly mutilated. While we were away they intermittently shelled Cooker's, Bus Farm and the D. Station and we had to stay away from 10 a.m. till 2.30 p.m. I had lunch when we got back and then went down to the D.S. and jove it had six very close ones around it. The Hun will never be satisfied till it is levelled. I just hope we are not in it at the time! The rest of the day has been peaceful and what a beautiful day it has been! Bus Farm was shelled again this evening. The N. Staffs relieve us to-night, a day earlier than usual, and we are glad. To be shelled with 5.9s is very trying.

Saturday 20.5.16.

We are back in Dranoutre again. We came out last night, there were very few strays about, luckily. Allam and I walked to Antiaircraft Farm and there I picked up my horse and Allam got a ride home in a mess cart. It was a beautiful night. It's been very hot to-day but I like it.

Sunday 21.5.16.

Went to church this morning in the Y.M.C.A. [Young Men's Christian Association] tent and took Communion and enjoyed it. This afternoon I walked over to Locre, a village about a mile from here to see Capt. W.H.D. Smith who is in the 7th F. Amb. 3rd Division. I found him alright and we had a long chat about our Varsity [university] days during tea time. Then we went to look for the S. African Heavy Artillery H.Q. and found them in Locre but Capt. Mullans, their doctor, had just gone out. He is an O.A.[31] and I badly wanted to see him. Then I saw some Lothian & Border Horse

---

31   An Old Andrean – a former pupil of Pirie's school, St. Andrew's College in South Africa.

about and recognised Ainsley Thin, whom I found out had just got his commission three weeks before and also that Charlie Brownlee was with the squadron. He had been brought from Salonika to join them. This squadron had come from Arras. I must try and see Charlie.

Monday 22.5.16.

This afternoon Capt. Barker, our Bde. T.O. [Transport Officer], Lt. Whiteman and I were to have gone into Bailleul to dinner but it rained and prevented us so we went to our Bde. Cinema in Dranoutre instead and saw Charlie Chaplin who was very funny. Then we had dinner at our Regt. H.Q. mess.

Tues. 23.5.16.

This afternoon I rode into Bailleul alone to do some shopping. I met Lt. Seddle, A.S.C., who supplies us with our grub and we two had tea at the Café in Rue du Collège. He was going on leave and was full of beans. I do envy him!! I came out in time to go to the Cinema at 6.30. A whole crowd of us went together, Lt. O'Brien, Morse, Metcalfe, Rivers, Pullan and self. After it I dined at D. Coy's mess (Vaughan's) and had a great dinner.

Thursday 25.5.16.

Last night the Regt. came in again. It was a late relief but Allam and I came up just at dusk and found the Dressing Station had been badly shelled and had some direct hits on it. One had burst at the door on the step but had scarcely touched Corp. Halliday's dug-out. The end gable has been knocked down more or less and a few holes all round the place. It's really a beastly unhealthy place now, so Capt. Waugh and I have decided on a new place and if only we can get the labour and material we shall soon put up new dugouts but labour is very short, at present all the men are needed to work on the front line trenches. Corp. and I were up at 6 a.m. and went round the trenches which had been left very dirty by the N. Staffs. It was quiet up there except for a few rifle grenades coming over, but one round of the Stokes trench mortar was sent over in return which quietened matters. On our way back it began to pour so we ran for it as we had no coats. It's rainy, dull and windy to-day, but we don't mind. It keeps Fritz quiet and his observation balloons can't go up, they always spell trouble!!!!

Satur. 27.5.16.

Yesterday was quiet on the whole. To-day Corp. and I went up to the trenches early and went all along the trenches and then had breakfast with Lt. Denny, D. Coy. and after it Vaughan came in and we had a chat and while with them C. Coy. had a few big shells behind their trenches but at once got retaliation [arranged] and fair strafed the Huns with whizz-bangs and shrapnel so they shut up. One fell between their front line and supports so we went along to see if there were any people hit but none were.

I then had lunch with C. Coy., Lts. Rivington, Amies, Ball and Jamieson. Amies, as usual, kept us in laughter, the other three are quiet fellows. We then went along to B. Coy. to see Lt. Field who was on the extreme left of our line as he was not feeling too fit. He has been temporarily attached to us from the 12th Sherwood's (Pioneers). Our 2nd in Command, Major H. Shirvell, is also from them.[32] We left B. Coy. and came home all along the front line, past C. Coy. H.Q., and down Cheshire Lane and down over the fields, not being molested at all. We got back about 4 p.m. and at 6 the trench mortars were registering on the Hun trenches so Fritz promptly retaliated with rifle grenades and unluckily one landed in one of the bays of C. Coy's trench killing one man and wounding three. Then we retaliated with rifle grenades and trench mortars and the Hun shut up. C.S.M. Flatt was in the bay at the time and wasn't touched luckily.

Sunday 28.5.16.

Just when I was thinking of getting up at 8 a.m. this morning we were shelled with 5.9s, one falling just in front of the dressing station so we all hopped up and collected in the dug-out and waited developments but only four fell and one was a dud. We think they stopped because of three of our aeroplanes [which] came overhead and I suppose the Hun battery was afraid of being spotted. We were glad as we expected it hot when they began. However we did our usual morning ablutions and had breakfast and then I went up to H.Q. at Cooker's Farm and spent the day there but no more shelling took place. While I was up there in the morning five of our big battle aeroplanes flew away over our lines towards Lille, evidently on a bombing raid. They were heavily shelled but just flew on. We watched one of our newest fast 'planes overtake a Hun plane the other day and expected it to bring it down any moment but it overtook it too late over the Hun lines and had to come back.

Monday 29.5.16.

We were up early to the trenches to-day and I first went to see Field in the right Company and then went all along the front line to C. Coy where I had breakfast with Amies and Ball and then went down Cheshire Lane and up Kingsway to D. Coy, spent the morning and afternoon and lunched with them and came home by Kingsway again at 4 p.m. We have been getting a lot of new officers lately so are nearly up to strength again. Last night after dinner I went up to R.E. Farm to see how our new D.S. was getting on and found it was being made all wrong and had to change the site of it. Crowds of Hun balloons have been up each day of late so we haven't shown a sign of movement outside the D.S.

---

32   This unit of 24th Division is probably best known for its production of the trench newspaper *The Wipers Times* and its various continuations, 1916-18.

Wed.31.5.16.

Yesterday began with being very wet and windy but it cleared up in the afternoon and about 3 p.m. a proper strafe took place in the trenches. It was no doubt the result of our trench mortars which had been registering at 3.30 a.m., just after 'Stand down'. The Huns sent over rifle grenades, 'Turnips' and 'Minnies' (i.e. Minenwerfers), H.E. shells, shrapnel and whizz bangs. The thirteen Minnies all fell behind B. Coy. the Right Company in D.3 and D.4., and at the barricade at the junction of Stretcher Lane and the Wytschaete Road and made huge holes. This strafe went on from about 3 to 6 p.m., and they also whizz-banged and shrapnelled R.E. Farm, the end of Durham Rd. communication trench and behind the support line. Needless to say we retaliated heavily, sending over rifle grenades, Stokes trench mortars, toffee apples (i.e. sixty pounder trench mortars) and whizz bangs and we kept it up after they stopped and so had the last word. The most wonderful thing of all was we hadn't a man hit. The Artillery F.O.O. [Forward Observation Officer] was slightly wounded. About 3.30 p.m. Major Shirvell and I had been watching the strafe from the visual signalling post in the trench at H.Q. (Cooker's Farm) and he had just remarked 'they may retaliate on us'. We had just moved to the dug-outs when we heard a crump coming and I bobbed into the signal dug-out, it bursting outside and I could feel the blast and earth falling about so we all cleared out up the trench at the double and they sent five more H.E. near Cooker's Farm. However they stopped, so we returned and had tea about which time (5.30 p.m.) Clark, our Adj. and a new officer Capt. Ferrers came back from the trenches. All the noise had died down when about 8 p.m. Ferrers and self were up the trench from H.Q. looking at a place where a screen was to be put up at, when all of a sudden four H.E. Shrapnel came along and burst near us and we down in the bottom of the trench without our steel helmets. It <u>was</u> a close business. I won't go anywhere without my helmet again. We were relieved last night. Capt. Waugh R.A.M.C. has gone sick so Capt. Hogg from the 72nd F. Amb. is with the N. Staffs. till he comes back. We are back at Wood Farm but instead of all four of us sleeping in the one room we each have a tent which is in the lee of a hedge and under the trees so as not to be spotted by planes. We mess in the room and the O.C. and Adj. work in it. A & B Coys. are at Antiaircraft Farm just down the Hill from us, C. Coy. further back in two farms and D. Coy. at Kandahar Farm.

Thurs. 1.6.16.

Last night after dinner I went down to A. Coy to play bridge. Lt. Gold and I played Capts. O'Connor and Buttle and took 1400 points off them. We two held all the cards. This afternoon I rode down to Locre to Capt. Rupert Mullins an O.A., but he was out. Just before dinner to-night at 7.30 p.m. we noticed one of [our] captive observation balloons over Neuve Eglise had broken away from its moorings and was gaily floating with the wind towards the Huns. They were firing heavily at it but as it was gradually rising they couldn't hit it. We just hope the observer managed to descend safely in his parachute. The last we saw of it was it floating very high away behind the Hun trenches.

Satur. 3.6.16.

Yesterday the guns around us were firing all day and all night a terrific fight was going on up the line. We heard this morning that the Huns had taken Sanctuary and Zouave Woods in the Ypres Salient which is just to the right of where we used to be at Hooge. It's quiet to-day. Had a nice ride into Dranoutre and a warm bath this afternoon. I hear the West Kents are to have a raid on the Hun trenches to-night. I hope it's successful.

Sunday 4.6.16.

The raid did come off last night. All the troops at Wood and Antiaircraft farms were taken into the trenches just between the two farms in case they were shelled. It was a very fine night and we were all in our places by 12 midnight and on the stroke of 12.30 a.m. our guns opened up a terrific fire on the Hun trenches just to the right of our line for forty minutes. It was something terrific, the shelling, everything from 12 inch to 18 pounders was turned on, the flashes lit up the country and trees and houses were silhouetted whilst the very lights (starlights) were extinguished by the bursting of the shells. About two minutes after our guns opened fire a red and green rocket went up which we took to be the German S.O.S. signal as their artillery at once opened with great vigour and then the noise was terrific. It was a wonderful sight and would have made a good film. It is the first night bombardment I have seen. We got to bed at 3 a.m. in daylight and the birds were singing most beautifully. We heard afterwards the raid was a failure. The torpedoes to blow up the barbed wire with didn't go off and so the men didn't get through the wire and had to bomb from no man's land. Luckily all got back including casualties, one officer killed and eight men wounded. The N. Staffs made a feint on the Kents' left by blowing up some land mines. We were all disappointed it was a failure. We have a Lt. Col. Bridge, H.L.I. [Highland Light Infantry], attached to us for a week for instruction on trench warfare. He is most interesting as he was in Gallipoli after I left and was present at both the evacuations and the Blizzard.

Monday 5.6.16.

I sent in my application for a regular commission in the R.A.M.C. to-day per the A.D.M.S. and got a very good recommendation from both Major Guyon (my late O.C.) and my present one, Lt.Col. de la Fontaine. We go into the trenches to-night again.

Tues. 6.6.16.

Last night Col. Bridge, self and Allam came up, just at dusk, to relieve; all was quiet. This morning early Corp. Halliday (who, by the way, has been awarded the Military Medal for bravery at Hooge) and I went up to the trenches. We went up via R.E. Farm, Durham Road to A. Coy. on the right, all along their trenches D3 and D4 and then down Stretcher Lane to C. Coy. and had breakfast with Hilton and Amies which consisted of porridge, kippers, bread, butter marmalade and tea – not bad for the trenches! Then I went down Cheshire Lane and along the support line and up the Kingsway to D. Coy. Vaughan's line D5 and D6. He has just won an M.C. for work at Hooge. I had a long talk with Cuthbert who had just come back from leave and very fed up. Then we went back by D5, D4, D3 trenches to A. Coy's H.Q. and had lunch with Lts. Gold and Ingrams – cold meat, apricots, toasted cheese and coffee, not to be grumbled at, is it? About 4 o'clock we came back via Durham Rd. and R.E. Farm. It poured all morning and my Burberry was soaked but the rain didn't come through. C. Coy's mess-dugout leaked like a sieve, nevertheless we enjoyed our breakfast.

Thurs. 8.6.16.

Yesterday was fairly quiet on the whole. While I was up at H.Q. a few shells fell behind it and we had visions of all having to clear out but they stopped. This morning Corp. [Halliday] and I were up at 7 a.m. and had breakfast and then went to the trenches via R.E. Farm and Durham Road and all along A. Coy. and then to C. Coy. where I sat and talked to Amies for a time and then went down Cheshire Lane and up Kingsway to D. Coy. I had lunch with them and came back about 3 o'clock. While I was up there General Capper,[33] our Divisional General, came round. It was quite quiet up there. Col. Bridge left us yesterday.

Friday 9.6.16.

Been wet this morning, with a high wind – but peaceful. About 12 o'clock I went up to R.E. Farm from the dressing station, Elbow Farm, to have lunch with B. Coy. Officers, Capt. Buttle, Lts. Lawrence, Castle and Royal.[34] I also went to see the new dressing station and it's going on very well. We shall soon be in it. Then I had tea with the Specialists-Officers, Lt. Youngman, the bomber, Pullan the machine gunner, and

---

33   Major General John Capper, born 1861, was the son of a civil servant in India. He served in India and South Africa with the Royal Engineers before commanding the Army School of Ballooning. He took command of 24th Division after Loos, where his brother, also a general, had been killed. His own son died on the Somme. Capper was later Director General of the Tank Corps and knighted. He was an energetic commander who also enjoyed preaching aggression and hatred of the enemy to his men.

34   James Royal was born in 1892. A clerk, he enlisted in January 1915 and was commissioned and joined 9th East Surrey in December. He left through sickness in May 1917, but returned in 1918 and became Brigade Intelligence Officer.

Hadenham the sniper, at their dug-out just below R.E. Farm. They have a gramophone with a fine selection of records.

Saturday 10.6.16.

This morning early Corp. and I went round the trenches and had breakfast with Vaughan and Morphy and then lunch at C. Coy. with Hilton, Amies and Picton[35] and came down Cheshire Lane to R.E. Farm to see about moving up to R.E. Farm in order to have the dug-out at Elbow Farm dismantled. It is all arranged that we moved up to-night and temporarily have the D. station in the farm itself and I am to sleep and mess with the Company Officers. The hole (9 ft. deep) is all ready dug with a drain and doorway to sink the French steel – Corp. Halliday and six men are to dismantle the dugout to-night at Elbow Farm.

Sunday 11.6.16.

We all trekked up to R.E. Farm last night at dusk, i.e. self, Corp. Halliday, the two medical orderlies, Allam and Rand, and my servant Croxford. The dug-out at the dressing station took the whole night to dismantle but is all ready to be brought up for [to-] night. Yesterday afternoon, after I had got back, a dickens of a strafe began, Minnies, rifle grenades and shell and shrapnel came over and we duly replied with force. We were lucky with casualties – two men wounded, including our best boxer Whitlock, and Lt. Ball, A. Coy., but he was only slightly hit on the forehead and is remaining at duty. For a wonder R.E., Cooker's and Elbow Farms weren't shelled.

Monday 12.6.16.

Went up to the trenches after breakfast via Durham Road. It was very wet and muddy. This morning Lts. Urban and Matheson were slightly wounded but Matheson had a lucky escape, the bullet went clean through his steel helmet but missed his head and only made a small slit over the bottom of his neck, and Urban was hit with a splinter on his nose. I had lunch with Vaughan and Co. and then came back. Pullan and I played Buttle and Metcalfe at bridge and took 1400 off them.

Tues. 13.6.16.

The last few days the guns have been very busy up Ypres way and we hear the Canadians have retaken most of the ground. The other morning the whole earth shook and we knew it was a mine going up. We since heard it was up the line on the Vierstraate-Wyschaete Road. Been very wet to-day again. We had word to take cover at 4 p.m.

---

35   James Picton was born 1893 and joined the Inns of Court O.T.C. in October 1914. Like Pirie, he joined 9th East Surrey in December 1915 and like him was killed in July 1917. He won an M.C. for the rescue of men in a tunnel collapse.

to-day as our 9.2 guns were to shell the Muskrat Mound in front of us which is in the Hun trenches and made of concrete. We shelled it for two hours and of course they replied shelling behind R.E. Farm. Our Adjutant, Lt. Clark was coming up while it was on and a shell landed right in front of him and for a marvel neither he nor the orderly was touched. The temporary M.O. of the N. Staffs., Capt. Hogg, relieved me early, so Pullan, Metcalfe and I left R.E. Farm at 8 p.m. in daylight and just as we got to Daylight Corner they began to shell Bus Farm so we took a short cut across fields to Antiaircraft Farm and we got home at nine just in time to miss a regular deluge.

Wed. 14.6.16.

Had a great sleep last night. It is fine to get one's clothes off after eight days!! We had the misfortune to have Lt. Amies and Sgt. Lines wounded by the same bullet and each through an arm. It was a stray bullet at Wulverghem Church. It is a wretched place for stray and machine gun bullets.

Thurs. 15.6.16.

I was invited to A. Coy. to dinner last night and before it Lt. Ball and I went to the Cinema which was very good indeed, then had dinner which was a most wonderful spread. Those present were Lt. Gold, O.C. A., Lts. Urban, Haines (a new arrival), Matheson, Ball and self. Last night the clock was put on an hour, 'Daylight Saving Bill' so we were done out of an hour's sleep last night. I received intimation from the A.D.M.S. to-day saying 'my application for a regular commission had gone on to the Surgeon General' so it looks hopeful. To-day is still very cold but luckily not wet. I rode into Bailleul this afternoon to do some shopping and had my first strawberries this season at the tea-rooms in Rue du Collège. My mare 'Corsets' was in great form and went very well, other days she's inclined to be lazy.

Friday 16.6.16.

We had a great rag at C. Coy's billet last night. I went down to D. Coy. after dinner and we then all went across to C. Coy. and dragged 'Buggie' Picton out of bed and Cuthbert douced him with tomato sauce!!! To-day I have been instructing all the officers' servants in first aid and bandaging. To-night I am to dine with B. Coy. The wind is N.E. so 'gas alert' is on.

Satur. 17.6.16.

We had a most wonderful dinner at B. Coy. last night. Those present were Capt. Buttle, Lts. Ingrams, Royal, Castle and Lawrence, while Capt. Barker, Lt. Rivington and self were guests. I left them at 11 p.m. and was just undressing when heavy artillery fire opened, so I hesitated about undressing further, as I had visions of a 'Stand to', wind being N.E. However I got into bed and fell asleep, only to be wakened at 10 to 1 by an orderly 'Stand to'. I was fed up as the guns were very busy and we were told the Huns had let off gas on our trenches so we expected to have to go up and reinforce. However I saw my staff all fixed up and told Allam to call me if we did move up and I got under the blankets with my clothes on and fell asleep to be wakened at 6.30 a.m. by Vaughan speaking to the O.C. next door so we had been saved moving up. We had two working parties of seventy-five men and two officers each working on the right and left of R.E. Farm. Vaughan and Morphy were in charge of the Right party and Schofield and Jamieson with the left. The gas was let off about 12 a.m. and they luckily got their helmets on in time and we only had one man gassed but Jamieson and about ten men were wounded by shell fire. Jamieson had his arm fractured. There were two waves of gas but they did not attack at all but shelled heavily behind R.E. Farm. The N. Staffs. who were in the trenches lost 134 men gassed which is very heavy. A very unfortunate incident took place this morning. Morton, one of my bearers, who was in all the gas came back with the others, went to sleep having hung his tunic on a nail above his head and while he was asleep it must have fallen down over his face as he woke up feeling very sick as he had been inhaling the gas from his saturated tunic for some time, so I had to send him to Hospital. He is a great loss to me. A lot of us went to the cinema to-night which was very good.

Monday 19.6.16.

Yesterday we got orders to move up and relieve the Staffs. It was bad luck on us as we had done eight days up – i.e. two day longer up the last time and we were only to have five days rest in Dranoutre when were expecting eight. Still, as the Staffs. had had such a rotten time up with this last gas attack we couldn't do otherwise than relieve them. I finished my course of instruction to the [officers'] servants yesterday. Allam and I left Dranoutre at 7 p.m. and got up here without adventure at 8.15 and so let Capt. Hogg R.A.M.C. away in daylight. When we got up here the wind was N. to N.E. which is the gas wind so we got our [gas] helmets on the new method, pinned on our chests under the tunic ready to be put on at a moment's notice. B. Coy. are at R.E. Farm this time, Lt. Gold, O.C., so I am messing with them. The Company came much later than we did and it was towards 2 a.m. before we went to bed. We hadn't been asleep more than an hour when we were suddenly wakened by the sentry: 'Gas hooters have gone, sir!' Allam and I got up at once and put on our helmets with terrific speed and came out of the dugout expecting to see the gas coming but when we got outside we were told 'it was a false alarm; the hooter was away up the line on our left', so we took our helmets off and we were glad. After the alarm we went to bed again and slept till 10 o'clock, then Allam and I went round the trenches, all was quiet up there but very dirty. Our light guns shelled the Huns while we were up there and about 3 o'clock they retaliated with crumps and shrapnel on R.E. Farm and the dug-outs below. We were lucky to only have two men hit. They kept it up for some time too. I hate these shells.

Satur. 24.6.16.

The previous days have been more or less quiet until yesterday and it turned out to be 'Hell'. I got up about 8 a.m., had breakfast and was just coming through the yard at R.E. from our mess when I heard an H.E. shrapnel shell coming so I ran out of the yard and it burst on Shell Farm behind R.E. Farm. They sent a few more on to it and then lengthened on to R.E. and one burst in our Regt. Sgt. Major's room, and killed him at once. He is a great loss as he was a very good fellow. His servant had just left the room when it happened, so poor R.S.M. [Regimental Sergeant Major] Ladd has gone west. They stopped shelling us shortly after that but our whizz bang batteries kept it up all day and then at about 5 a.m [p.m.] they sent over two Minnies. We didn't go up to the trenches after all. Then about 8 p.m. the real strafe began. It was wet and misty and they sent over Minnies and H.E. on our front line, also on R.E. Farm. It was absolute inferno and the ground fair rattled. This went on till about 10 o'clock and then the whole night through every now and again they would send over Minnies. These beastly Minnies bashed our parapets badly and buried a lot of men who came down very shaken with shell shock, some raving mad and had to be lashed to the stretcher. It was pitiful to see them. We had remarkably few wounded almost all shell shock. One very sad incident was Lt. Youngman, M. Cross being killed while digging out buried men. He had got two out of three unearthed when he was shot through the head. His death was met in a manner typical of him, absolutely fearless he was. He's a very good bombing officer gone.[36] He succeeded poor Howell. Spurling succeeds Youngman. We were up all night attending to casualties and to add to it, it was a filthy wet night and mud galore but we got all the cases away by about 6.30 a.m. to-day. Then I had breakfast at 7 and to bed at 7.15 and slept pretty well till 2 o'clock, only our guns woke me up every now and again. They have been very active to-day, they make one's head feel dull and heavy. I hear the breaches in the trenches have all been built up again which is jolly good work as the bombardment was awful. Some of the men who were partly buried came down with the yarn 'that in the badly wrecked part of the trench two Hun officers came over and began to dig them out and at first they didn't notice they were Germans till they spoke amongst themselves as they had khaki on just like our officers but their caps were fawn coloured with black shining peaks. One man said they read the name of the Regt. on his shoulder and while one was digging him out the other kept watch then suddenly they left him, fired a few rounds with their revolvers over the parapet and went away taking his rifle with them, the shots evidently being a sign they were about to return'.[37]

36 John Youngman, born 1896, had been with the battalion since October 1915. He won his
    M.C. for an earlier gas attack at Wulverghem.
37 Although Pirie was sceptical and it is not mentioned in the battalion war diary, this
    curious story seems essentially true. According to Makoben's regimental history of RIR
    212, around this time a reconnaissance in force by this unit overran a British sap, and
    brought back a booty of rifles, helmets and equipment, but no prisoners.

Monday 26th June, 16.

Here I am at No. 12 Casualty Clearing Station, Hazebrouck, France. Yesterday was quiet after the strafe and last night gas cylinders were brought up to put in ours and the West Kents' trenches. At about 10 pm. last night when I was having the sick parade, a message came saying an M.O. had come to relieve me so I went to see him and found Lt. Gough from the 73rd F. Amb. He said he had been sent up because I was reporting sick which was the first I had heard of it and as I thought he had made a mistake I 'phoned up Clark, the Adjutant who knew nothing about it so then the O.C. came to the 'phone and he said he had arranged with our Brigadier, Mitford,[38] to send me down for a rest without my knowing about it. I didn't want to go but he insisted so I stayed all night and got things in place for Gough and at daybreak after 'Stand Down' walked down to the F. Amb. Dressing station at Kandahar Farm where I picked up a motor ambulance and drove to Dranoutre via Neuve Eglise and on to here which was an hour's run through very pretty country, arriving here at 7 a.m. I was very tired so went to bed at once and slept soundly till lunch. This is a very nice place, holds forty-two beds and is a rest station for officers only. There are officers from all along the 2nd Army line.

Friday 30.6.16.

Still having an excellent rest, have breakfast in bed every morning and just loaf about during the day but have to be in bed by 9 p.m., rather early but we are resting, aren't we!! We have been playing some bridge and for a wonder have held quite good hands. Four of us, Capt. Riley, R.F.A., a Canadian, an Irish M.O., an Australian and self have what we call our parades twice daily, i.e., strawberries and cream and jove they are excellent and quite cheap. There is lots of fruit at present, apricots, peaches and cherries. This is quite a big town with good shops but very little doing in it. Yesterday a Col. Barclay took Riley and I out for a motor run after lunch through most beautiful country. The crops are looking very fine and promise an excellent harvest which is wonderful when every available man is with the colours. We went through Zuytpeene, Nordpeene, and Arnèke and returned by Cassel which is perched on top of a high hill. We went up by the car and then climbed to the top of the Casino which is the H.Q. of the 2nd Army and had a most wonderful view of the surrounding country. You could see the Belgian dunes, Dunkirk smoking, Poperinghe and all along the front for miles. I have never seen such an expanse before. The weather has been very wet and cold these last few days.

---

38   Bertram Mitford, born 1863, served with the Buffs and East Surrey Regiment, and saw much service in the Sudan and South Africa, where he won a D.S.O., before retiring as a Brigadier General in 1910. He commanded 72nd Brigade from 1914. His extensive diaries are at the N.A.M.

Sunday 2nd July, 16.

We heard of the great offensive on the Somme to-day which began yesterday. This afternoon Whitehead got up a very fine garden party which was held in the C.C.S. garden. He had the 16th Lancers band which was excellent, also a very funny comedian from the Lancers. He sang, so did an A.S.C. Lieut. and an R.E. Corporal. Then half time we had tea, cherries, peaches and strawberries. Luckily it was a fine afternoon and I enjoyed it muchly.

Tuesday 4.7.16.

Here I am back with the Regt. again. I left Hazebrouck at 6.30 p.m. and came up by train to Bailleul where Baker met me with my horse and we rode out to find the Regt. at Locre, a village about two kilometres from Dranoutre. They had a lot of shelling after I left them but were lucky with casualties. Lt. Denny was slightly wounded and went to the base. Lt. Morphy was gassed a little from our gas which was let off when the [8th] Queen's made the raid and it affected his heart so he is now in Hospital at home. The Regt. came out of the trenches on the 29th night and went to Aircraft farm and then came down here on Saturday night. This is quite a nice place, the men are in tents and we H.Q. are in a big hut with a veranda. We have our mess on the veranda and I sleep at the other end.

Thurs. 6.7.16.

Weather has been fair to medium, pretty wet. Last night Capt. Hilton, Lts. Pullan, Gold, Spurling, Hadenham, Whiteman and self dined at the convent and had a good dinner and then a sing song after it. This afternoon Capt. Heales, our 2nd in command and I rode over to the A.S.C. billets to see Capt. Barker's Wanderers play cricket against the A.S.C. Coy. The former won. This evening I had dinner with Capt. Mullins who is M.O. to the S. African batteries. He is an O.A. and we had a long chat about college.

Satur. 8.7.16.

We got a sudden order last night to move into the trenches to-night. We were to have gone into huts behind Mount Kemmel in a few days time but instead are now going into trenches on the River Douve just north of Plug Street Wood (Ploegsteert). We are rather fed up as our rest has been cut short by a week and the week we have been out has been spent in very strenuous working parties for both officers and men.

Sunday 9.7.16.

The Bn. moved away from Locre last night at 8.30. I rode as far as Neuve Église via Dranoutre, and then Baker, my groom, took the horse back. I had sent Corp. Halliday and Bearer Wright up to reconnoitre and they met us at Neuve Église and guided me and Allam up. We turned right from the village (which, by the way, has its end towards the Hun in ruins but the far end is in good repair and people still living in it. It is famed for its lace), and went down a mud road which we floundered about on and eventually got on to a good main road arriving at Red Lodge in Plug Street Wood about 11 o'clock feeling very tired. We relieved the Australians. We didn't worry to go to bed as I wanted to go to the firing line to arrange about getting casualties out. Corp. Halliday, Lt. Metcalfe and I started off at 3.30 a.m. just in grey dawn and reconnoitred our way up. It was some walk as we didn't know the way. Red Lodge stands right under the steep slope of Hill 63 in the Bois de Ploegsteert. It is a very fine wood and on the hillside are very fine dugouts, hold many men and absolutely safe from shelling. We left Red Lodge and walked up through the wood over Hill 63, passing Forts Glissold and Eberle and struck the Cellars, Le Rossignol Road at right angles. We crossed that rapidly as you are in full view of Messines and are liable to be shelled and went through a crumped barn called Fletcher's Post – at right angles to the Cellars Road is another one running down to Ration Farm and La Plus Douve Farm and Fletcher's Post stands on the angle of the two roads. A trench runs from Fletcher's Post to Ration Farm which we went down but it wasn't pleasant as it's in full view of the Hun line. However we reached Ration Farm alright and went between it and La Plus Douve Farm and then turned right and followed the River Douve in the cover of the trees and finally got into a communication trench called Currie Avenue, passing first Stinking Farm and then Gooseberry Farm on your left through very much shelling and then went into Spring Trench on the right which leads into Winter Trench where Gold and his Coy. are. We then had to come back to Currie Avenue to get up to the Front Line and passed Gabion Farm on your right and then got into the line. Jove it was an endless walk up that Currie Avenue; it took two hours to get to Ingrams and his Coy., and while we were there three 'Dud Archie' [faulty antiaircraft] shells came down and fell just near us and 'put the wind up' us. We then retraced our steps and got home at 7 after getting into a trench with mud and water up to nearly our knees. We went to bed at once and slept till 12 noon. This place, Red Lodge, is the Lodge for a chateau which stands on the hillside and the Lodge is a jolly fine billet. I have a spring bed to sleep on.

Tues. 11.7.16.

The last two nights we have been sleeping in the dugouts because we had a number of raids on the Hun trenches and expected retaliation. The first night they gave nothing back but last night they did in a hut and a good deal of shrapnel came over but as everyone was in dugouts no one was touched. Last night after dinner I went along to see Lt. Harold Mitten who is in a battery quite near here. Allam and I were to have gone up to the trenches at 3 a.m. this morning but the sentry failed to wake me and when I woke it was 4.20 so we fled up to Winter Trench, getting up there in the record time of 30 minutes, did the sick, (only nine) and came back arriving back at 6.5, and went to bed and slept till 11. We move from Red Lodge to-night as the Bn. takes over more trenches and Red Lodge becomes Brigade Reserve. I am to have my dressing station at La Plus Douve Farm with Waugh of the N. Staffs. It doesn't look a healthy spot at all – rather shelly!! I'm sorry we are leaving Red Lodge, it's very nice here.

Wed. 12.7.16.

It is with great regret that I read of Major Guyon being killed while O.C. of a West Yorks. Bn. in the Somme Battle. He was my O.C. in Gallipoli and a nicer man never lived. Then Win in her letter last night said Will had been wounded so I just hope not severely.[39] The price of life down there is high but well worth it. Allam and I trekked from Red Lodge last night at dusk to La Plus Douce Farm where our Aid Post is. It's in a dugout behind the barn, quite a good place. I sleep in a dugout next door to it with Capt. Waugh of the Staffords. It appears that Ration Farm's proper name is La Plus Douve Farm and what I took for La Plus Douve Farm is La Plus Douce Farm. La Plus Douce is very pretty indeed with an old moat round it. It is only about 50 yds. from Ration Farm .Both these farms have been badly shelled, especially Ration Farm. Our H.Q. is in Stinking Farm at present. It's a wretched place, daren't move there by day, otherwise you are shelled.

Thurs. 13.7.16.

Last night the Hun Machine Gun was very active along the Douve River and between Ration Farm and La Plus Douce Farm – three casualties from it. Corp. and I were up at 4 a.m. this morning to go round the trenches. It was cold, drizzly, and windy. However it was very quiet except for one near bullet. We started up along the Douve River, Douve Brook would be better nomenclature and walked in the open under cover of the trees along it, crossed it after about 900 yds. and got into the communication trench, passing Stinking Farm on our left and just beyond it turned right down a short trench to the Douve Dugouts which are on the Douve back [bank?]. Two platoons of C. Coy. are in them. We then went back to the C.T. and after a short walk turned right into Spring Street and it took us to Winter Trench where I met Lts. Castle and Lawrence, commonly called the 'Bing Boys',[40] and they told me Lt. Ingrams had won an M.C. He well deserves it. I had a cup of coffee with him and congratulated him.[41] Then we went back along the trench into Currie Avenue, the C.T. to Well Avenue, where the specialists are in dugouts. Then on along Currie Avenue to the line past Gabion Farm. We did our tour of inspection and got back to bed at 7, slept till about 12. Then had breakfast. I mess alone here as our H.Q. are too far away so I have three

---

39   Both unidentified.
40   From a popular musical of the time.
41   Frank Ingrams, born 1896, was a student when he enlisted in September 1914 and was commissioned later that month. Joining 9th East Surrey in December 1915, he won an M.C. for restoring the defences and rescuing those buried when his trench was destroyed by shellfire at Wulverghem. He was to die at Delville Wood in September.

meals a day, breakfast at about 12 noon, tea at four and dinner at 7 p.m. Croxford cooks for me and he does me quite well. We had a few whizz bangs about us this afternoon but no damage was done. I don't mind them but I bar 5.9 crumps!!

Satur. 15.7.16.

Rand and I went up to the trenches this morning. It was a most beautiful morning and very quiet. Things are still going well down South [i.e. the Somme]. I noticed Major Cripps, D.S.O., our late Adjutant out East[42] is amongst the wounded.

Monday 17.7.16.

L/Cpl. Allam and I went up to the trenches this morning. It was a wretched misty damp morning and the duck boards were most hopelessly slippery. It was an awful walk up to the line. I have had Lt. Snowball, R.F.A. of the trench mortar battery in to see me. His dugout is quite near by mine. He is an Australian and was in Gallipoli.

Tuesday 18.7.16.

While I was playing bridge with the Staff's Coy. Officers the O.C. 'phoned down to say Hadenham had been badly hit in the head. It was an awful shock to me as he was such a good fellow. When they got him to the dressing station he was mortally wounded in the head and we heard to-day that he died in Bailleul. Well, a good friend and a very fine soldier has gone. He has been out here sixteen odd months, first as a Sgt. with the 8th Bn. and since Xmas with the 9th Bn.[43] We are being relieved to-night by the 8th Queens and we go into Red Lodge, Plug Street as Bde. Reserve for eight days. Lt. Patch, R.A.M.C.[44] will relieve me. On the walls of this farm we are in are some drawings by Bairnsfather, the famous 'Bystander' artist. They are quite good. He belongs to the 1/5 Warwick's.[45]

Wed.19.7.16.

Patch relieved me early last night at 8.30 in daylight so we left before the machine guns got active and got to Red Lodge in peace. I found the specialist officers here so sat and chatted to them till about 12 and then went to bed but was up for sick parade again at 9, to find no sick, much to my disgust. Just when I was having breakfast Clark came in and said we were to be ready to move from here at 2 p.m. being relieved by

---

42   2nd Royal Fusiliers, Gallipoli.

43   Lawrence Hadenham was a waiter, aged 19, when he enlisted in September 1914. He was commissioned in November 1915.

44   Lieutenant later Captain C.J. Lodge Patch, M.C., born 1887, was R.M.O. to 8th Queen's 1915-18. His short memoir is at I.W.M.

45   Bruce Bairnsfather, creator of the famous cartoon character 'Old Bill', had served here with 1st Royal Warwickshire during winter 1914-15.

the 20th Division. The Bn. to relieve us is coming in buses and we return in them. We go to behind Meteren at first for a few days and then where – no one knows – great conjectures are the order, may be South to the Somme battle but personally I think Ypres Salient. I would rather go south and take my chance than go to Ypres again. However if it's to win the war soon I don't mind where we go!! We are all sorry we are leaving this area as it's very quiet and peaceful on the whole.

Thurs. 20.7.16.

We were relieved by the 11th Rifle Brigade last night at 10 p.m. We marched back to the village of Romarin about four kilometres from Plug Street and then got on to the buses. Soon after the buses started an overhead telephone wire nearly lopped off our heads on top of the bus. It came all of a sudden and as a great surprise. Q.M.S. Bates and I got cut about. O' Connor and the others got nothing so for the rest of the journey, an 1½ hrs. run we spent on the bottom of the bus!!! We came via Bailleul and Meteren to near Flêtre and then marched about two miles to our billets. We are in the same billets except H.Q. as we were in when we came from Ypres. I am billeted in a farm alone just below H.Q. and there is a most amusing girl here. She speaks quite good English too. The country looks beautiful, crops just turning colour and trees looking beautiful. I just hope we have a decent rest as it's most peaceful here. Each Coy. has a farm as a billet. We don't know where we are going but we all think to the Somme battle, I don't mind if we do, may get a 'blighty' wound[46] and get home for a change!!!

Satur. 22.7.16.

Still having a fine rest, doing the men a world of good. Each morning after sick parade at 9 I ride round the billets – it's great! Yesterday afternoon Clark and I rode to the top of Mont des Cats which is very near us. We had a wonderful view from there of Ypres, St. Eloi, Poperinghe and in fact all round. On top of Mont des Cats is a windmill and along-side it a nephew of the Kaiser's[47] was killed with shrapnel during a skirmish with our cavalry early in the war (13th Oct. 1914). Last night we heard that we are going South to the Somme on Monday. I'm glad and quite looking forward to it. I just hope the Regt. does well but I hate to think of the casualties. We shall now leave the 2nd Army, 5th Corps and go to the 4th Army, 9th Corps.

---

46   One requiring return to the U.K.
47   Prince Maximilian von Hesse, born 1894, was also a great grandson of Queen Victoria
      and the brother of the Empress of Russia.

Sunday 23.7.16.

We are off to the South to-morrow to the Battle of the Somme and I'm looking forward to it, for after all 'Who dies if England lives'.[48] I just hope I manage to do my part properly and not be a funk. We had a ripping rest here and I have enjoyed it very much. To-night I'm having a dinner as to-morrow is my twenty eighth birthday. Capt. 'Baby' Hilton, O.C. [C] Coy, Lt. Whiteman, our R.T.O and Capt. Heales, 2nd in command are my guests. We entrain at Bailleul to-morrow at 2.28 p.m. and have eleven hours in the train but where we go to I don't know.

---

48   A reference to Rudyard Kipling's 1914 poem, *For all we have and are.*

2

Somme and Vimy, July–October 1916

Wed. 26.7.16.

On Monday we all fell in at 11 a.m. from Noot Boom, near Mont des Cats and marched about 3-4 miles to Bailleul Station and got on to the train and left at 2.28 p.m. and came via Hazebrouck, St. Pol, Doullens, to a siding Longueau on the east side of Amiens and detrained there at 10.30. Rivers, Metcalfe, Pullan and I played bridge most of the way. It was a wonderful change in the country coming from North to South, very good to poor, chalky country, poor crops and few farm houses. We had a dickens of a march from Longueau through Amiens to this village Saisseval where we are billeted. It was about 12-13 miles march and we arrived here at 6.30 yesterday morning, feeling very tired. We found it a very pretty little village in a hollow surrounded by trees and hills but very few people in it and a very poor class of people. There are lots of billets for men but very few for officers and the people are very inhospitable. We H.Q. have quite a good billet and are very comfortable. I went to bed yesterday at nine and slept like a log till 3.30 p.m., and then tested two wells and saw the sick and men with sore feet. There were a lot with sore feet. Had an early bed last night and to-day did sick at 9 a.m. and then inspected billets and then watched an instructor showing the men about bayonet fighting, it was very interesting. We are only to be here a few days and then go into the Somme battle.

Sunday 30.7.16.

The order has come at last to move up to the great push to-morrow. We have spent a quiet time but I have enjoyed the peace and quiet of it all. The other afternoon I went with Whiteman when he was exercising his mules. We went for a jolly fine ride through a number of villages, first Seux, then Fluy, Quevauvillers which was quite a big place and then back by Revelles, Pissy, and Bovelles. The people in the villages turned out to see us as if it was a circus!!! The weather has been very fine here and very hot. We have had a good deal of fruit in this village, red currants, peaches, grapes, etc. The transport trek to-night and go by road all the way to our destination Morlancourt, while we march to-morrow from here (Saisseval) to Ailly (10 K. away) and there go by the train and pass through Amiens to Mericourt l'Abbé, where we detrain and march to Morlancourt about seven Kil[ometres]. It's very hot to-day so the march will be trying. Poor Lawrence is to go on ahead with the 'Toughs'!! I pity him!! We'll soon be near the big push. I wonder what our fates are to be!! I hope for a 'blighty'!!

Thurs. 3rd August.16.

Here we are in rear of the big battle. We marched out of Saisseval on Monday at 2 p.m. to go to entrain at Ailly sur Somme. It was about six miles and beastly hot and dusty. We were to entrain at 5.30 p.m. but on arrival at the station we were told all trains were five hours late so we marched down to the Somme canal and had a ripping swim which put new life into us again. We managed to raise an omelette and some tea in the Café Batteux and then marched to the station again expecting to go any minute but instead we were on that wretched station from 8.30 to 7.30 next morning and it was hopeless, couldn't sleep as trains were passing every five minutes. In the early morning it got so cold that Major Heales and I went off and lay down in the waiting room, certainly warmer but a beastly hard floor. Eventually we got our train at 7.30 a.m. Tues. morning, feeling grumpy from want of sleep, and we reached Amiens at 9.30, although it was only about eight miles away – a typical French train! Finally we reached Mericourt l'Abbé about 11. We travelled by train all up the Somme River past Corbie and there the railway leaves the Somme and follows the River Ancre and all along it is very pretty. We saw lots of Hun prisoners working along the line. They looked very fit and happy. We detrained at Mericourt and there had breakfast, washed and shaved in the Ancre, oh, we were filthy from the train!! We marched out of Mericourt at mid-day in awful heat and dust, and a whole crowd of Hun prisoners watched us go by, they looked very sullen and never smiled, all were fine men. We had a very dusty march (to Morlancourt) of four miles and I had to send some men to Hospital with heat stroke.[1] We had reckoned on being three days at Morlancourt so as to rest before going in to the show but as soon as we reached it we had orders to move again to the sand pits near Méaulte which is just behind Albert at 8 p.m., another four miles – we were fed up !! Morlancourt was a wretched village, poor and nothing to buy. We reached Morlancourt about 3 p.m., had something to eat and on we went again, and on our way up we met the Bantam division[2] coming out from the Battle. They were full of beans, singing and laughing. We reached the Sandpits about 10 p.m., and found it consisted of a huge camp, the men in bivouacs and officers in tents. I can tell you we did sleep that Tuesday night – tired, I think so!!! When we woke yesterday we found the country stiff with troops and it seems so funny that what was dangerous ground to wander about on is now safe for we are in a valley close behind our original

---

1   The temperature on 1 August reached 86 degrees Fahrenheit.
2   35th Division's infantry was made up of 'Bantam' battalions from recruits who were below the Army's standard height requirement.

trenches. We can see Albert with the hanging statue of the Virgin Mary from the church steeple. It's most wonderful the way it is hanging. The French say when it falls the war will end.[3] We are now about 6-7 miles from the front line, and expect to go up to-morrow night. Last night the guns went all night, 'some' noise, so that there must have been a show on. Yesterday afternoon Major Heales, Whiteman and I rode through Méaulte to the Ancre, about two miles from here and had a fine bathe, only the water was a bit cold. One can quite easily realise where the five millions [pounds] a day goes when you see the organisation for a battle like this, the transport, both horse and motor, new laid railways, the huge number of guns and the tons on tons of shells fired, and the number of men in it. It is a most wonderful show.

Thurs. [Friday] 4.8.16.

We are still in camp at the Sandpits on the Albert-Bray Road. Yesterday afternoon Whiteman and I rode up to Albert, about two miles off, to see the famous leaning statue of the Virgin Mary with the Child in her arms. It is leaning over at less than a right angle to the spire and she is looking down at the ground. The church has been shelled a good deal and has many holes in it. The French say when the statue is knocked down the war will end!!! Albert hasn't on the whole been shelled much, it's not a Wipers!! A few civilians had stayed on in the place and they were doing a roaring trade with the Tommies. It was most extraordinary on the village green were a lot of caravans with all their scenery etc. on them, just as they had been left two years ago when war broke out. All round the town it was stiff with troops.

Satur. 6.8.16. [5.8.16]

Yesterday was an appalling day of dust. The wind was high and with that and the traffic dust it was the limit. Yesterday afternoon Whiteman and I rode over to see Bray-sur-Somme and on our way over we were nearly drowned in dust. Bray isn't much of a place but the river is very fine. Gilbert [Ormsby] used to have his Field Ambulance there. After tea Major Heales and I walked over to see the village and trenches around Fricourt which we had captured the first day of the Somme battle.[4] It was a ¾ hour's walk but well worth it. The village was absolutely past its best, worse than Wipers and the Hun trenches had suffered very badly too so our shell fire must have been terrific. As usual the Huns held all the high points and vantage ground. But what beats all creation is how we ever took that maze of trenches. It is all chalk country and the Hun trenches had been very deep and their dugouts were marvellous, so deep that they would defy any shell on earth. One dugout I went down into was a most elaborate affair. It consisted of three stairs down into it for a depth of 30-40 feet

3   It fell in April 1918.
4   This had been one of the few British successes on that notorious day.

La vierge dorée du clocher de la basilique d'Albert.   D'après l'Illustration.   21₁
The golden virgin on the bell-tower of the basilic church at Albert.   I. M.
Золоченная статуя Богородицы на колокольнѣ Альберта.

Figure 18. The 'Leaning Virgin' of Albert. (Author's collection)

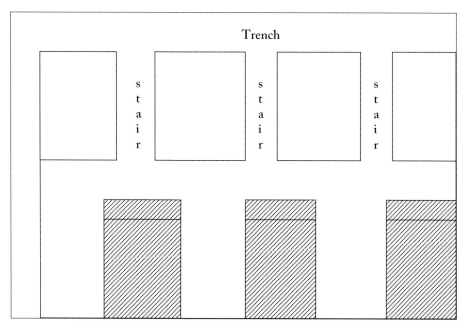

Diagram based on version appearing in Pirie typescript.

and than at the bottom was a long passage with small rooms running off it like this [see above diagram].

It would have held a large number of men. They also had sentry boxes lined with steel girders and likewise with sand bags on top so that in a strafe the man could stand inside just having a look out every now and again and keep watch while everyone else was safely down in the dugout.[5] We had the good luck to meet an R.E. officer who had been on that very part of the front for a year and had made and blown up the mines in this Fricourt salient. He pointed out his mines (or rather craters now) which they had blown up the first day, three of them. They were anything from 50-80 feet deep and a diameter of 30-40 yards, a colossal piece of work. He also pointed out the V shaped trench called the Tambour which Hadenham used to talk so much about. He had been in this very part of the line. Another interesting thing was to see how our Engineers had repaired the road and railway which had been in the Hun hands. Just behind the village of Fricourt stands Fricourt wood and behind it Mametz wood and to the right of that is the village of Mametz and then to the right of that stands Bernafay Wood, all in our hands now [see reproduction of typescript diagram on next page]. Wonderful are our men to have taken such strongholds.

5   The German dugouts at Fricourt were widely visited, including by officers and men of 9th East Surrey on 6 August and by King George V on 10 August.

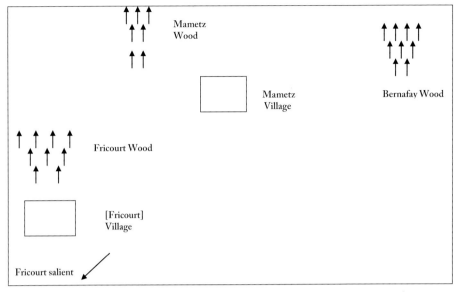

Diagram based on version appearing in Pirie typescript (see previous page).

Sunday 6.8.16.

This morning our Chaplain, Rev. Poole,[6] had his usual open air service. Then after it I took Communion. After lunch Whiteman and I rode over to the River Ancre to just below the village of Méaulte and had a fine bathe. Then after tea we rode over to see the trenches on the hill to the right of Fricourt and got Cooke (W's groom) to hold our horses while we had a look at them. As usual the Hun held the crest of the hill and all No Man's Land was a long strip of mine craters which both sides had blown up at different times, forming a deep valley on top of this hill. You got a very fine view of the country from the top. You could see Fricourt village and its wood behind with Mametz village to the right of it and its wood behind Fricourt Wood then behind that stands Contalmaison in absolute ruins. Then to the right and behind, to the right of that, is High Wood (Fourcaux Bois) and to the right of it again you can see Delville Wood. It was a wonderful view and you marvel more than ever at us taking all the ground as it is covered with lines of chalk trenches. Like elsewhere they had a regular maze of trenches on this hill and the dugouts were more elaborate than the previous ones. One had three stories, the bottom story must have been about a hundred feet down. The top flat contained an officer's bunk with curtains on it and a table and a cupboard and the table was still laid. In another very deep dug-out they had a hand grenade and trench

6   George Poole, born 1881, served as the Brigade's chaplain from summer 1915. He was to win an M.C. for maintaining morale and evacuating wounded in the Great Retreat of March 1918.

mortar factory. They had made a lot of 'canister or oil drum' trench mortar shells and hand grenades. Then outside, behind the trench, we saw a *Minenwerfer* trench mortar gun which had been halved by a shell. It was a very simple affair, made of wood, lined with tin and bound with wire like an old fashioned cannon. On one dugout was written 'Germans buried here', and had been filled in while from others an awful odour evolved from dead Huns in them. This is a weird war!

Tuesday 8.8.16.

We leave the camp on the Albert Bray Road and march to the old Hun front line trenches in front of Carnoy and go into Hun dugouts to be in support to the front line. The 2nd Division were to take Guillemont last night and it sounded like it too and we are to relieve them. This Regiment goes into the line eventually between Delville Wood and Waterlot Farm. God grant I may see this affair through safely!

Friday 18.8.16.

Here we are out again after some strenuous days. We moved up to dugouts between Maricourt and Carnoy on the 10th and then had three days there, the Companies doing working parties at night in the front line in front of Guillemont and each night we had some men put out with the shelling going up the Valley of Death[7], it was a H--- of a place. Captain O'Connor was wounded in the knee and has gone home, lucky devil! We went into the line on Sunday night last. I went up early between five and seven p.m. and escaped without a shell. We left dugouts at Talus Boisé and went up via the Briqueterie and up the Maltz Horn Trench on the right side of the Valley of Death, it has been crumped [shelled] in, and we legged it up that and then into a sunken road, which is a very shelly place, and then up Scottish Trench to our H.Q. in the line opposite Guillemont. The front line only being about 150 yards from there. It was a wretched dugout about as large as a rifle grenade [sic.]and three of us used to sleep and eat in it all like sardines, it was beastly uncomfortable. We got shelled all day and night except as a rule between 7-9 p.m. and 5-7 a.m., when there was a lull and it was heavenly after the awful noise. My head ached all day. We were lucky with casualties till C. & D. Companies attacked,[8] a strong point 130 yards in front of us on the 16th at 5.40 p.m. Then it was worse than Hell. I was dressing wounded in the trenches – enough said – <u>awful</u>!! Our men advanced very well but the attack failed and we lost Capt. Vaughan, Cuthbert, O'Brien, Matheson, Spurling, Lawrence killed, Denny and Metcalfe wounded.[9] Capt. Hilton and Lt. Schofield and Picton got back safely and about 150 men wounded and killed. The saddest part of all was Corp. Halliday was mortally wounded in the abdomen whilst getting away the second

---

7   So named as it was continually shelled.
8   From Lamb Trench in front of Arrowhead Copse.
9   Lieutenant W.C. Metcalfe died of wounds 19 August.

last stretcher case; that finished me off, I wept then. He's an awful loss to me. I don't know what I shall do without him. I am so sad at losing all these officers as we were just like a big family and I loved Vaughan and Cuthbert.[10] We moved back to Talus Boisé yesterday morning at day break after getting the cases all away and came back via Scottish Trench and Irish Alley to the Briqueterie feeling dirty, unshaven, foot sore and oh! so tired and sleepy, very little sleep for four nights and three days so we didn't half sleep last night. We moved to-day about a mile away from Talus Boisé in the afternoon to the craters in our old front line in front of the village of Carnoy. We are under orders to be ready to move at a ¼ hour's notice to the line as our Division is trying to take Guillemont to-day, it's not a village as there's not a wall standing. Well, I have been lucky, may I be so again!

Sunday 20.8.16.

On Friday evening about 9 p.m. we got sudden orders to move up to reinforce so we hurriedly packed up C. & D. Companies from the craters at Carnoy and we picked up A. & B. Companies at Montauban who were holding the defences there. I marched up with Lt. Rivers, O.C., D. Coy. Montauban is absolutely in ruins. After we joined A. & B. Companies we marched up towards Bernafay Wood and then turned off to the right to the Briqueterie and spent a most miserable night on the roadside. It was bitterly cold and wet and in the end it turned out we shouldn't have moved up, it was a mistake. Still it's only one of the rigors of the campaign. In the early morning of Saturday we moved into Dublin and Casement Trenches near the Briqueterie and H.Q. into some artillery dugouts so weren't so badly off. We had some shells very close and I nearly got a 'blighty' one. It was bitterly cold last night but we made a bed of many sand bags and put our feet in sand bags so we didn't do badly. To-day has been windy and cold. We move up to the trenches at Guillemont to-night, only it's to the left of our last position, and the 35th Division (Bantams) take over our trenches. I'm hoping for good luck again.

Wednesday 23.8.16.

Here we are back at the Citadel out of the strafe once again. It's heavenly to be out of it again. To go back a bit – the Battalion moved up to the line last Sunday night, an hour's interval between each Company. Hilton asked me to go with him and we moved off at 2.30 a.m. on Monday morning. We went up via Irish Alley, walked along the parapet as it was quicker and then crossed the Sunken Road into White Horse Trench which is an old Hun one and has been hopelessly shelled so is very exposed, and full of broken telephone wires which impede you badly underfoot. We had got well along it

---

10   Vaughan was clearly a popular and well-regarded officer. Brigadier General Mitford, who had seen much death in his time, recorded his particular distress at Vaughan's death in his diary.

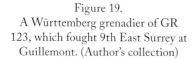

Figure 19.
A Württemberg grenadier of GR
123, which fought 9th East Surrey at
Guillemont. (Author's collection)

when a block occurred, B. Coy's guide had lost his way, couldn't find Sherwood trench which we had to file down so I left Hilton and went ahead to see what had gone wrong and just as I got to the head of the Battalion I met the O.C. at the head of Sherwood Trench and at that moment the Huns began to shell us and the poor men in that beastly open White Horse Trench – no cover whatsoever – so we quickly filed into Sherwood Trench, diving the shelling but unfortunately D. Coy. was at the end and had Lt. Rivers killed, Lt. Lillywhite wounded and D. Coy. Sgt. Major Tanner.[11] I very nearly came up with Rivers as he asked me to come with him just a second after Capt. Hilton did. I got down in the Sherwood Trench and the trench was blown in by a shell quite near. This shelling was in the early morning as it was then just 4 a.m. He shells every morning at that time. I feel sorry for Rivers as he is married and has a kiddy. We then turned out of Sherwood Trench into a beastly shallow half dug trench called Brighton Alley and in it was our H.Q. C. and D. Companies held Sherwood, and A. and B., Edwards and Knott trenches which was just in front of H.Q., whilst the [8th] Queen's

11   Second Lieutenant, later Colonel, Geoffery Lillywhite survived, as do his letters at IWM. John Tanner returned to the battalion and was killed in August 1917.

Regiment held the front line. We and the Queen's shared the H.Q. dugout so it was an awful squash. On the 21st afternoon the Queen's and 12th Royal Fusiliers attacked at 4.30 p.m., and were successful but in the end, through a mistake, retired. We, who were behind them, got an awful shelling for four hours. It seemed worse than the day of our attack on the 16th as our men were in deep trenches and we had few casualties and so I hadn't work to occupy my mind. We had Capt. Hilton wounded that afternoon and I was glad as he had been out seventeen months and he deserved a rest. The Queen's were relieved by the N. Staffs the night of their attack and we stayed in during the 22nd which was comparatively quiet and then were relieved that night by the 11th K.R.R. [King's Royal Rifle] Corps, 20th Division. We filed out down Brighton Alley, Sherwood Trench and down a very deep trench through Trônes Wood and across to Bernafay Wood and down all of it. Just as we entered Trônes Wood we had a lucky escape from two shells, they burst in the trench just in front of us so we all got down and then marched on like fury. We came out of the wood at the end and down through Montauban to the Craters where we all had tea and then past Carnoy to our camp at the Citadel which we reached at 4.30 a.m. this morning and oh! we were glad to get safely out of it. We all tumbled into bed and slept till nearly 12 noon, hadn't had much sleep up front. Had a good sponge down and a complete change of clothing when I got up. We are very comfortable here, all the men and officers have tents or huts. The Citadel is a series of dugouts and tents on the Fricourt Bray Road. We hope to be out now for a decent rest, in fact, not go up again.

Thursday 24.8.16.

Still resting at the Citadel. Went for a bath in the Somme at Bray with Clark and Gold. It was top-hole.

Friday 25.8.16.

This morning Whiteman woke me at 6.30 and said 'pack up', and at once had visions of going up to the line again but to our joy found it was to go back a bit. We marched from the Citadel at 10 a.m., via Morlancourt and across the Ancre at the village of Ville sur Ancre to a place below Dernancourt in the fields on the Albert-Amiens road, about an eight mile march. It was a deuce of a roundabout way to come and we got here at 3 p.m. Just as we fell out to settle down we were greeted by a solitary shell alongside the road but it did no damage. The officers are in tents and the men in bivouacs. It is showery so I feel sorry for the men.

Saturday 26.8.16.

Got orders to-day to say we go into the line again to-morrow at Delville Wood so we haven't had much rest. Am not looking forward to it. The C.O. and Lt. Pullan have gone up to see the line. There is one consolation if we survive this third trip we probably won't have to go up again, and none of us will be sorry!! Very showery and windy to-day.

Monday 28.8.16.

We didn't go up yesterday after all, much to our joy. In the morning at 8.30 a.m. General Capper, our Divisional Commander, inspected our Brigade, the 72nd. He also thanked and congratulated us on our work while in the battle. It rained while he was inspecting us so we got a bit wet. We had an early lunch and then fell in and marched down the Albert-Amiens Road to Ribemont sur Ancre which is a village just off the main road. It was quite a short march and we did it between some very heavy showers. This is quite a nice village and we are all very comfortable and to add to it all, it's peaceful, no sound of guns to be heard. We hear we are due to go up again on the 30-31st night to Delville Wood.

Tuesday 29.8.16.

Got orders this afternoon to leave here (Ribemont) to-morrow morning at 5.30 a.m. We march to Fricourt where we camp for the day and then move up to trenches near Montauban where we are Brigade reserve. The Queen's will be in support and the N. Staffs and W. Kents in the front line at Delville Wood –not a healthy spot from all accounts. We have had an excellent rest, been out just a week and it's been heavenly back here, no noise of guns and had some excellent fruit, peaches, apples, pears and grapes. The weather has been very showery, had a terrific thunderstorm to-day. I expect the trenches will be awful, mud and water. Here's for hoping for good luck again!

Wednesday 30.9.18 [30.8.16.]

Here we are in old Hun dugouts at Montauban. We left Ribemont at 5.30 a.m. this morning. It had been raining heavily all night but it was dry for our march to the camp outside Fricourt. We marched via Buire-sur-Ancre, Dernancourt, Méaulte and just as we got to our camp at 8.30 it began to pelt and as the tents were still occupied we got nicely soaked till the other Regiment went out. We stayed in the camp till 3.30 p.m. and then marched up to here and oh! the roads were too appallingly muddy for words, up to the knees in places. I rode up with Clark the Adjutant, and Major Ottley, second in command[12] so was alright but the men were in an awful state. Our H.Q. dugout is an old Hun kitchen but we are quite comfy. It is on the North side of the village and looks towards High and Delville Woods.

Thursday 31.8.16.

The Hun shelled all round us to-day and one 12" shell just missed our dugout but gave it a good shaking. The N. Staffs have had a bad time already so A. Coy. under Lt. Gold and D. Coy. under Lt. Royal with Major Ottley, go up to-night to reinforce

12   Sent from the Royal Fusiliers with Major Heales sick.

them on the East edge of Delville Wood and the rest of us move up to-morrow after-noon and relieve the Staffs. It has been raining hard and everything is mud. We hear we only do twenty four hours in which isn't so bad.

Wednesday 6th September, 16.

We moved up to Delville Wood on the afternoon of the 1st and went up past Bernafay Wood and all along the top of York Alley trench and into Longueval Alley to H.Q. which was in old German Alley. We were shelled going up but were lucky. Fortunately for us we had a very fine deep Hun dugout as our Aid Post, and H.Q. also had one. Our Aid Post was in an old Hun trench just on the edge of the Wood and oh! the shelling was terrific, much worse than at Guillemont. We had not been settled long when casualties began to come in from all the Regiments around and we were kept busy till we came out to-day. On the 2nd the O.C. [de la Fontaine] led a bombing attack and was badly wounded in the chest but is doing well. Major Ottley and Lt. Ingrams, Lt. Haines and Lt. Urban killed, while Lts. Monro, Grant, Gold, Castle, Pullan were wounded. On the 2nd [3rd] the Divisions on our right took Guillemont and Ginchy and Leuze Wood so we came in for less shelling. We had a good deal of rain so the trenches were too muddy for words and getting out stretcher cases was very difficult. I lost four bearers wounded and one killed and was lucky at that. The Regiment came out last night about 12 a.m. but Allam, Rand, Croxford and I came away at 6.30 a.m. so as to make sure all our wounded had been got away. Those four days and five nights were the most trying I have ever spent, very little sleep and very heavy shelling. I don't know how anyone got out alive. The wood was so heavily shelled by day and night that all wounded were stored in Hun dugouts all day till between 5 and 8 a.m. and 5 and 8 p.m. during which periods the shelling seemed to die down and so allow the cases to be got out to my aid post then they were carried from me by R.A.M.C. bearers to a dressing station at the Shrine and from there by another relief to the quarry at Bernafay wood and from there by horse or motor ambulance to Mametz. My regt. bearers did very fine work, especially Mead, Trish,[13] Oyston and Hardiker, they were fearless and worked like slaves.[14] When we left the Aid Post at 6.30 a.m. we brought L/Cpl. Lennard with us and as he was exhausted we had to lug him out. It was very muddy so we wound sandbags around our legs to keep them dry and as it was misty the Hun balloons couldn't see us but as our guns were shelling heavily and we expected a reply so we just walked outside the trench as it was quicker and we didn't wait for a rest till we got past Bernafay Wood as you were very liable to be shelled. (I forgot to mention we got a lot of tear [gas] shells while at Montauban and Delville Wood, it <u>does</u> make your eyes smart!) It was an extraordinary sight to see the crowds

13   Lance Corporal Alfred Trish was later awarded an M.M. for saving wounded in the March 1918 Retreat.
14   For Pirie's letter which describes his experiences at Delville Wood in less restrained terms see Appendix III.

of men walking about behind, some carrying water and food up, others digging and such like, just as if nothing was happening. Tommy Atkins is a marvel!! After our rest we went on to Montauban and then on to the main road to Mametz where we raised some tea from some gunners and it <u>was</u> welcome as we were exhausted from want of sleep and ploughing through the mud. At Mametz we picked up a G.S. [General Service] wagon which took us down through Fricourt and just beyond was our camp. We were awful sights when we got in at 9 a.m., dirty, covered with mud and unshaven for five days so I had breakfast and then shaved, a hot sponge down and a complete change of clothing. We had to march to the camp on the Albert – Amiens Road at 2 p.m. and when we arrived there (a four mile march) Capt. Hilton ('Baby') and I rode down to Heilly to see our C.O.[15] We found him doing very well indeed. We had a bottle of Phys [Champagne] at Heilly then Hilton went on to see his old Regt. 19th County of London and we got back at 9 p.m., dead beat, and didn't I sleep although it was on the ground! We have got a lot of new officers including an O.C., Lt. Col. Tew, very quiet and dry but nice.[16] Our 2 [nd]/ [in] command is a Capt. Jackson, a huge fellow, ex-cavalryman.

Thursday 7.9.16.

We entrained at Dernancourt-sur-Ancre at 12 p.m. to-day and had a five hours run all along the Somme to Longpré, and the Regiment marched from there to Francières, about six miles. I came on in advance in a motor ambulance and I was glad of it as I was very tired. H.Q. are billeted in a fine Chateau owned by the Count of St. Pal. [St. Pol?] He and the Countess are staying in it at present and are very decent to us. We have our mess in the Curé's house. This is a very pretty village situated in a deep valley with heavily sloped slopes. Jove it's blissfully peaceful here!!! The poor Regiment is reduced to about two hundred odd out of eight hundred, sad but true.

Sunday 10.9.16.

We had an open air church service this morning and then communion after it. Padré Poole is our Chaplain. We often see him in the trenches. This afternoon Capt. 'Baby' Hilton and I rode down to the Somme Canal at Pont-Remy about three kilometres from here and had a fine swim.

Tuesday 12.9.16.

This afternoon the Division had a horse show for all the transport of the various units in it. It was a fine turn out. Then there was some flat racing. The divisional band turned out and tea and drinks in a marquee, so really one might have been at

---

15   De la Fontaine – badly wounded at Delville Wood.
16   Harold Tew was born in Scotland in 1869. Commissioned in 1889 he had seen much action in the Boer War. In 1914, he had served as a major at Mons with 1st East Surrey.

an agricultural show at home. The show was simply stiff with 'Red Hats'- our Corps commander (by the way we now belong to the X Corps), Lt. General Morland and our divisional commander, General Capper were there to say nothing of our Brigadier, General Mitford and crowds more.

Wednesday 13.9.16.

This afternoon Hilton and Warre-Dymond,[17] now O.C. B. Company and I rode over to Bellancourt which is on the Amiens-Abbeville road to see the N. Staffs. about a Lewis gun and then to Buigny l'Abbé to the Queen's. We at Francières are about five miles from Abbeville. I am having my sick parade at 7 a.m. and the mornings are simply perfect. After breakfast I inspect all the billets. We are having lots of fine fruit here, pears, apples and grapes. Autumn is just beginning to show its appearance – some of the leaves are turning yellow. I'm not looking forward to the winter at all. (I have quite forgotten to record the fact that while we were in the line at Delville Wood one morning about 7 a.m. we saw a Hun 'plane swoop down on five of our latest and largest aeroplanes and bring one down by machine gun fire. It was a fine piece of work on the Hun's part but it was a ghastly sight to see this 'plane nose-dive to earth just in front of the Wood.).

Thursday 14.9.16.

To-morrow Hilton and I go to Paris for forty eight hours leave. I'm looking forward to it. It ought to be fine. Yesterday 140 men and four officers were sent to the seaside for three days at Ault on the Channel. The men thoroughly deserve it too.

Monday 18.9.16.

On Friday morning Hilton and I rode into Abbeville, had lunch and then the train to Paris via Amiens. The train was a very good one, left Abbeville at 2.30 p.m. and got to Paris at 5.30. We first reported ourselves to the A.P.M. [Assistant Provost Marshal] who is Major Hon. Maurice Brett (Zena Dare's husband) then got rooms at the Hotel 'Continental'. We went to Les Folies Bergère theatre that night. A Revue was on. We didn't understand much of the show but the music was very pretty. After that we went to see some of the sights of Paris, but they weren't very exciting so came back to the hotel. Saturday morning we just loafed about the hotel and in the after-noon took a taxi to see the Eiffel Tower and then out to the Bois de Boulogne which is very fine. In the evening, after a good dinner, we went to the Tobarin Skating Rink but it was very feeble so taxied to the Olympia Theatre, a music hall, which was quite

---

17   Godfrey Warre-Dymond, believed to be the model for Stanhope in R.C. Sherriff's *Journey's End*, had joined the battalion on 1 September. Sherriff considered him inspirational. He distinguished himself at Ypres in August 1917, won an M.C. in the March 1918 Retreat and was taken prisoner in the battalion's last stand there.

good. One would scarcely say a war was on, as the Restaurants are as good as ever and theatres etc. all going, only the girls aren't so brightly dressed as in peace time. Sunday afternoon we went to the Jardin des Tuileries to hear a Servian band and then at 7.15 p.m. caught our train at the Gare du Nord and after a beastly slow nine hours journey got off at Pont-Remy at 5 a.m. this morning and walked the three kilometres back, getting back at 6 a.m., then we went to bed and had a good sleep. The Regiment was to have moved to-day to Abbeville to entrain there for Berguette which is near Loos way but instead we go to-morrow. We are jolly glad we aren't going back to the Somme again. We expect to be a little time round Berguette and then into the trenches somewhere for the winter.

Wednesday 20.9.16.

We left Francières yesterday at 1 o'clock mid-day. It had been raining hard all the previous day and night and up till about 11 a.m. when it cleared up and we had a beautiful afternoon to march to Abbeville, a ten kilometre march. We left there by train at 5 p.m. and all thought we were to detrain at Berguette seven hours later but instead were suddenly ordered (at a station called Brias) to detrain and there our advanced party met us and guided us to this village, Valhuon, about two miles from the railway. We no sooner had settled in our billets when it began to rain torrents again and it's hard at it to-day. In our train journey we came via Auxi-le-Chateau, Frévent and St. Pol, arriving at Brias at 9 p.m. We understand we are only to be here a few days and then go on to Berguette as it is full of men at present.

Thursday 21.9.16.

We are not going to Berguette after all, (it would have taken us somewhere near Armentières had we gone there) but now find ourselves opposite the Vimy Ridge and Souchez, not an area with a good reputation!! Beastly wet again to-day – raining torrents.

Saturday 23.9.16.

Yesterday and to-day have been very fine but quite autumn in type, fresh in the morning and the leaves are changing colour rapidly. I have been busy here inspecting drafts and training six new stretcher-bearers, Allan and Wain of A. Coy., Sellis, Banister, Treby and Bladock of B. Coy. All are of recent drafts but seem useful fellows. Yesterday Whiteman and I rode into St. Pol, about six kilometres from here. It's quite a decent place, very pretty down in a valley. We had a nice tea at the Mikado tea rooms, and then rode home slowly. We move up to Bruay to-morrow, a twelve mile march, and then into divisional reserve for the Vimy Ridge just south of Souchez.

Sunday 24.9.16.

We were up early this morning and moved off from Valhuon about 8 a.m. It was a perfect day for a march and the whole country was smiling, and people in their Sunday best going to church. We came through two villages in which were billeted the Royal Naval Division. In one I ran across Capt. Taylor of one of their Marine F. Ambulances. The last time I met him was in Gallipoli. He's an O.A. We had a dickens of a long and steep hill to climb a short way from Bruay but the men marched well and got up alright. We reached Bruay about 12 p.m. and found it was a very spread out mining town. We had the best billets I have seen in France, very clean, nice white sheets and the people were most hospitable. Worse luck we are only to be two nights in such comfort!

Tuesday 26.9.16.

Yesterday we had jolly fine hot baths at the colliery baths. We were up beastly early this morning, 4.45 a.m., had breakfast and moved off at 6.30 a.m. We had about 10 miles to march but it was a fine day and got here, Estrée Cauchy at 10 a.m. via Houdain and Rebreuve villages. We had a fiend of a hill to climb near here, worse than Sunday's one. This village is the Divisional Reserve Area and is on the main road from Bruay to Arras but it's a poor village and the billets aren't up to much. We are about ten miles from Arras. We are to be in D.W. [Divisional?] Reserve for six days and then go into the line. There was a terrific cannonade on the Somme to-day about lunch time; we could hear it very distinctly.

Friday 29.9.16.

We are still at Estrée Cauchy in D.W. reserve but move up on Monday 2nd October to Bde. Reserve, just behind the line. Nothing whatsoever doing here – very quiet village. I lectured all the officers yesterday on Trench Feet and First Aid-work. My Medical Orderly, L/Cpl Allam, has been awarded the Military Medal.[18] He thoroughly deserves it for he's an excellent fellow. The leave has started again and I hope to get mine in during the coming month, only our O.C., Col. Tew, C.M.G. [Companion of the Order of St. Michael and St. George], doesn't seem keen on officers going on leave. This afternoon I rode over to the 72nd F. Amb. at Les Quatre Vents, a tiny village about a mile from here and had tea with Capts. Groves and Webster, two very nice fellows.

Saturday 30.9.16.

This morning the O.C., 2nd in command, Capt. Spencer, and O.Cs. of each Company and myself went up to see the reserve trenches which we take over on Monday. We rode

18   Presumably on Pirie's recommendation.

Figure 20. Estrée Cauchy, 9th East Surrey battalion headquarters in September/October 1916 – a 2012 photograph with the author and his son, Andrew. (Author's collection)

to a village Villers-au-Bois, about four miles from here and there left our horses. The village had been shelled a bit but there were still a few inhabitants in it. Bde. H.Q. are in it. Then we walked across country and at a sunken road behind Berthonval Wood, picked up a guide who was to lead us to Cabaret Rouge where the trenches were. He led us to 130th Road but lost his way and took us all down it to Daly's – so called as it's a spacious dugout – Daly's is just at Hospital corner where the Motor Ambulance picks up the wounded. Then we had to climb up 130 Road again and turned into Cabaret Road communication trench and after a mile of it came to the Cabaret Rouge line. It <u>was</u> a trudge on those duck-boards. Two Companies are to be there. Then we came back by Boyau 123C. Trench which brought us out on the Maestre Line about a mile by trench behind Cabaret Rouge. At Maestre Line we and two other Companies are to be with Batt. H.Q. This line runs just in front of Berthonval Wood. Whiteman went with us so when we had finished our jobs we came back to Villers au Bois, picked up our horses and came home. The trenches and dugouts are very good and it seems extraordinarily peaceful.

Sunday 1.10.16.

We had a very nice open air service this morning and the Divisional Band played the music. Our Chaplain, Capt. Poole preached. It was a year ago on the 25th September since this battalion was in action at Loos so our Brigadier General, Mitford, is having a social gathering of all the survivors of the Brigade at Les 4 Vents to-night. We move off early to-morrow morning to go into Brigade reserve for eight days.

Monday 2.10.16.

We were up with the sparrows this morning at 5 o'clock and the Battalion marched off at about 7 a.m. up to the reserve trenches via Villers-au-Bois and got up here about 9 a.m. It was a beautiful morning with a dash of frost in the air but when we got up here it began to rain and now the mud is awful. Truly winter is coming!! Two Companies, B. and D. are here in a line of trenches, the Maistre Line just in front of Berthonval Wood and Batt. H.Q. are just behind them in artillery gun pits. We have a fine big dugout for a mess, lined with canvas and a proper house fireplace built in. Our bedroom consists of a dugout halved and lined with canvas. The Colonel has one half and the Adjutant and I the other half. Our beds consist of wood frames with rabbit netting wire across it and then covered with canvas and it's most comfortable. The other two Companies are a good half hour's walk from here up a Communication trench called Boyau 123 in the Cabaret Rouge line. I went up to see them this afternoon in awful rain but my Burberry held it out. They are quite comfortable up there, everybody in dugouts.

Thursday 5.10.16.

Been raining off and on each day since we arrived in this line and each morning I have been walking up to Cabaret Rouge to see the other two Companies' sick. To-day I had lunch with Capt. Lang and Eberts of our F. Amb. up there then after lunch went up to see the front line. We went up Wortley Avenue which turns off Boyau 123. When you get to the far end of W. Avenue you find yourself in Zouave Valley in which my aid post will be and our Batt. H.Q. Then we trekked up the other side of the hill into a C.T. called International Avenue and into the front line which is quite good but very muddy. I quite enjoyed watching our Stokes and 60 pounder (commonly called Toffee-apple) trench mortars being sent over to the Hun. You could follow their flight the whole way. Just after we left, the Hun began to reply with Minnies which are huge trench mortars. On our way back Lieut. Warre-Dymond and I had tea with A. Coy. at Cabaret Rouge.

Saturday 9.9.16. [7.10.16.]

Bad weather still continues so I'm afraid our offensive on the Somme may have to cease if it continues. This afternoon Allam and I walked over to a village, Mount St. Eloi (not the St. Eloi in the Ypres Salient). It has been knocked about a good deal, the interior of the church is especially wrecked, shells must have all burst inside. There is the remains of a fine old church spire in the village which I hear was ruined in 1870.

Monday 9.10.16.

Weather been much better to-day, looks like improving again. To-morrow we go into the front line of the Berthonval sector for eight days. This afternoon Baker, my groom, brought my horse up and I rode into Villers-au-Bois for a bath.

Tuesday 10.10.16.

To-day we moved up to the line. Allam and I left H.Q. at Berthonval Wood at 9 a.m., and came up via Boyau 123 and Wortley Avenue. Our aid post is in Zouave Valley and we are very comfortable. I have a dugout to myself while Allam, Rand and Croxford sleep opposite in the Aid Post dugout. Besides that we have two other dugouts, one for drying wet clothes in and the other for greasing feet in – a prevention against frost bitten feet. Then we have four R.A.M.C. bearers who convey the wounded from us to the F. Ambulance advanced dressing station. After lunch I went round all the trenches. They are quite good but the left Company is badly minenwerfered at times. While Croxford and I were up there one of our 'planes brought down a Boche one. The Boche just managed to fall in his own lines. At one time I thought he would fall in No Man's Land. It was fine to see him come down. It's been a beautiful day and fine moonlight to-night.

Wednesday 11.10.16.

Been trying hard to get away on leave but can't get an M.O. from the A.D.M.S. to relieve me, over six months since I went. Went round the trenches this morning with Lt. Thomas, our bombing officer.[19] We went up to B. Coy's H.Q., via International Avenue and then from there up Gordon trench into the front line, starting along Mandora South trench past the bombing sap then along Mandora Central and South and along Hartung and Bamburgh Trenches down to C. Coy's H.Q. in Brown's Burrows which are very deep dugouts. Leading off the junction of Hartung and Mandora North is a trench leading out to Ersatz Crater. That trench, Hartung and Bamburgh and the Communication Trenches, Blue Bull Alley and Ersatz Alley are continually being minnied – most unpleasant! The Huns made a raid on Ersatz Crater two nights before we came in and captured one of the Queen's but left behind a dead under officer so we scored as much as they did. To-day I have had our carpenter on to lining my dugout with green canvas and the dressing station dugout is also being done, as they both looked so filthy and dismal.

---

19   Second Lieutenant Lechmere Thomas had joined the battalion at Delville Wood aged 18. He was to make a name for himself, winning an M.C. and Bar for raids, before being seriously wounded in the German March 1918 offensive. He later distinguished himself in the Second World War, becoming a Major General and was interviewed by Peter Liddle in 1976 about his Great War.

Thursday 12.10.16.

Round the line as usual this morning, all was quiet but this afternoon there was a proper trench mortar strafe. It began at 2 p.m., we, with Stokes Mortars, toffee apples, so called as it consists of a round 60 lb. shell on the end of a three foot steel stick, and with our raw huge '¼ to 10 gun' (so called as it's a trench mortar with a 9.45 bore and it throws a huge shell 194 lbs. weight and makes a 14 ft. deep hole). Fritz replied with Minnies but we soon shut him up, because for every one he sent over he got at least four back. You can follow the flight of all these shells in the air, all the strafing seems to be done by mortars here, very few shells.

Monday 16.10.16.

Things are livening up a bit on this sector of the front. I thought it wouldn't remain quiet when our artillery got into position. On Saturday night some Regiment had a bombing raid just south of us and the Huns dropped some shells on our trenches and the valley. Then yesterday morning he just missed our H.Q. Mess dugout called the Tank with a 4.2 shell and hit another dugout to bits with another one. It's all the result of us strafing him with trench mortars and our guns and if he becomes angry he will make it very hot for us in Zouave Valley. The weather has been much better these last two days but it's very cold to-night – a good dash of frost in it. We are in the Berthonval Sector trenches on the Vimy Ridge just South of Souchez and in front of Lens, both of which we can see. Behind Souchez in our ground lies Ablain St. Nazaire with the high ridge. The Lorette Heights to the left of it. The French drove the Huns out of Ablain St. N. and Souchez over the L. Heights and on to the top of this Vimy Ridge at the same time as the Battle of Loos. It is some feat as these are terrific ridges to have to storm. Souchez and A. St. N. are in ruins and we can see them from our trenches. The famous sugar factory of Souchez which the French and Huns exchanged so often is between A. St. N. and Souchez and the German maze of trenches called the Labyrinth is on the left of Souchez. The French took it at the same time as the battle of Loos.

Tuesday 17.10.16.

This morning Allam and I went down the valley to see the Aid Post we will take over when we come up the next time. It is the extreme left of the Carency Sector of the Vimy Ridge and is bang in front of Souchez. It's quite a good Aid Post but not such a good one as our present one but much safer as they are all deep dugouts. When I got back to our H.Q. at lunch I was told we were to shift to the Bully Grenay Divisional Sector about the 23rd which is about one divisional front up the line from here and is next the Loos salient, so we won't come back to the Vimy Ridge. I'm sorry as it's a nice piece of the line, good dugouts and such like. We are to be relieved by the Middlesex to-morrow afternoon and go into Divisional reserve at Estrée Cauchy till we move to our new area. The weather has turned wet again.

Wednesday 18.10.16.

We were relieved this afternoon at about 3.20 so started off at once via Wortley Avenue and Boyau 123 to the Maistre Line where my horse was to be, but on arriving there, there was no sign of it, so had visions of a long walk back but by luck caught an artillery mess cart and after getting on to the main road met Baker with my horse so rode back and just got to Estrée Cauchy at dark. [Lieutenant and Quartermaster] Birch and I share the same billet over the Ordnance office.

Friday 20.10.16.

Yesterday afternoon in spite of much rain Hilton and I rode into Bruay (about 8-9 miles away) in the afternoon, had tea, did some shopping and had dinner with Capt. Teddy Price, R.A.M.C. who was at the Varsity with me. We had quite a good time, nice change after the trenches. We started back in the dark at 9.25 and our horses went like the wind, got back in 1¼ hours. This afternoon I rode over to see the A.D.M.S. at Camblin l'Abbé, about two miles from here and at last he said I would get away sometime next week and jove it's <u>great</u> to look forward to! On my way back I ran across Gilbert [Ormsby], Alice's husband, in a motor car. He had just come from our village looking for me. He is just close to us at Aubigny about four miles away so I'm going to have lunch with him to-morrow. He is O.C. No. 42, C.C.S.

Saturday 21.10.16.

Had a great day to-day. Rode over to Aubigny, through Villers Châtel and had lunch and tea with Gilbert and saw over his C.C.S. I got back in time for our concert at 6.30 which was a huge success.

3

Loos and Lens, October 1916–April 1917

Tuesday 24.10.16.

This morning we marched off from Estrée Cauchy at 9 a.m. to Noeux-les-Mines via Grand Servins, Petit Servins, Gouy Servins, Bouvigny, Boyeffles, Sains-en-Gohelle, P[eti]t Sains. It was about a ten mile march and it would have been a very pretty one but for a heavy mist which hung low and obscured the view. The roads were muddy and wet but the men marched very well and we reached here N[oeux]-les-Mines at 1 p.m. This is a straggled out mining town and has been shelled in parts but the coal pits are still gaily working and it's full of civilians and very good shops in it. The men are all in big huts but the officers are billeted on the people. I have a most excellent billet in the chemist's house. It's the best I have had in France, much better than my Bruay one. It's a huge room with a carpet, marble wash stand, spring bed and sheets!! Worse luck we are only here for one night. I'm afraid such billets would soon ruin us for trench warfare. We go into trenches to-morrow just north of Loos, bon eh!!

Wednesday 25.10.16.

We left N-les-Mines at 10.45 a.m. with about 200 yard intervals between each platoon so as to avoid a large body of men being spotted and shelled as they can observe you from the village of Hulluch. I came along with Capt. Baby Hilton. The roads were very muddy and dirty. We marched through Mazingarbe, a mining place and it has been shelled at times too. Then we came to a ruined and deserted village, also mining, called La Philosophe, which we come to for our divisional rest – not a very bright spot. From Mazingarbe we had a wretched march on cobbled roads – they are very trying on one's feet. Shortly after La P.[hilosophe] we entered Vermelles, quite a big ruined town. It is a second Ypres. The French drove the Huns out of it in December 1914 on Xmas Day. It must have been a wonderful effort! On the far side of the town we entered a communication trench called Le Rutoire Alley which took us parallel to the Hulluch-Vermelles road, passing the farm of

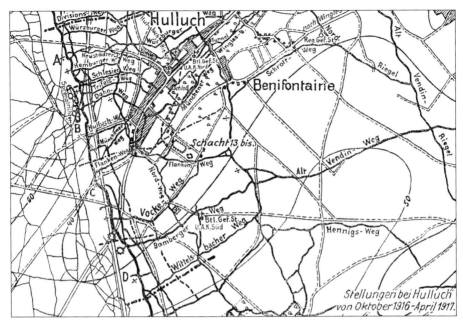

Map 9. Hulluch –German positions October 1916 to April 1917. The thick black line marks the German front line, from Gruson *Das Königlich Preussische 4. Thüringische Infanterie-Regiment Nr.72 im Weltkrieg.*

Le Rutoire on our right. Jove that was some march up Le Rutoire Alley, it seemed as if it would never end as it was over two miles long with hundreds of windings. It was raining and the duckboards in the trenches were slippery and at last, when we turned into Tenth Avenue on our right and reached H.Q. we were fed up and weary for it was about 3 p.m. My Battalion is in Brigade Reserve in Tenth Avenue and we are all in dugouts and are fairly comfortable. Tenth Avenue used to be the Hun front line trench before the battle of Loos and it was just at this spot that this Battalion was cut up at Loos. The famous Lone Tree which was cut down after the battle owing to being such a landmark on this plain is just outside our Batt. H.Q. The wounded were collected around it during the battle. It is now just a scrubby bunch of short branches. I have no dugout owing to mine falling in so I'm going to get L/Cpl Webb, my stretcher-bearer corporal to make one for me. He's a miner and is excellent at such jobs. We relieved the 12th [11th] King's Own Royal Lancs. (Bantams) of the 40th Division. Funny little fellows but very sturdy. They would put five men in a dugout where we could only get three!!! We are to be six days in Brigade Reserve and then six days in the front line and then six days in Divisional Reserve at La Philosophe. This is a wretched looking country, flat and nothing but dirty coal mining villages with crowds of huge slag heaps and chimney stacks. No word of leave yet.

Thursday 26.10.16.

Still wet and muddy. My dugout is to be started to-night near H.Q. Mess. I'm full of excitement and glee. I'm off on leave beginning on Monday so my relief is coming up on Sunday morning so as to let me get away to the Transport lines at Les Brebis, a tidy walk, to change out of my trench togs and get my things together and leave for Béthune where I catch the train at 8.30 a.m. on Monday. From our trenches in Tenth Avenue you get a wonderful view of the Loos salient. Behind and to the left you can see the Hohenzollern Redoubt, then the famous Quarries, then the village of Hulluch with the huge Tower Bridge works of the Société Metallurgique de Pont à Vendin behind it, to the right of that is the famous Hill 70 which we captured and lost at the Battle of Loos. In front of it and in our hand is the battered village of Loos and to the right of it is Bully Grenay, once a garden city, also in our hands. It is just opposite the extreme right of the Loos salient.

Saturday 28.10.16.

Just received news tonight that Lieut. and Adjutant Clark and Lieut. Gold of this Battalion have been awarded Military Crosses.[1] Both good men and well do they deserve it. I have got my leave warrant to-day and am off to-morrow, jove I am looking forward to leave to Edinburgh. It will be nearly seven months since I last went – 6-15th April was the last time.

Monday 30.10.16.

Here we are in Boulogne. My relief, Lieut. O'Donnell, R.A.M.C., instead of coming in the morning yesterday, only arrived at 3.30 p.m. I was fed up because I wanted to ride into Béthune in daylight and get a bed at the Station Hotel. However, as soon as he arrived I was off like a hare over the open, didn't worry about Communication trenches, to La Philosophe, where Baker met me with my horse and we rode to the Transport Lines at Les Brebis where I changed out of my trench togs and rode into Béthune via Mazingarbe. We got to Béthune at 7 p.m. but couldn't raise a bed for love nor money so just slept on a bench. As a matter of fact I didn't care where I slept for I was off on leave!! The leave train left at 8.49 a.m., and Lt. Botham travelled down with me. We got to Boulogne at 2.30 and found the boat had gone in the morning so would have to wait till to-morrow but we got our leave extended by one day. The weather is very boisterous for crossing!!!

Wednesday 1.11.16.

Back in Edinburgh, jove it's great!!! We had a fiend of a crossing yesterday but after we got on to the train everything was O.K. again. We arrived at Victoria Station at 4.30

1   For the Somme.

p.m. and at once got a taxi across to Campden Hill Court to see Alice [my sister] but much to my disgust she had gone off back to Dublin that very day, after having waited the whole of October in London to see me. I was disappointed! Then I went to Queen Ann Street to see Lieut. Castle (Snag) who was in Hospital there and he too I just missed so in disgust went to the Piccadilly Restaurant and had a great dinner, worse luck alone! I caught my train at 11.30 p.m. from King's Cross and had a good sleep as I had a sleeper. I'm afraid my eight days leave will fly!

Thursday 9.11.16.

Feeling too downhearted for words. I left Edinburgh last night and here we are stuck a whole day in Folkestone. We were unable to cross to-day, submarines I suppose! Luckily I met Capt. Park and Lt. Small, R.A.M.C., Edinburgh fellows, so have some company. We are staying at the Pavilion Hotel. We are going to see 'The Whip' to-night. It's a very fine day.

Saturday 11.11.16.

Back with the Regiment again. We crossed yesterday; had a good crossing and came up by train with Lt. Greathead, R.E., and Capt. Impey, R.A.M.C. (Little Bob). The latter is in a F. Ambulance at Wipers. We got to Béthune about 2 a.m., and were lucky to get a bed at the station hotel and then came out by the mess cart and luckily found the Regiment out of the trenches at a small shell-swept mining village La Philosophe. I found Hilton had gone on leave while I was away. The new O.C., Col. Swanton has been making himself objectionable and seems to be loathed all round.[2] He ordered my stretcher-bearers to carry rifles and bayonets so I had to see him about it, but he gave in to me and was quite decent. I bar anyone interfering with my department. Worse luck we go into the trenches to-morrow again. Capt. Anslow, who used to be with us has returned and taken over B. Company from Lt. Warre-Dymond.

Sunday 12.11.16.

We are in the line again, took over from the Queen's. We marched up from La Philosophe via Vermelles and then up that fiend of a 2½ mile Communication trench, Le Rutoire Alley to 9th Avenue, jove it was a wearisome trek, luckily it was a fine day. I went round the Reserve trench line this afternoon, entering it from Essex lane and back home by Wingsway C.T. The Reserve line is in fairly good order.

---

2   Thomas Swanton had been commissioned in the East Surrey Regiment in 1910, aged 22. He joined 1st East Surrey at the Front in May 1915. Sherriff, in *Memories of Active Service*, confirms he was a martinet, who soon made himself generally unpopular with 9th East Surrey, with whom he served from 25 October 1916.

Monday 13.11.16.

L/Cpl. Webb of the S.Bs. took me round the line this morning as I did not know it. It's in a wretched state, mud galore and parapets all falling in. It will take months of work to repair it.

Thursday 16.11.16.

Nothing much been doing. It has fortunately remained dry but very cold and frosty so the men have done a dickens of a lot of work in repairing the trenches. We have seen a couple of big flights of geese flying westward which the O.C. says 'is a sign of snow and cold weather'. The Huns and our men in the trenches were firing at them and brought down two. They just fluttered down like pieces of paper. I have been going round the trenches every morning and either Croxford, my servant, or Rand or Corporal Allam accompany me. One day I visit the left Company which was D this time and the Company in reserve (A Coy.) and the next day the right (C Coy.) and centre Coys. (B Coy). When we went to the left Coy. we went from Bn. H.Q. in 9th Avenue up Wingsway to the line along it and then back to the Reserve Line which is at right angles to Wingsway and home by Essex Lane. The next day we would go down Essex Lane to C. Coy. along the front line to B. Coy. and back by Hay Alley. It's not very healthy at the top end of Hay Alley – the home of Minnies and Aerial darts!!! This evening Lt. Thomas, our bombing officer, is going out with some of his bombers on a small raid to try and capture a Hun sentry[3] in a sap which runs out from the Hun line. Rand, my medical orderly, and I are going up to the front line to be on the spot in case anyone is wounded while on the raid.

Friday 17.11.16.

There was no luck in the raid last night. Thomas, Sgt. Summers, D.C.M.,[4] L/Cpl. Husk (Taffy), Pte. Brunt, a red headed fellow and six others went out, crawled right past the Hun wire and lay in waiting for three hours to catch the Hun but he never came along so they had to come in as it was fearfully cold and the moon would soon be up. We were in the front line and were about frozen but they must have been frozen meat, lying out in No Man's Land!! They were awfully fed up at not getting him, however they are to have another shot to-night. Very overcast to-night, looks like snow.

---

3   To identify his unit and obtain any other useful intelligence.
4   Walter Summers enlisted in October 1914, giving his age as 21 and profession as cinematograph producer. He joined 9th East Surrey in October 1915 and was soon promoted to sergeant. He was outstandingly brave and won a Distinguished Conduct Medal and then an M.M., largely for patrolling and raiding. Commissioned in 1918, he won an M.C. with 12th East Surrey. After the war he directed many films.

Figure 21. A German outpost in *Trichter 1,* a fortified crater in front of Hulluch, manned by IR 72 which faced 9th East Surrey here, autumn/winter 1917. (© Andrew Lucas)

Saturday 18.11.16.

Fearfully cold last night and when we woke up this morning it had snowed a little. No luck again last night. They lay waiting for two hours but it was so cold had to come in. We are back in 10th Avenue to-day in Brigade Reserve and the Queen's have taken over the front line from us. I'm glad we are back as the men are worn out with work and the cold. We have had three cases of Trench Foot[5] during the six days in but luckily only slight ones, so we kept them in a dugout for twenty-four hours then they were quite O.K. again. It was wonderfully quiet in the line except for a few Minnies and Aerial darts. Pte. Lambert, one of my ex- stretcher-bearers was killed this trip in.[6]

---

5   A disease arising from men in the trenches having their feet continually wet whilst circulation was restricted by boots and puttees. If not adequately treated gangrene could develop. Various preventative measures were recommended. The High Command took trench foot very seriously and saw its incidence as an indicator of a unit's morale and efficiency.

6   Robert Lambert died as a machine gunner, aged 35. Some others of Pirie's stretcher-bearers also moved to combatant roles. Lambert's brief diary of service abroad with the battalion from 31 August 1915 is at I.W.M.

Monday 19.11.16. [20.11.16]

The thaw has set in so everything is greasy and muddy. L/Cpl. Webb, Ptes. Truss and Rolls of D.Coy. are building a dugout for me in Wingsway, near the Aid Post. My old one was a pokey effort and too far away from the Aid Post.

Friday 24.11.16.

The Regiment moved up to the front line again for another six days tour and the Queen's took over 10th Avenue from us. The dugout is nearly complete and hope to get into it tomorrow. After these six days in we go back to billets in La Philosophe for six days rest.

Monday 27.11.16.

I trekked into the new dugout last night. The table and bed and one shelf has been put in but we must still have another shelf for books and a washing stand, then it will be complete. The canvas door was put on to-day. The stove did not prove a success last night as the ring on top has been lost and the tin (top of an oil drum!) we put on top didn't fit and so it smoked furiously. However to-night we cut the tin to fit the top and glued it down with clay so now the smoke <u>has</u> to go up the chimney, and it's burning very well and gives off a splendid heat. Croxford and I went round the whole line to-day. It was a fine day, frosty. There is still a good deal of mud in the trenches after Saturday's rain.

Thursday 30.11.16.

Here we are back in La Philosophe in billets after eighteen days in the trenches. It's great to be back and be able to roam about wherever you like. The dugout was completely furnished before we left and we threw out the old French stove as it persisted in smoking furiously and got a sort of oil drum stove made by the R.Es. but it's about as bad as the other one. I have made all arrangements for the inoculation of the whole of the Battalion and am to do A. & D. Companies to-morrow.

Friday 1.12.16.

Corporal Allam and I did the two companies this afternoon, but found about forty men in each company who had recently been done which reduced our work.

Saturday 2.12.16.

This morning we did C Coy. and in the afternoon I rode into Noeux-les-Mines via Mazingarbe to see the A.D.M.S. on business. Then had tea with the 72nd Field Ambulance and got back at 6 p.m. in time for a concert given by some R.G.A. [Royal Garrison Artillery] men at La Philosophe in the Recreation room. It was jolly good.

Sunday 3.12.16.

Went to early communion this morning and had the sick parade at nine instead of 7 a.m. Then inspected a draft of 69 men at 11 and inoculated B. Coy. at 2 p.m. so it was quite a busy day.

Monday 4.12.16.

I rode into Les Brebis via Mazingarbe this morning to have a bath and in the afternoon Whiteman drove 'Baby' Hilton and self into Béthune via Sailly la Bourse and Beuvry. We had tea and did a deal of shopping and then had dinner. Lts. Thomas, Ellis and Webb joined us and later on Lts. Warre-Dymond and Churcher joined us so we were quite a merry party. Béthune is quite a decent sized place and has good shops in it. I ran across Capt. Paul Little R.A.M.C. who was in my year at the Varsity. He has just got an M.C. We came out with the mess cart, but oh, it was cold, in fact every day has been since we have been in billets.

Tuesday 5.12.16.

A draft of 70 arrived to-day so had to fit each man with a new small box respirator. They arrived too late to be medically examined so shall have to do that later. This evening the 'Snipers', i.e. our divisional Follies Troupe gave a splendid concert in La Philosophe. One fellow, Sapper Shackleton of the R.Es. was excellent.[7]

Wednesday 6.12.16.

This morning at 5 a.m. I was awakened by a rifle shot and yells and was called to see the sentry on H.Q. guard who had been wounded in the leg and found it was broken. At the time it happened a party of East Yorks who were returning from a working party were coming out of the Divisional soup kitchen and someone had fired the rifle. The man who did it hasn't been traced, but it was found he had taken the Sergeant of the guard's rifle out of the guard room, fired it and thrown it down near the sentry, between two houses. The Battalion moved up again this morning and we relieved the 8th Queen's. I came up with C Coy. with Capt. Hilton at 8 a.m. It has been raining to-day. The oil drum stove isn't a success so Webb, Truss, Hardiker and Croxford are going down to Le Rutoire Farm to get bricks to-morrow and make an open fire for me.

---

7   Most divisions and many smaller units formed concert parties of serving soldiers, who were inspired by music hall entertainers.

Thursday 7.12.16.

Rand and I went round the Centre Coy (C Coy.) and Right Coy's. (B.Coy.) trenches this morning. The new fire place is in and alight. It's a huge success, no smoke now. It's made of a base of petrol tins filled with clay and the upper part of bricks. It gives out a splendid heat so the dugout is completely furnished now. There is a nasty smell of tear gas shells about. The Huns let loose with them when the Queen's were in and the smell hasn't died away yet.

Saturday 9.12.16.

It has rained all day to-day and the whole place is just mud and water, filthy it is. Croxford went round with me this morning. Just as we got to the top of Hay Alley Fritz was busy with his Minnies all around Hay Alley and Hilton's H.Q. so we waited a bit till he had finished sending over his issue and pushed on but just as we reached the dugout he sent over one behind the dugout – maybe for luck!! After I had seen Baby I went along the line to Anslow's area. At one place a Minnie had fallen right in the trench so had to scramble over the top in full view of the Hun. This afternoon I went up to D. Coy in the Reserve line to see Ellis (Lt.) who had influenza and then I had tea with Tetley and Co.

Monday 11.12.16.

Rand and I went round to-day and as we were in the Right Coy. front line one of our aeroplanes flew over the Hun lines and we could see him dropping bombs on a village behind, you could see the bomb drop. It's been a fine clear day

Tuesday 12.12.16.

The Queen's relieved us to-day and we are in reserve in 10th Avenue trenches. I'm feeling rather like Flu but it is so rife in the Regiment I daren't go to bed.

Friday 15.12.16.

I was compelled to go to bed after all yesterday but am up again and feeling pretty fit. I have got Webb and Truss on to enlarging my dugout as it is beastly small. The weather is vile, very wet.

Monday 18.12.16.

The Regiment is back in the line again and I have trekked back into my dugout in Wingsway. I much prefer when we are in line to being in 10th Avenue as our dugouts are much more comfortable. While the relief was taking place to-day the Hun greeted us with some shells along Le Rutoire Alley and Hay Alley and around Hay Dump in 9th Avenue but no one was hurt.

Tuesday 19.12.16.

Rand and I were round the centre Coy. and Right Coy. this morning. Just as we were in the front line of the centre Coy. our trench mortars started a strafe and I knew there would be some retaliation so quickly went along the support line which was full of mud and water and one place absolutely flattened out by Minnies, to the Right Company. No sooner had we reached it than showers of aerial darts and Minnies came over on to the way we had come so we just missed it. We saw a big flight of geese this morning and to-night it's snowing. This is the 3rd time flights of geese have been followed by snow.

Saturday 23.12.16.

The weather has been very wet the last few days and the trenches are afloat. We had a man killed yesterday in Green Curve – a beast of a place. It's very bad luck considering it's so near Xmas. Then two men were wounded on one of the Crater posts by a bomb. To-day at 8 a.m. punctually the Hun Minnied and shelled the front line with whizz bangs and we back at H.Q. got whizz bangs and tear shells and all our eyes were smarting furiously. They kept it up till about lunch time but we have been very lucky with casualties, none killed and only about a dozen walking cases, all slight. We are to be relieved to-morrow by the Queen's and go back to La Philosophe for six days so we mean to have a good Xmas Day.

Sunday 24.12.16.

Here we are back in billets at La Philosophe and it's great after eighteen days in the trenches. Unfortunately just as all the men in B.Coy. in the Right Coy. area were about to move out an aerial dart landed amongst them and killed Sergeant Parsons and three men and wounded my stretcher-bearer Sillis and another man. As Allam and I were coming down Le Rutoire Alley the Huns were shelling a battery on the outskirts of Philosophe and we afterwards heard they had put out a gun and killed two officers.

Xmas Day 1916.

Went to early Communion this morning which was held in the Recreation Room by our Chaplain Capt. Poole. Had sick parade at 9.15 and then was free for the day. All the officers subscribed towards the men's dinners and they had Pork or Beef and plum puddings, oranges and beer so they didn't do so badly. This evening there is to be a concert given by B & D. Coy.s and after it all the officers are to dine together.

26.12.16 Boxing Day.

The concert last night was a huge success, especially the Trio Hilton, Tetley and Lindsay when they sang a parody on 'Another little drink wouldn't do us any harm.'[8] Half way through the concert there was an interval when beer and sandwiches were handed round to the men. Our Xmas dinner was a huge success-twenty-six officers sat down together and Lt. Mase[9] provided an excellent dinner and most wonderful programmes were painted (water colours) by Pte Cole, one of our men.[10] The dinner party eventually dispersed at 12.30, Clark having been in great form. A and C Coys held their concert this evening and after it I dined with the officers of the 103rd Coy. R.Es. In it I know Lt. Greathead very well. I was at school with three of his brothers in the Cape.

27.12.16. Wednesday

Xmas Day was a vile day of wind but it's very fine to-day. Hilton, Tetley, Whiteman and I drove into Béthune to see Lt. Yalden who was wounded with us and is now with the 1st E. Surreys. He had tea and dinner with us, also a jolly good feed of oysters. When we came back it was an awful job to see our way as there was a dense fog on and only the trees and houses on the roadside guided us home.

Friday 29.12.16.

The weather has been very wet again. Last night Major Anderson,[11] Capts. Barker, Hilton, Tetley, Lt. Mase and I had a real good dinner together at the officers' restaurant in Mazingarbe. But I'm off to bed early to-night as I'm dead beat with all these late nights and besides we move up again to-morrow afternoon. We always used to relieve in the morning but the Hun got to know of it somehow and shelled us, hence the change to afternoon, I'm not looking forward to eighteen days in.

8   W.H. 'Harry' Lindsay, born 1894, attended public school before becoming a meat broker. He was commissioned after being wounded serving in the ranks of the Rifle Brigade, arriving with 9th East Surrey in September 1916. He won an M.C. for the January 1917 raid and was later Adjutant. He was killed, as a captain, in September 1918, resisting a German trench raid at Loos. Some light-hearted letters of his survive in Sherriff's correspondence.

9   Arthur Mase had joined the battalion in August 1916 and left it, through sickness, in March 1917. He later served with the Rifle Brigade.

10   Edward Cole, whilst serving with the battalion produced a number of artistic works during late 1916 and 1917, including Christmas cards, programmes and caricatures of officers, examples of which are included in this book. At the time of writing I have two forthcoming articles on him and his work for *Stand To!*

11   Major, later Lieutenant Colonel William Anderson was born 1881 and a chartered accountant and stockbroker. He served with 9th East Surrey for around four months. He won a posthumous V.C. with his regiment, the Highland Light Infantry, in March 1918.

UNDERSTUDY

2. Lieut. W.H.Lindsay. M.C.

Figure 22.
A caricature of Second Lieutenant
(later Captain) W.H. Lindsay, by
Private Edward Cole, early 1917.
(© Surrey History Centre)

Saturday 30.12.16.

Here we are in again, and I hear the Huns did shell this morning as usual so he was diddled this time. From all descriptions the trenches are in an awful state, mud and water up to one's knees and most of the trenches are 'minnied'. He has certainly taken the upper hand with trench mortars off us.

Sunday 31.12.16.

Didn't go round the line to-day as we were to strafe the Huns with our heavy guns and the front line was to be cleared – the strafe however didn't come off so I went up to the Reserve line where I met Hilton. He has been sent to the R.Es. to give him a rest as he has done twenty two months in the trenches. The Hun has been very quiet to-day so I am wondering if we are for it to-night at midnight or to-morrow. He's sure to give us a New Year present. I'm not worrying to sit in the New Year, bed's the best place.

New Year's Day 1917.

I went to bed at 11.30 p.m. last night and all was very quiet except that the Hun was raking Le Rutoire Plain with his machine guns but at 8 a.m. this morning he strafed the front line and rear with all sorts of stuff till about 9.15 pretty heavily and then slowly till about one o'clock. Then our heavy guns strafed him so he hasn't had it all his own way. To-day like Xmas Day has been a dismal bleak one but not so windy. The entrance to the Right Coy. H.Q.s deep dugout was squashed in by a Minnie bursting on the parapet alongside the entrance and a man who was taking shelter in the entrance was crushed to death. D Coy. is holding the Right and Capt. Tetley was rather badly shaken so is resting at H.Q. and Lt. Mase is running the Coy. The Crater Post[s], (five in number) on the Hulluch Mine Craters, have been badly knocked about – a Sgt. Chinnery and two men were killed on the extreme left one No.5 by a Minnie. The left Coy [front line]. held by C. Coy. has been very badly smashed in by Minnies, in all it has been a wretched New Year!

Tuesday 2.1.17.

Rand and I went round the centre and right Coys. this morning and the top of Hay Alley is knee deep with mud and water and in all the trenches are in a bad state. We came back by Essex Lane and it was very muddy at the top end also. Six days in such a piece of line is far too long a period both from a mental and physical point of view.

Wednesday 3.1.17.

Last night No. 2 Crater Post and No. 1 were badly strafed with aerial darts and we were up at 2 a.m., 4 a.m., and 7.30 a.m. to see three stretcher cases (bad ones) and two slight walking ones, and to-day has been one worry after another over cases of threatened trench foot and amongst them are three cases of trench foot. The Centre Coy. who are holding most of the crater posts are the chief victims. I marvel that there hasn't been dozens of cases. In all it has been a very trying day, full of worries.

Friday 5.1.17

Went round the centre and right Coys. yesterday, all was quiet. This morning when I went round to breakfast I was told I was being relieved by a Lt. C.P. [sic.] Hartley[12] who is to take over my job to-day and I am to go to the 74th Field Ambulance for duty. I have now been just short of thirteen months with this Regiment, the 9th East Surreys and have sort of grown to be one of them and am most downhearted at leaving them for I'll miss Hilton, Tetley, Whiteman and Clark badly, still I need a change

---

12   Lieutenant later Captain George Hartley was a Scot, born 1887. From engineering he moved to medicine, graduating in 1916. He won an M.C. and became a Midlands general practitioner after the war.

badly as I'm warworn and nervy so it's for the Regiment's good to get someone fresh and full of energy. I wish I could take Corp. Allam with me. He's a most excellent medical orderly. Funnily enough I leave to-morrow which makes it just a year since we moved into the line at Hooge in the Ypres Salient.

Saturday 6.1.17.

This morning after having handed over everything to Lt. Hartley, I went round all the Regiment and said au revoir to all the officers, stretcher-bearers and Corp. Allam and when I finally left the Battalion in Tenth Avenue I just felt as if I had left my home. I came down with Clark and Thomas and Lt. Hills of the 72nd Brigade Staff. We came down Le Rutoire Alley till we got opposite Le Rutoire Farm and then struck through the farm which is in ruins, across Le Rutoire Plain to La Philosophe where I went in to say au revoir to Capt. Hilton who is attached to the 103rd Coy. R.Es. He was very sick at my going away but I had had quite enough of our O.C., Col. Swanton, he's a swine. Then I had lunch at Brigade H.Q., and said au revoir to them. The General [Mitford] was awfully decent to me and asked me to be sure to come back to his Brigade. My horse was waiting for me at Bde. H.Q., and I rode to Les Brebis to pick up my kit and the ambulance car to bring me to my new unit. I found Birch, the Quarter Master in bed with Flu. and Whiteman was on leave. The run from Les Brebis to here, Labeuvrière, was about an hour and I arrived at the 74th Field Ambulance just at tea time, so now I'm safely with my new unit.

Sunday 7.1.17.

My new O.C. Lt. Col. Rose, D.S.O.[13] seems a very decent sort and so are the other officers, Capt. McKnight an Irishman,[14] Capt. McCurrick, Capt. McPherson and Lt. and Q.M. Merryman. I have quite a decent billet with a spring bed and sheets, a thing you seldom got with the Infantry. This unit is stationed in a village, Labeuvrière, about three miles away from Béthune and is running the 1st Army Corps Rest Station which only takes in patients who need a rest or won't take longer then fourteen days to recover. It consists of an old monastery and huts. I have been put in charge of the huts called 'B' Block and have about ninety patients to look after, all minor ailments. I have to visit the three huts each day at 9 a.m. and it takes about two hours to get round them, and after that have nil to do so it's a very slack job, and we are miles away from the guns. I'm Orderly Officer to-morrow so will be a bit busier.

---

13   Alexander Rose, born 1878, had been commissioned in the R.A.M.C. in 1905.
14   Matthew McKnight had been in France since March 1915. In 1919 his Medal Card indicates service in India and a home address in Dublin.

Monday 8.1.17.

I was Orderly Officer to-day so after I had done my wards I went round with the Orderly Sergeant and inspected the whole Rest Station. Then this afternoon, I had to pay all the patients, some 350, but Capt. McKnight helped me so it didn't take so very long. Then my last job was to inspect the men who were to be discharged next day at 6 p.m.

Tuesday 9.1.17.

While I was doing my wards this morning we had Surgeon General Pike[15] who is the Director of Medical Services for the 1st Army. He was accompanied by Col. Buswell, C.M.G., our Divisional A.D.M.S.[16] This afternoon I went for a ride on my new horse Ginger. He's a fine big chestnut and goes very well, fast and comfortable. McCurrick, Merryman and I went for the ride together along the Béthune Road and back through Annezin and Fouquereuil, both coal mining villages.

Wednesday 10.1.17.

This afternoon Capt. McKnight and I rode into Béthune, did some shopping, had tea and came out again in time for a very good Cinema show in the Rest station hall.

Friday 12.1.17.

This afternoon the Ambulance's new Pierrot Troupe,[17] 'The Yellow Birds' gave their first performance. Some of the nurses and M.Os. from No.18 C.C.S. at La Pugnoy came to it and then had tea with us. It was a huge success.

Monday 15.1.17.

On Saturday afternoon McKnight and I went for a fine ride all down the eastern side of the Bois des Dames, through a village, Hesdigneul, where the 1st Corps Field Cashier was. There we drew some money and then rode back along the western side of the Bois, through Lapugnoy. On Sunday, King, McKnight and I rode over to the 21st Welsh Mobile Laboratory at Chocques and then all through a wood to Allouagne and thence back through Lapugnoy. My horse was going very well indeed. To-day I was Orderly Officer and was a little more busy than usual.

---

15 William Pike born 1860, promoted Major General 1918 and made KCMG 1919.
16 Colonel Ferberd Buswell, C.M.G., born 1864, was A.D.M.S. from November 1915 to April 1918.
17 Pierrots were entertainers with white faces wearing white French pantomime costumes, as seen in many British music halls.

Thursday 18.1.17.

We had a very heavy fall of snow yesterday and it's still snowing to-day.

Friday 19.1.17.

It's still snowing a little and the ground is white and it's very cold. This afternoon the 5th Divisional Concert Troupe 'The Whizz Bangs' gave us a show and it was top-hole, in fact the best I've seen in France. We had some of the staffs of No.1 C.C.S. at Chocques and No.18 C.C.S. at Lapugnoy over to see it.

Tuesday 23.1.17.

Yesterday I had tea with Whiteman and Webb[18] of the E. Surreys in Béthune. We also went to the 'Whizz Bangs' which is excellent. I heard all the news of the Regiment and that poor Lt. Trench had been killed. He hadn't been long with the Regt.[19] The Regiment is to do a daylight raid at 12.30 p.m., just to the right of Hulluch Craters. Lts. Thomas and Lindsay and fifty men are going over. I hope it's a success. I heard during the weekend that I had been granted a commission in the R.A.M.C. regular army with the temporary rank of Captain, but all my previous service counts so I have got two years in which will help towards promotion. This evening the O.C. had a big dinner party for a lot of his friends Colonel Winder etc.

Thursday 25.1.17.

Our Ambulance Pierrot troupe the 'Yellowbirds' gave a performance to-night. It was quite good. We had Lt. Grant of the East Surreys who is at the Army Corps sniping school up the road and Lt. Hoggan, one of the instructors, down to dinner to-night. We also heard that the raid had been a huge success, at first it was reported they had taken three prisoners and the raiders had had four wounded, then later we heard they had taken forty prisoners.[20] The snow is still lying and we are having very heavy frosts so it's bitterly cold.

Saturday 27.1.17.

Still bitterly cold and snow lying. I was over at the Corps Field Cashier this after-noon at La Buissière to draw cash and while I was in his office I met a fellow from

---

18   Lawrence 'Jimbo' Webb had joined the battalion in September 1916. He was Assistant
      Adjutant for some time. He was with de la Fontaine when he was killed in August 1917 and
      won an M.C. for restoring positions after the German attack. He left in December 1917, sick.
19   Nugent Trench, born 1887, had been living in Australia, but enlisted with the Canadians.
      Commissioned in the British Army in 1915, he joined the battalion on 27 November
      1916 and was killed on 16 January.
20   IR72 opposite reported two dead, three wounded and three missing. 9th East Surrey and
      the R.E. had three killed and four wounded among the fifty-nine participants.

Figure 23. Another photograph of men from IR 72 in the crater front line area west of Hulluch. (© Andrew Lucas)

Edinburgh, Teddy Price, who is in a C.C.S. near here. After I got back I paid out the patients. Captain McKnight is laid up with Flu just now so we are a little more busy. The Division was to have come out on the 29th for a month's rest and the 21st Division was to relieve it but the 21st has suddenly been moved to Ypres so the rest is off. I'm very sorry for the poor men, as the cold must be terrific. Rumour hath it that the Huns are expected to attack up there.

Tuesday 30.1.17.

Still very cold and snow lying and it has snowed again to-day. I have got a beastly boil near my right eye which is beastly painful.

Friday 2.2.17.

The boil on my face is considerably better to-day but still painful. I had a great surprise to-day; after I had done my wards at 11 a.m. who should I find waiting for me but Lieut. Whiteman, the East Surreys' Transport Officer. He gave me all the news of the Regiment and I was glad to see him. It was just like old days again. This afternoon No. 18 C.C.S. from Lapugnoy gave a show in our hall and brought some of their nurses but I didn't go with my face in bandages. The O.C., Col. Rose went on leave to-day.

Tuesday 6.2.17.

My boil has gone, thank goodness, and am O.K. again. This afternoon I rode into Béthune through Annezin and had tea with Capt. Gibb, R.A.M.C. He is M.O. to the 5th Divisional R.Es. We used to be at school together at St. Andrew's in the Cape. We went out to tea but to our disgust we couldn't get any tea cakes as every Tuesday and Thursday now it's a meatless and sugarless day in France. While at tea I met Lt. Douglass from the E. Surreys[21] and we had a chat together. He is to have dinner with me to-morrow night. Then I went to the barber's and then ran across Lt. Blower of the E. Surreys He gave me a graphic description of the raid. Snow still lying and extremely cold with bitter frosts.

Wednesday 7.2.17.

Still very cold. To-night Douglass came over to dinner and after it we had some bridge. He and I played King and McCurrick but we went down badly, couldn't hold any cards.

Thursday 8.2.17.

This morning I went to the No 18 C.C.S. dentist at Lapugnoy to see about a stopped tooth so he bored it out and I am to return on Sunday to have it restopped. As soon as I got back King and I went to Aire via Lillers by car to have lunch with Capt. Caher of the 74th F.A. who is running the first Army Corps Officers' Rest Station. He was for a long time M.O. to the 12th Royal Fusiliers in this Division. We had lunch with him and in the Rest Station which is a top-hole place I ran across Lts. Cowper and Sherriff of the E. Surreys.[22] After lunch we went for a stroll round the town. It has a very fine old church dating from 1735. The Tower and roof had been rebuilt then, as when the Duke of Marlborough attacked the town[23] he shelled the tower and roof and you can still see an old round cannon ball sticking in the brick wall of the church. The old custom house is very quaint too. After tea we returned to Labeuvrière. It's about an eight mile run. We have a Capt. Shuttleworth of the D.L.I. [Durham Light Infantry] messing with us just now. He is a great old boy and is the 21st Divisional Claims Officer.

21   Archibald Douglass, the son of a clergyman, had been serving with the battalion since June 1916 and was nicknamed 'Father'. Sherriff had enormous respect for him and he seems to be the chief inspiration for 'Osborne' in *Journey's End*. As a captain, Douglass died of wounds, aged 30, in April 1918.
22   Robert Sherriff was an insurance clerk, born 1896. He joined the battalion 1 October 1916 and left it in August 1917, through wounds. He later used these experiences in writing *Journey's End*, and subsequently wrote about some of his time with the battalion in a series of articles, an essay and an unpublished memoir. His papers are at Surrey History Centre. He had been at the Rest Station since 24 January through severe nerve pain, which he believed was psychosomatic.
23   In 1710 during the war of the Spanish Succession.

Friday 9.2.17.

Just after lunch to-day Capt. King, our O.C., got a wire from the A.D.M.S. to detail an officer for duty for a few days with the 73rd F. Amb., and to take over St. George's Aid Post in 10th Avenue which is behind Hulluch and he asked if I would care to go so I jumped at it and got my things packed and my servant Horne and I were off at once. McPartlan, my real servant is soon to go on leave, so I have Horne temporarily. We first went to Noeux-les-Mines to report to the O.C. 73rd F.A., Capt. Cunningham, but he was at the Philosophe Aid Post so motored on to there and found him there with the officers of the 37th Division F. Amb., who are to take over from us on the 12th. Horne and I walked up along the light railway and got up here (St. George's) about 6 p.m., and relieved Capt. Brisco who was ill with Flu. Much to my joy I found my old Batt., the East Surreys were still in the line so I went round to the H.Q. in 9th Avenue and walked in in the middle of their dinner and a regular cheer went up. Jove, it was like old days being back with them again. I long to get back to them. I found Major Anderson in command, Col. Swanton is at an O.C.'s course at the base, but Col. de la Fontaine was expected back any day. We had a great talk; Major Anderson, Lt. Clark the Adjutant, Lts. Grant, Lindsay, Ellis and Hartley the M.O. were there. They unfortunately go back to Philosophe to-morrow but as the whole division is going out to rest behind Béthune I shall go and see them there.

Saturday 10.2.17.

Last night about 1 a.m. I was called up to see a wounded E. Surrey and at 7.30 a.m. I was up to see more wounded. The Huns had raided the N. Staffs who are on the right of the Surreys at 4.30 a.m. and the first to be brought in was a Hun with a broken leg. He was a boy of twenty but of fine physique and well clad but almost pulseless with cold as he had been lying in No Man's Land for two hours in the snow and it freezing hard. However we dressed his wounds and warmed him with hot bottles, whiskey and blankets. I later heard the Staffs were on the watch and caught them with Lewis guns and killed a lot on our wire as well as capturing an unwounded Hun officer and man, a slightly wounded man and this badly hit one. (They were Prussians).[24] At 9 a.m. Corp. Allam came in to see me and we had a long talk. Then Capt. Patch, the 8th Queen's M.O. came round so another chat followed. About 12 o'clock I had a note from the O.C. 73rd F. Amb. telling me to make arrangements with the M.O. of the N. Staffs. as they are to have a raid to-morrow night and see about supplying him with bearers. So I at once went up Pont Street Communication Trench and turned into Curzon Street where their H.Q. is and Col. Dugmore was awfully decent. The raid comes off at 7.15 to-morrow night and Lt. Blythe, their M.O., and I are to have our Aid Post in the support trench where there's a deep dugout between Essex Lane and Vendin Alley

---

24   According to 24th Division's war diary, WO95/2190, at T.N.A., the raiders were from IR 72 and the more seriously wounded prisoner died a little later.

and I shall bring up twelve bearers to carry the wounded away. Blythe and I have been reconnoitring the route of evacuation after dark to-night. I am going to dinner with the N. Staffs to-night in Tenth Avenue. They were relieved to-day by the West Kents.

Monday 12.2.17.

On Saturday night about 12.30 a.m. I was wakened to read an urgent note which ordered me to proceed to Loos on Sunday and report to the 3rd Rifle Brigade not later than 3 p.m. to help them with their raid. On Sunday morning Capt. Renwick and his men of a 37th Div. F. Amb. came up to relieve me so I left the dressing station in charge of him and I got a guide to show me the way to Loos. We went along 10th Avenue and at Blighty Steps we turned into Chalk Pit Alley which is a very long Communication Trench and then turned right into Gun Trench (the end of which brought us into Loos) and then turned left along English Alley and then right into Dot Way and Hants Lane which brought us to the Post Office and Square and finally to the Main advanced dressing station St. Patrick's, which is in the cellars of the ruined convent. I saw Capt. Brown in charge of the A.D.S., and he gave me a guide across to the R.B.'s [Rifle Brigade's] aid post which is in Loos, up towards the famous Tower Bridge. I saw Capt. Fawn, the M.O., and we arranged everything but much to my disgust he was to do the forward work and I the back, just what I didn't wish, and besides I was to miss the N. Staffs' raid. However I was to have dinner with the R.B.'s at 7.30 so I returned to St. Patrick's and had tea with Brown, who told me that the 8th Buffs' raid was cancelled and as he was to run it I got him to take on the R.B.'s one and I hurried back to the North Staffs' one. We had just got into the support line to the right of Essex Lane when the Huns shelled us with whizz-bangs (18 pounders)[25] but did no damage. The raiding party went over at 7.15 p.m. and as soon as they called for bearers, myself and twelve R.A.M.C. bearers went into the front line to get away the wounded and dead. The trench was very low in places and as heavy machine gun fire was going on you had to be careful to keep low. When we got into the front line we found four killed and fourteen wounded, and later on I heard an officer and three men were missing, the officer and one man were thought to have got into the Hun trench so in all the Raid was a total failure. The Hun must have guessed it was coming off for no sooner than the party went over they opened up with very heavy machine gun fire and whizz bangs. The men were fearfully disappointed it had failed! We had a dickens of a job to get the wounded and dead out on account of the low trench. On my way back I reported to Col. Dugmore, O.C. N. Staffs that all the wounded and dead were out and then back to the A.D.S., and to bed about 10 p.m., absolutely dead beat after a very strenuous day of it, but I thoroughly enjoyed the excitement.

25   Actually the Germans used 77mm field guns with somewhat lighter shells than the British 18 pounder field gun.

This morning my servant and I walked back to Philosophe where we got a car to Noeux-les-Mines. I had lunch with the 73rd F. Amb. and then they gave me another car back to my unit at Labeuvrière and I'm now ready for bed.

Tuesday 13.2.17.

When I got back yesterday I found Capt. McCurrick had gone to No 18 C.C.S. at Lapugnoy so we are an officer short now. I saw him down there to-day when I went to the dentist.

This afternoon I rode over to see the East Surreys at Bas Rieux on the Béthune-Lillers Road. I went round and saw all the Companies, also Allam, and had dinner at H.Q.s, and asked the O.C. to apply for me to come back which he said he would help me to do so I am going to see the A.D.M.S. about it.[26] The whole 24th Division have been relieved by the 27th from Neuve Chapelle and the Division is now resting in this area.

Thursday 15.2.17.

Last night we heard Lts. Thomas and Lindsay and Lt. Hartley, R.A.M.C., who succeeded me with the E. Surreys, each got M. Crosses for good work in the raid.[27] This morning I rode down to the dentist and he finished off my tooth for which I am thankful. Our O.C., Col. Rose returned from leave to-day and while Col. Buswell, A.D.M.S. is on leave he is to do his work so I'm not moving in the matter of returning to the Regiment till Col. Buswell comes back. This evening the 24th Divisional concert party 'The Snipers' gave a performance to the patients which was quite good. I saw Thomas at it. He is at present A.D.C. [Aide de Camp] to the divisional general [Capper] and is having a great time.

Friday 16.2.17.

This morning we were up at 6 a.m. for an inspection. Capt. King and I took 100 men over to a neighbouring village, Hesdigneul, about three miles away, to represent the R.A.M.C. on Brigade inspection by General Nivelle the Commander-in-Chief of the French armies. It was fortunately a very fine day and I quite enjoyed it. Nivelle seems quite a young fellow with lots of character, energy and go.[28] The thaw has set in again and the intense cold has gone.

---

26   On the face of it, Pirie had swallowed his objections to Swanton, such was his eagerness to return.
27   The 25 January raid.
28   Robert Nivelle was actually born in 1856. With the French government having lost confidence in Joffre, Nivelle was appointed commander in chief in his place at the end of 1916. Nivelle's self confidence, energy and fluent English helped him win over Britain's new Prime Minister, David Lloyd George, to his plans for offensive action on the Western Front. Unfortunately Nivelle's offensive in April on the Chemin des Dames was to prove a disaster and he was quickly replaced by Pétain.

Sunday 18.2.17.

I rode over to see the E. Surreys this afternoon and to congratulate Hartley and Lindsay, but found them both out. The thaw has set in alright now and it looks like rain. I have been put on as chairman of the F. Amb. Sports Committee and we are to play our first match on Tuesday against the 129th Field Coy. R.E. We are also supplying four men to represent the F. Ambulances in the Cross Country Four Miles, the other two F. Ambs. also supply four each.

Tuesday 20.2.17.

We won our match to-day by four goals to one. It has been an awful problem to get a field as it has been raining torrents and as it's a low lying country and very little pasture, everything is under water. However, we borrowed No.1 C.C.S. field at Chocques and played there. Capts. King and McKnight and I had to sit on a Court of Enquiry which took us from 2 till 7.40 so I did not see the match. We got a new officer yesterday, a Lt. Cook, but he's too old for forward work.

Friday 23.2.17.

I rode over to see General Mitford this afternoon to ask him to get me back to the Regiment which he said he would and wanted me back very badly. He also complimented me on my work in the line the night of the N. Staffs' raid. I had tea with him.

Saturday 24.2.17.

We played the 2nd round of the Bde. football tournament this afternoon vs. 73rd Brigade H.Q., but lost on extra time by 3-1. The ground was in a shocking state.

Sunday 25.2.17.

It has been a very fine day to-day. I rode over to Bas Rieux to see the E. Surreys and had tea with B. Coy officers and was back in time for dinner at 7.30.

Monday 26.2.17.

The divisional Cross Country Run was run off this afternoon. It started near Allouagne and went through the Bois du Reveillon to St. Saveur village and finished just outside Labeuvrière. It was a very good race. The 3rd Rifle Brigade won it, 8th R. West Kents 2nd, 13th Middlesex 3rd, 7th Northants 4th, and the R.A.M.C. 5th, so we did much better than I expected.

Tuesday 27.2.17.

This afternoon the 74th F. Amb. played us at football but we lost by 2 goals to nil. Our team played very badly. Col. Cunningham and Capt. Biden the O.C. and 2nd in command of 74 had dinner with us afterwards, they are two very nice fellows.

Wednesday 28.2.17.

This afternoon, being orderly officer for the day, I took the unit for a short route march through Lapugnoy as we are shifting to Aix-Noulette to do forward work on the 4th March.

Saturday 3.3.17.

This morning Capt. King and I, with 35 men, marched from Labeuvrière at 12.30 p.m. via Gosnay, Hesdigneul, Vaudricourt, Drouvin, Noeux-les-Mines, Petit Sains to Aix Noulette, which is on the Béthune-Arras Road. We arrived here at 5 p.m. and took over from the 2nd Canadian F. Amb., 1st Canadian Division. It was about a fourteen mile march. I was rather tired at the end but I have had so little exercise at Labeuvrière. This is the same division as we took over from last March at Messines.

Sunday 4.3.17.

This morning Capt. Kelly, the Canadian M.O., took me round the trenches and we took up our men to take over the Bearer Posts. This village is very prettily set in a hollow but has been battered about a good deal. We have the advanced dressing station in the brewery and strange to say it has been scarcely touched. It has huge cellars which are ideal for our work and they afford a good deal of safety. There are still quite a number of civilians in the village who run shops and estaminets (pubs). When Kelly and I went round this morning we walked up the Arras Road and just before we got to the top of the hill we got into the Arras Road C Trench which runs alongside the main Béthune-Arras Road. The first bearer post was just at the beginning of the C.T. The next post was at the Pump House, a ruined house up to which water is pumped. Then we continued up the trench past a ruined house called The Colonel's House, and leading off to the left from it is a trench Cooker Alley. Eventually at the very top of the Arras Road C.T. is No. 3 Bearer Post at a place called French Dump where the rations come to at nights for the right and centre Brigades in the line. The division is now in the Bully Grenay Sector which is just south of Loos and north of the Vimy Ridge. At French Dump which lies on the Arras Road [and?] is under the Notre Dame de Lorette Ridge we turned half left into Ration Trench and at the top end of it was No. 4 bearer post just next to a R.A. [Regimental Aid] Post. It took an hour to get to No.4 post. From it we went into H. Quarters Trench to another R. Aid Post and then when each post had taken over we came back to Aix-Noulette. Everything was very quiet up the line to-day. This Bully Grenay Sector is right in front of Lens, the suburbs of which you can plainly see.

Wednesday 7.3.17.

King and I have been going round the bearer and Regt. Aid Post on alternate days. To-day I went to the 8th Buffs' Aid Post to see Capt. McKnight, to get to it you turn off at the Pump House on the left and go along Cap de Pont trench and then turn left again into Cap de Corons trench. He has quite a good aid post. This afternoon I walked over to Bully Grenay which is a big mining town to see Brigadier General Mitford about getting back to the E. Surreys and he said he would go and see the A.D.M.S. about it. Bully has been shelled a bit but nothing to talk of, and there are a lot of civilians in it yet, with quite decent shops. All between here and Bully the country is simply stiff with guns. Yesterday I went for a wander up behind the Noulette Wood and there are crowds of guns there too. In the wood there are a lot of wooden huts, a regular encampment, just like Ploegsteert (Plug Street) and the huts are called the Noulette Huts and contain a Machine Gun Coy. and the Trench Mortar Battery. We have had Harris, Merryman, Cahir and McPherson up to visit us and they had tea with us. A new officer, Capt. Davidson, a regular, has joined the F. Amb. with the view to taking over command of it. (We hear our O.C., Col. Rose is to get a C.C.S.) Davidson comes from No. 18 C.C.S. at Lapugnoy and seems a very decent fellow. Lt. Cook has gone to No. 18 C.C.S. in his place.

Saturday 10.3.17.

Last night Lt. Bourdillon, a S. African, who is in the [Royal] Sussex and is acting Town Major of Aix Noulette came in to see us and told me that 'General Mitford had got the 42nd Division and was leaving soon', so I tore over to see him this morning on a push bike and found him and he was going off at 10 a.m., but said he would write to the A.D.M.S. about me.[29] Then he told me Col. de la Fontaine had rejoined the E. Surreys two days ago and as they were in Bully Grenay I promptly went and saw him to get him to help me to get back to the Regt. and he said he would go and see the A.D.M.S. to-morrow, so I am anxiously waiting the result. He is looking awfully well in spite of being so badly wounded. I have never seen him look so fat [fit?]. The

---

29   Mitford was not a success as a divisional commander, losing his command after six months. His new division, of Territorials from Egypt, resented the supercession of their old commander and did not perform well. Mitford seems to have been seen as a driver by the division, rather than a leader, and his replacement by Solly Flood was welcomed. On the other hand, Brigadier General Johnston, taking command of a brigade in the Division in September 1917, found the officers 'fearfully inexperienced' (Astill, *Diaries of Alexander Johnston* p.228). *The B.E.F. Times*, produced by soldiers of 24th Division, saw Mitford's softer side, regretting his departure in March and describing him as 'our oldest friend in the Division' Westhorp, *The Wipers Times* p.182.

42nd Division is the East Lancashire Territorial Division that was in Gallipoli with us (the 29th [Division]).

Monday 12.3.17.

I was up round the line yesterday and Capt. King and Sgt. Todd went to-day (and got shelled along Ration Trench and French Dump with 5.9s). Col. Buswell the A.D.M.S. and Capt. Russell his D.A.D.M.S. came up to the A.D.S. this morning and took careful note of the number of wounded we could take in and it was estimated that we could accommodate 200 lying cases and 100 sitting, so I'm afraid the spring show isn't far away. Just as he was driving off he said Col. de la Fontaine had asked for me and asked if I was keen to go back and I said yes, so he said he would send me back. On Sunday night the Huns tried to raid the Royal Sussex but failed badly and got beans but we were busy at the A.D.S. I was up at 12 midnight and was busy till 5 a.m. with cases from the Leinsters and R.B.s. Then King took on, as I was going up the line, and I found him still busy at 12 noon when I got back. He had had a number from the Sussex.

Tuesday 13.3.17.

I was up the line to-day with Sgt. Todd, a very fine fellow and it was beastly wet in Ration Trench, water up to your knees in one place. This evening I got a notification from the A.D.M.S. to rejoin the E. Surreys to-morrow and Lt. Hartley, M.C. who is with them was to rejoin the 74th F. Amb. I must say I don't regret having spent these nine weeks with the Ambulance because I have got an insight now of its working and I shall be sorry to leave Capt. King who is a topper.

Wednesday 14.3.17.

Here I am back with the Regiment again. I drove from Aix Noulette this morning by motor to Bully Grenay, and took over from Hartley who was very downhearted at having to go back. I went round all the Companies to see them and they were all surprised to see me back but seemed glad. Allam is awfully pleased. I now have a new servant, Pte. Mountford, a regular soldier, as Croxford, my old one was returned to duty and then went sick and [has] gone to C.C.S. Mountford seems quite a useful fellow. The Battalion goes into the line to-night again, a beastly night relief, worse luck. We relieve the Queens as of old.

Thursday 15.3.17.

Allam and I came up last night after dinner starting about 7.30 p.m. and it was a pitch-black night. We came up a road to Calonne which is, or rather was, a mining village and the road was ankle deep in mud, then we got into a trench Essex Trench, but it was so muddy we just walked on top and risked the Boche machine guns. I took over from Capt. Patch. This morning I went round with an orderly, Green, and located each of the four Company H.Q.s, but didn't go round the front line. It is a

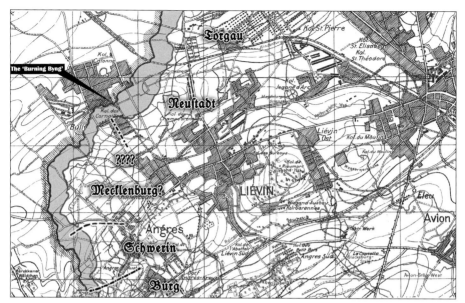

Map 10. Lens immediately preceding the Battle of Arras , annotated to show German
defence sectors and the position of the 'Burning Byng', from Behrmann,
Die Osterschlacht bei Arras 1917, I.

most intricate line as it runs amongst the houses. This must have been a fine model
village in peace time. The Huns shelled the village this morning and killed one and
wounded four men in a cellar. We are all living in cellars and are quite comfortable
but they wouldn't hold out anything heavy.

Friday 16.3.17.

This morning the famous orderly Kimber[30]and I went round the line. We started from
Bn. H.Q. in York Street, then turned right into Hougomont Street, which runs on
top of the ground behind the houses and along past the left of the two Mine heads,
and then got into Temple Street, which is a trench and very muddy, and then turned
left into Boyau Thomas which brought us into the Rt. Coy. support line which is
behind a row of houses and is called Morgan Trench and the Coy. H.Q. is in one of
the cellars of the house. There I saw Tetley (Capt.) and his lot. Then we turned left
into Boyau 214 which brought us into the Rt. Coy's front line which consists of houses
and sandbags as parapets, a most extraordinary line. On the right of the line is another

---

30   This cannot be the same Kimber who had served under Pirie at Gallipoli. Private Henry
     Kimber's first overseas service, according to his medal card, was France 31 August 1915,
     when he presumably landed with 9th East Surrey. He had won an M.M. for the Somme.
     He survived the war.

Figure 24. The canal on the far side of Lens circa 1916. The handwritten note by
the arrow indicates the location of the *5. Batterie*, so evidently this is in the
German artillery lines. (© Andrew Lucas)

Mine-head and on the left a high railway embankment called the Burning Byng as it
smokes away all day long and gives off tarry fumes. The trench runs up the Byng along
the top and down the other side. The stones in the trench on the Byng are quite hot
and the men like that trench on cold nights. On top of the Byng are a lot of railway
trucks and an engine (now in a ruined condition), evidently abandoned there when the
war zone reached this region. From the top of the Byng you can get a good view of the
surrounding country, nothing but coal mine-heads and model villages to be seen all
around you. This is the Black Country of France. As you go down the side of the Byng
you pass Pit Prop Corner and then Mersey Tunnel which passes through the Burning
Byng. This railway embankment also runs through the Hun lines and opposite the
Rt. Coy. it is very hard to make out where the Hun line is as it's amongst houses also.
After the Byng the front line runs straight to the left in open country and is about
300 yards from the Huns. When we reached the Left. Coy. H.Q. we returned to Bn.
H.Q. via Porthcawl Trench and Horse Guard's Avenue (both very muddy, in fact so
bad that I wear thigh gum boots) to Durham Quad and thence into York Street again.
My Regt. Aid Post is in a cellar just at the junction of York Street and Essex Trench,
the latter leads to the Square of Calonne village. Having the line amongst the houses
it makes it a most difficult business to find your way about in the trenches. It's great
news our now being beyond Baghdad![31]

31   After the Kut disaster in 1916, the British had now advanced in Iraq, seizing Baghdad on
     11 March and pressing on beyond.

Figure 25. A ruined pithead at Lens (Fosse 16), summer 1915. It was still largely intact in spring 1917 and would have been clearly visible from the 'Burning Byng'. (© Andrew Lucas)

Saturday 17.3.17.

This morning I first went to the Reserve Coy. in Temple Street. They have a very cosy H.Q. in a cellar. I am busy just now about getting the cellars and dugouts made gas proof with blankets. Each entrance has two blankets with an interval between so that when you open one blanket you have still to reach No.2 and by the time you reach No.2 No. 1 is closed so very little gas gets into the cellar or dugout. After I left the Res. Coy. in Temple St. Green, my orderly, and I continued along it and then turned left opposite the right Pit head into Oxford Street, then went under a battered railway bridge called Marble Arch and into Brick Walk and then left into Morgan Trench and saw Tetley. Then we went up Boyau 214 into the front line and over the Byng and along part of the centre Coy. front and then turned left into Boyau 224 which brought us to the Centre Coy. H.Q., Lt. Warre-Dymond is O.C. Coy. just now while Capt. Hilton is at the base training men.

Sunday 18.3.17.

I went round the centre and right Coys. this morning. The trenches have dried a lot after yesterday's wind. [A] Boche plane was very active yesterday and all our planes seemed to funk tackling him. He was observing for a 5.9 battery which was shelling one of our batteries. We heard to-day that they had put a gun out of action and caused some casualties amongst the battery's personnel. The Hun has a new aeroplane called the Rumpler which is very fast and it's a question who has the absolute supremacy of the air. We still have it in numbers anyhow.[32] Our trenches are on the edge of Calonne village so after I had been round the line I went over to the village square to inspect the Company cook houses, also to see my small hospital where I keep slight cases. It can hold about five cases and Pte. Simpson, my medical orderly looks after the men. The area round the square is the portion of the village we go back to when the battalion is Brigade support and as the N. Staffs are there at present I went in to see Lt. Blythe, their M.O. Capt. King is very keen to exchange with him and Blythe, from this morning's talk, seems keen to do so. Capt. Tower, our new B[riga]de. Major was up this afternoon and he told us we had occupied Bapaume.[33] Tower[34] succeeded Nelthorpe who has gone to the 1st Army. We also have a new staff Capt. Ward from the Sherwoods. He succeeded Major Fox who has also gone to the Army.

Tuesday 20.3.17.

I didn't go round the line this morning as I had a deuce of a dose of Influenza taking hold of me and I feel rotten to-night. The Queens relieve us to-night and we move back into the centre of this Calonne village and act as the Battalion in Brigade support. We have three Coys. in Calonne and one in the village of Maroc which is to our left. We relieve the N. Staffs in Calonne and they move into the line on the left of us. The Hun got the 'wind up' last night because we put up some red rockets for a test to our artillery. These beastly red rockets are evidently the Hun S.O.S. signal because he promptly opened out on us with heavy machine gun fire and artillery and we had a few casualties. He must have thought he was to be raided.

---

32   It would soon be 'Bloody April', with the R.F.C. having superiority in numbers, but the Germans having the edge in aircraft quality. The R.F.C. was to take heavy losses in support of the successful British ground offensive.

33   From 16 March the Germans retreated from their lines between Arras and Soissons, to a new, much shorter line, the Hindenburg Line, devastating the area left behind.

34   Captain, later Lieutenant Colonel Kinglake Tower had taken over in January. He admired Brigadier General Mitford's exceptional bravery, but found him difficult to work with, unlike his friend Sweny, Mitford's successor. He left the brigade in August 1917 after being badly gassed. His short memoir is at I.W.M.

Figure 26. 9th East Surrey officers, March 1917 - front row: first left G.W. Warre-Dymond;
fourth left H.V.M. de la Fontaine, fifth left C.A. Clark, sixth left G.S. Tetley; second row:
centre R. C. Sherriff; extreme right W.H. Lindsay; third row: first left A.H. Douglass; third
left H.W. Kiver. (© Surrey History Centre, ref.,ESR/25/CLARK/7)

Tuesday 27.3.17.

I am feeling much better now but the night we moved to Calonne I went to bed with
a Temp.[erature] of 102.4 [Fahrenheit] and was there for four days, feeling very cheap
and nasty. It has left me beastly weak and heady. There are a number of cases in the
Battalion. We relieved the Queens yesterday afternoon, making it a daylight relief
which is always preferable to a night one. The weather has been shocking these last
few days, snow, sleet and rain alternately.

Friday 30.3.17.

I am feeling ever so much better now, in fact, quite shaken off the Influenza but I still
have a rotten cold in my head. However I have been going round the line daily and as
I am O.C. of gas curtains on dugouts, I am pretty busy. In spite of the bad weather we
have been having very few sick and so far only one casualty and at that a self inflicted
one.[35] On Wednesday morning, just after I got back from the trenches we witnessed
a most exciting aeroplane fight. A very fast Hun plane swept down on a slow patrol

35   Liable to face a court martial.

one of ours and really, everyone thought our plane was a goner, but instead, by most wonderful flying and manoeuvring, after about fifteen minutes he outwitted the Hun who had the advantage over him of speed and being above him. But every time the Hun got over him, he, by very steep banking, and on one occasion looped the loop, always got away.

Sunday 1.4.17.

Didn't go round the line to-day but instead spent the whole day till after tea time in superintending to build a gas proof porch to the entrance of signaller's cellar of the Centre Coy. and got it practically finished but as we are being relieved to-night and go back to Bully Grenay as Divisional Reserve for six days, the Queens are to finish it. There has been more snow to-day again.

Monday 2.4.17.

The Queens relieved us by day yesterday and we moved back to Calonne till we were relieved by the 8th Royal West Kents and Corp. Allam and I got away about 11.30 p.m. and walked down by the Transport Road to Bully and just as we reached the Bully end the Hun sent over some 5.9 shells but well in front of us and did us no harm. We have just done 18 days in the line and are now back here for six days but from all accounts he has been shelling Bully Grenay quite a lot in retaliation to our heavy guns which no one can marvel at because we have been shelling him day and night of late and he's having a very thin time of it. I have got a very good billet, spring bed with sheets and it's great to get your clothes off as all the eighteen days up the line I never had them off at nights beyond my boots and tunic and then ten days previous to rejoining the Regiment on the 14th March, I didn't have them off at the F. Ambulance so in all I hadn't had them off at nights for a whole month. We had a terrific snow storm this afternoon and the streets were all rushing torrents.

Tuesday 3.4.17.

This morning was bitterly cold, all the streets were frozen when I went to my sick parade at 8 a.m. After breakfast I went round to see Capt. Milne of the 73rd F. Amb., who is running the dressing station in Bully Grenay. After lunch I rode over to see the 74th F. Amb. at Fosse X Petit Sains and saw Capts. King, Cahir, McPherson and [the] O.C., and had tea with them, and a hand at bridge. They were saying that Aix Noulette village is being shelled now and a 5.9 shell had dropped in the yard of the A.D.S.

Thursday 5.4.17.

Yesterday evening, Capt. Tetley and I had dinner with Capt. Barker, our Brigade Transport Officer, at Les Brebis. He is a most amusing fellow and kept us in roars of laughter. While we were at dinner with him the Huns shelled Bully Grenay badly and wounded one of our signallers and I was sent for. Les Brebis and Bully join up with each other and are no distance apart. This afternoon I rode over to Fosse X and put up my horse there and then got a lift in a motor to a gas lecture by Col. Saltau in Noeux-les-Mines. It was most interesting and was all about the treatment of various gas poisoning. Then we came back to the 74th F. Amb. and had tea. After it I rode back and went to a jolly good concert given by the Regiment. Our Brigadier General, Sweny, was at it and he dined with us at H.Q. afterwards. He has been wounded three times and is a most interesting fellow.[36]

Sunday 8.4.17.

Here we are back in the trenches again. We came in again last night and I don't mind being here at all because Bully was getting a bit hot with shells flying about. Allam and I started away last night just about eight when it was twilight and came up by Pont Grenay and the sunken round [road?], everything was quite quiet and it became bright moonlight. The Queens, whom we relieved are not looking forward to going to Bully.

Monday 9.4.17.

This morning I was woken up at 5.30 a.m. by a terrific bombardment on our right and later we heard that there had been a huge attack from the Vimy Ridge down to Arras and we had been very successful taking all our objectives and some 5000 prisoners and many guns, so now we hold the Vimy Ridge the Huns may retire in front of us.

Wednesday 11.4.17.

I have been busy getting our mess strengthened with pit props and brick rubble on top because it was such an egg shell of a place. The dressing station we have also considerably strengthened. The Vimy Ridge Battle has been a huge success, 12,000 prisoners and much booty.[37] We can see the Ridge quite plainly from here, it's only about two miles from us. The C.O., Col. de la Fontaine and Corp. Allam have been laid up with 'Flu'. We now have Swanton back, the late C.O., and he is now Major Swanton and 2nd in command, and as unpleasant as ever. 'Baby' Hilton is back and is as cheery as ever. He has been away at the base training men for two months. He is 2nd in Command to D. Coy. under Tetley.

36   William Sweny, D.S.O., born 1873, had been commissioned in the Royal Fusiliers in 1893. He had been promoted Major in 1910 and temporary Brigadier General in March 1917.
37   According to its war diary, WO95/2215, the Battalion erected a notice board in No Man's Land with, in German, 'We have captured over 10,000 prisoners and 100 guns at Vimy. Will you surrender too?'

Friday 13.4.17.

The O.C. and Corp. Allam have both been laid up with Influenza but are better again. Things have been fairly quiet except that we had 2/Lt. Trenchard wounded in the face. He has only been with us about three weeks.[38] We were to have been relieved to-night by the Queens and were to go to Calonne but we received a message this afternoon that patrols sent out on our right have found the Hun trenches unoccupied so they are evidently retiring as the result of Vimy Ridge being taken as we now hold all the points of observation. So we are to remain in the line and at present we have sent patrols out to see if they have retired in front of us. It is now 4.30 p.m. Their line was still occupied last night because Lt. Thomas and Sgt. Summers heard and saw the Huns in their trenches while patrolling No Man's Land last night. It has certainly been quiet to-day and our aeroplanes have been flying very low and not been fired at by either [anti]aircraft guns or machine guns. Our men are all in great spirits and eager to get into the open fighting again. The Hun is far from going strong at present. The weather has been atrocious, snow galore, but luckily to-day is fine and clear for observation, just the thing we need most. Last night many explosions were heard in Lens which is just opposite us, also there have been fires in it for the last few nights so I expect he is destroying it before he goes. Two churches which we used to be able to see yesterday had disappeared from view this morning when we got up – destroyed, I suppose.

Saturday 14.4.17.

The patrols got over safely yesterday afternoon, opposite the left and centre companies and they had to cut a way through the barbed wire entanglement but on the right it had been destroyed by our shell and mortar fire. Not a shot was fired at them. When the right patrol got into the Hun line they just saw the last Hun bolting over the crest, and all of the patrols pushed on followed by a platoon of men from each Coy. without any opposition, well into his support line. Then the whole of the three companies followed on and took up a position in his reserve line which was on an average depth of 900 yards from our front line, by dark and remained there till morning and then pushed on further after daylight, patrols feeling their way forward and the companies followed them and by evening had got forward another 200 yards in depth. As our men went forward the West Kents on our left and R.M.L.I. [Royal Marine Light Infantry] on our right went forward too and it was extraordinary after all these months of Trench Warfare, to see men running about in No Man's Land and places where it was formerly certain death. Our Right Coy. captured a *Minenwerfer* – which is a heavy Trench Mortar. The N. Staffs. came up and occupied our old front line after

---

38   Cecil Trenchard, born 1881, was a stock agent in Australia. He had joined the battalion 16 March. He lost an eye and served on in England. He is believed to be the model for Trotter in *Journey's End*.

we went forward. This evening the Battalion was relieved in their forward positions by the N. Staffs and we moved into the support line which the West Kents used to hold on our left. It is just in front of the village of Maroc and alongside the famous two coal slag heaps which we call the Double Crassier. As we were going across to take up our new position we saw a Hun plane brought down. It just spiralled down and then landed with a crash behind some houses. It has been a fine day.

Sunday 15.4.17.

We all slept in deep dugouts and as we had no blankets we had to improvise something so I slept with sand bags on each leg and both legs in a mailbag and then a waterproof sheet over me so I was really quite warm and as we were all very tired we slept heavily. It was pouring when we got up at 8 a.m. After breakfast Allam and I started out to test a well which was supposed to be in the German old front line and after a deuce of a hunt up and down his old trenches we found the place and it turned out to be a beastly mine sap so having got our feet very wet, we trekked back for lunch. It is wonderful to see how rapidly the men can make a road over the trenches. They have been making one from Maroc past Fosse 16 to Cité St Pierre. This afternoon I went in advance with the servants to our new H.Q. in Cité St Pierre, a mining village we had taken. We got there safely amidst pouring rain and got a good cellar for an Aid Post and a cellar for Lt. Webb and I to sleep in. These cellars are regular fortresses, tons of bricks on top of the roof. In our cellar they have made an extension in the shape of a deep dugout in which we shall sleep. The Battalion moves up to Cité St. Pierre to-night to be in reserve and the Staffs and Kents are advancing to-day. We are to be here two days.

Monday 16.4.17.

The whole Battalion were safely housed in cellars last night and had a good night's rest. We shift up to-night and take over from the West Kents who are on the edge of the town of Lens and just in front of Cité St. Pierre. This morning Lt. Lindsay and I hunted round for a place for Batt. H.Q. and a dressing station. We found splendid cellars on the eastern edge of Cité St. Pierre which had been the Hun Brigade Commander's place. The cellars all have tons of concrete on top and nothing on earth could come through. The Hun General's cellar is luxuriously got up, but they have hacked everything to pieces in their mess, chairs, tables and a piano are in ruins. He certainly didn't mean us to use it but they must have retired very rapidly as they haven't blown up the cellars. The cellar where four of H.Q. officers sleep in was pulled to pieces too and the servants found a trap set, a wire attached to a bomb but luckily they spotted it and cut the wire. I have my dressing station in a cellar of the Bureau de l'Octroi. [toll house] It is small but strong, except that the door faces the Hun which is bad if we are shelled as they could drop one into the doorway. We got back to lunch after our hunt and the O.C. said 'the H. Quarters we had selected were too far back and he had seen a likely place near the Church' so Lts. Lindsay, Picton and I with Sgt. Ericson and some men went to reconnoitre it. We went past the church which the Hun had blown up, before he went, but it was far from a healthy spot as he had plastered that area with shells and we had one very close to us and had to take cover behind a house. Eventually we found the house but it was far too small. We had to wait a bit till the shelling wore off and then nipped back quickly, but it was a very hot corner. There has been no move forward to-day as the division on our left i.e. in front of Loos, have been hung up and we must all conform to each other's movements. The Hun is holding the line around Lens strongly with snipers and machine guns but he is still burning the town and he must eventually give it up as the people on our right are gradually getting round it. They have shelled Cité St. Pierre a fair amount to-day but we were lucky only to have two Sgts. hit, Lennard and Rymills and not bad at that. It is not to be wondered at that he shells the place as there is so much movement in it which he can see from the church tower of Lens.

Tuesday 17.4.17.

We moved into the New H.Q. and the Batt. into the trenches last night. No sooner had we got settled than he shelled all round H.Q. all night till 10 this morning but we didn't have a single casualty – wonderful luck! He was quite quiet till 5.30 p.m., but since, he has been shelling us again off and on. It has been raining these last two days with touches of snow, truly miserable and it's impeding us getting our guns up. I sleep in the dressing station so as to be on the spot.

Wednesday 18.4.17.

The Huns shelled H.Q. and around it again up till 10 o'clock last night and unfortunately killed 2/Lt. Kiver who is the musician and songster of the Battalion. He is a great loss to us all.[39] Things are stationary in this area at present. The Huns are holding a line in front of us and as the 6th Division on our left cannot progress owing to the enemy holding on to Hill 70 in front of Loos we are totally hung up at present but the German will have to give up Lens soon as we are working round him on the south. Our trenches are most peculiar as they run amongst the houses and the Hun's are likewise. Both sides have been active with their snipers. We have bagged some Huns and they have bagged some of ours, killed Sgt. Harris who had just been awarded the Military Medal and they wounded Pte. Pearce, one of our snipers. Still, considering the shelling, we have had very few casualties and what casualties have occurred, have unfortunately been killed. I had an escape this morning. Word came over from the dressing station that there was a man wounded, they were shelling all round H.Q. and the dressing station at regular intervals so I waited till one dropped and then ran across the open square to the dressing station and just after I got in they dropped a 4.2 inch shell just outside – still, nearly dead never helps the kirkyaird!!! [churchyard]

---

39   Hubert Kiver was born in 1893. His father was a professor of music and he became a professional vocalist. He had only arrived with the battalion 27 February.

Figure 27. Germans in the main street in Lens, June 1917. (© Andrew Lucas)

Thursday 19.4.17.

He shelled us round H.Q. again last night at 9 and again at 2 a.m., but we had no casualties. He is a little quieter than he was the first night. The division is being relieved by the 46th Division which is a Territorial one. The West Kents and Queens who were in reserve were relieved last night and we are to be relieved to-night by the 5th Lincolns. We trek back to Fosse X at Petit Sains which is on the Béthune – Arras Road and then to-morrow have a ten mile march to Lozinghem and thence to behind Lillers where we are to rest, which will be great. This division of ours (the 24th) has got great praise for its work in following up the Hun. We advanced on a 6 ½ mile front and took the big mining town of Liévin, Bois de Riaumont, and smaller mining villages, Cités de la Plain, Cornailles, St. Pierre, and our line is all around the western edge of Lens which they are still burning. The church spire in Lens hasn't disappeared yet but it will no doubt be blown up before we get it. They are no doubt using it as an artillery observation post.

Friday 20.4.17.

The Lincolns relieved us last night and luckily he only sent a very few shells over so had no casualties. The relief was very well carried out and eventually Allam and I, who waited till everybody was clear, got away at 12.30 a.m. and walked down by the new road past Fosse XVI to Maroc but it was an awful march as the road was ankle deep in sticky mud and progress was very slow, then on top of that it was pitch-dark and every now and again, just as your eyes were getting used to the dark the guns would fire and the flash absolutely blind you again. However, after we got to Maroc the road was hard and good but although we meant to come back by Bully Grenay we took the wrong turning and landed in Les Brebis, much to our disgust as it took us a long way round. We eventually got back to Fosse X at 3 a.m., dead beat and feet soaking. Then our billets weren't to be found and no food to be had beyond some tea and a spot of cake. Oh, it was a mess up and we all cursed royally. In the end billets were found and we got to bed at 25 to 5, dog tired and slept till about 9. After lunch we fell in again and marched off at 2.30 p.m. via Hersin, Barlin, Bruay, Marles-les-Mines and got here (Lozinghem) at 7.30. We had a couple of fiendish hills to climb at Marles-les-Mines but although the men were very tired they managed it. After we got here I had a foot inspection and doctored the sore feet, as we have an 8 mile march to-morrow. We did 12 miles to-day.

Figure 28. British shells exploding in Lens, June 1917. (© Andrew Lucas)

4

To die in Flanders, April to July 1917

Saturday 21.4.17

We fell in this morning at 9 a.m. and marched from Lozinghem to another village Auchy-au-Bois via Marles-les-Mines, Cauchy, Ferfay, Amettes. The men again marched splendidly and luckily both days have been good for it – no rain! We had fine billets at Lozinghem but we are equally lucky here. Lt. Thomas and I are billeted in the school master's house and they are awfully hospitable people. This is a most peaceful village set down in a valley surrounded by a wood. We are about 8 kilometres from Lillers. We are only to be here two days, worse luck, and then go further back to another village.

Sunday 22.4.17.

One of my ears has got cold into it and as it was singing and making me deaf I rode into Lillers this morning via Lières and Ecquedbecques about 8 kilometres to the West Riding C.C.S. to have my ear examined. But they had no ear specialist so I rode back to Ecquedbecques and got Capt. King of the 74th F. Amb. to look at it. We had lunch first, and then after, King prescribed for me and as soon as I got back I used the stuff and it cleared my ear at once. It's a great relief to get rid of the singing and deafness. To-day has been beautiful so it was top-hole out riding. The French people are all very busy ploughing and harrowing, after the rain.

Monday 23.4.17.

Another beautiful day. Went for a ride to St. Hilaire this afternoon which, on the map looks a big place, but it's a wretched little town. We are on the move again to-morrow further away from the lines. We march off from here at 9 a.m. to Coyecques about 15 miles from here and according to the map we have some fine hills to get over. We are shifting because there is better training ground round Coyecques, but I'm sorry we are shifting as we are very comfortable here.

Tuesday 24.4.17.

The move for to-day was cancelled, and we go to-morrow. To-day has been absolutely perfect, it was real spring weather. This afternoon, Tetley and I rode over to see a fellow Wright in the 7th Northamptons. They are in a village, Febvin -Palvart, about 5 kilometres from us. We had tea in his mess, A. Coy. and had quite a jolly time. After dinner this evening, Homewood and I played Douglass and Tetley at Auction Bridge in C. Coy's mess but we lost badly. We have an early rise to-morrow, reveille at 5.30 a.m., and march off at 9.

Wednesday 25.4.17.

We started punctually this morning and got here at one o'clock. It was quite cold to-day so marched most of the way. It was only 11 miles, not 15, as first thought. We came through Ligny-les-Aire and then Cuhem and Erny St. Julien. There were two fine steep hills just as we got to this side of the two latter places as both the villages lie in very deep valleys. There is a dickens of a steep hill down into Coyecques where we are now resting. This village is situated on the River Lys and is very pretty, with high hills on both sides. We are all very comfortable, personally I have a top-hole billet. We have H.Q. mess in an estaminet and just opposite is orderly room, in the Mairie (town hall). My Medical Inspection Room is in a room of a house occupied by refugees from Bully Grenay. He was the chemist there. The people in the village are all very nice. A. Coy (Capt. Taylor's Coy.) are billeted in a small hamlet called Crocq, about one kilometre from here. The rest of us are in the village. We are on a narrow gauge railway which goes to Aire. There is splendid trout fishing in the river.

Saturday 28.4.17.

The weather is still very fine, real spring is here but the trees are very behind. Yesterday Whiteman and I rode over to a town Fauquembergues, about six kilometres away and did some shopping. This afternoon the 103rd Coy. R.Es. had sports at a neighbouring hamlet and we beat them at tug of war and horse wrestling but lost the bolster bar contest. After it, we had tea with them and in all spent a very amusing afternoon.

Sunday 29.4.17.

We had a very nice open air service in a field and after it Holy Communion in the village school, this morning. In the afternoon Whiteman and I rode down the valley of the Lys River to Thérouanne and meant to have tea there but it's a poor village and full of Portuguese[1] so we just returned to our own village, Coyecques.

1   A Portuguese Corps arrived to support the Allies in 1917. The soldiers were neglected and unenthusiastic. Their resistance to the German Lys offensive in April 1918 was ineffective.

Sunday 7.5.17. [6.5.17.]

This last week the weather has been very fine. After our daily parades which end at 4 p.m. there have been great inter-company football and tug of war contests. Being a more or less unbiased member of the Battalion I have been refereeing a lot of the matches and have thoroughly enjoyed it. So far C. & D. Coys (Capt. Warre-Dymond and Capt. Tetley's) have ended up in the final for the football and it's to be played on Thursday evening as we have some officers on leave to Paris for four days just now. The final of the Tug of War is between C. Coy and the transport section. Our Batt. sports are to take place on Wednesday afternoon. Pte. Cole has sketched a very clever programme for us. On Wednesday afternoon all officers of the Batt. had to go over to Div. H.Q. at Bomy to meet Major General Jacob, the Army Corps Commander of the II Corps in which we now are. After that we came back to Coyecques and then rode over to Delettes, two kilometres away, to see a contest, boxing between ten of our men and ten of the 8th R. West Kents. There was some very good boxing especially between Pte. Clark of ours and Pte. Lodbury of the Kents, ex Fly weight champion of the world. We won the match 6-4 contests. On Saturday morning Lt. Picton, our Lewis Gun Officer, was thrown off Major Swanton's horse and broke his thumb and got his face bashed so had to go to Hospital. 2/Lt. Ellis is to succeed him from D. Coy. During this week Capt. O'Connor rejoined the Batt. He was wounded the first day after we went into the Somme Battle. He was also wounded at Loos.

Tuesday 8.5.17.

Yesterday the Batt. played the 196 Coy. A.S.C. at football and won by 3 goals to 1. To-day has been a very busy day for me. We put the whole Batt. through the gas chamber with tear gas in it to see if the box respirators were in proper order. We started at 9.30 a.m. and got finished at 5.45 p.m. My voice was about done after the day instructing the men. Then at 7 p.m. I had to see all the crocks or bad marchers because we got a sudden order to march off to-morrow from Coyecques to a village Rely just about a kilometre from Auchy-au-bois where we were before. We are all very, very sorry to leave Coyecques as we have had a very jolly time here. After Rely, we go to somewhere north of Aire and then up near Hazebrouck which I am afraid means our going to the Ypres Salient. Goodness, I never wish to see that place again!

Wednesday 9.5.17.

We marched off at 10 a.m. to-day from Coyecques, much to our sorrow. It was a broiling hot day and plus that, some very steep hills, especially at Coyecques. We marched via Erny-St. Julien, Cuhem, Fléchin and La Tirmande to Rely. We got to Rely about 3 p.m. We were longer on the march than we should have been as Lt. Thomas, who was leading the column, misread the map and took us round by Fléchin. General Capper, our Div. Commander, inspected us at Cuhem while marching.

Wednesday [Thursday] 10.5.17.

We marched off from Rely this morning at 10 a.m. via Linghem, Lambres, Aire and Boeseghem, and got here, Les Ciseaux at 1.30. It was a very hot day again but a much more level road. Still, a lot of men fell out and I had the joy of seeing them at 5 p.m., and only got finished at 8 p.m. D Coy. especially, excelled themselves. We are to be here to-morrow and then go on the next day.

Thursday [Friday] 11.5.17.

This is a very straggling village but we are all very comfy and it's beautiful country. Worse luck, it's the edge of French Flanders. I have never seen so many men sick just when we were about to march off and it has been very trying to get them along. Our Div. General inspected and addressed us to-day. To-morrow we march to Steenvoorde which means a long march.

Friday [Saturday] 12.5.17.

This morning we were up at 4.20 a.m. and marched off at 6.7 a.m. (minus packs, thank goodness!) via Steenbecque and Morbecque (both on the main Aire- Hazebrouck Road), through Hazebrouck and St. Sylvestre Cappel. Just outside the latter place we halted from 12 to 2 p.m. to have dinner and rest. We were marching as a whole Brigade. N. Staffs first, then us and then the Queens and last R.W. Kents, with 100 yards interval between each Coy. It was nice and cool when we started but became very hot and in the afternoon, when we started off again, it was terrific. We marched through Steenvoorde to an inn called Rattekot Inn, just across the Belgian Frontier on the Watou-Abeele Road. We reached our destination at 4.45 p.m., very hot and tired and I had a huge foot inspection.[2] Outside St. Sylvestre I ran across Giff van der Vijver's Bde. but he was still in the line. In Steenvoorde I saw Capt. King, R.A.M.C., and had a chat.

Sunday 13.5.17.

We started off, marching at 10 a.m. this morning, but only had eight miles to go. It was a twenty odd stunt yesterday. It was very hot again. We marched through Poperinghe to A Camp, just outside Poperinghe so we are back to our old haunts where I first was with the Batt. Pop. is just the same as ever. To-morrow night we go into the trenches at Hooge in front of Ypres, also an old haunt. Oh, I do so hate this area, and 'Hooge' means shells all day long! Just after we reached this camp a Hun plane swept down on one of our observation balloons and brought it down in flames. During lunch hour we had a nice shower which cleared the air and cooled it.

---

2   The battalion war diary proudly records twenty-two miles were marched in ten hours with only four men falling out.

Tuesday 15.5.17.

We entrained at the level crossing below A Camp last night on the Pop.-Ypres (Wipers) express which took us up to just short of the Asylum at Ypres and there guides brought us by the Ypres-Roulers railway which runs round the outskirts of the city. Then just before we got to Hell Fire Corner where the railway crosses the Menin-Ypres Road we turned off right and came up by the China Wall (which is made of sand bags) past Gordon Farm to Half Way House which is our Bn. H.Q. We weren't molested at all. We relieved the 9th Yorks and Lancs. 23rd Div. last night and are now in the Hooge trenches in front of Ypres. We were in this line from January to March 1916, but things have changed a good deal. The Huns have pushed us back from Hooge and they now look bang down the Menin Road to Ypres and the Aid Post which used to be at the Mill on the Menin Road is now at Halfway House where our H.Q. is. The dugouts at Halfway House are miles better than they used to be, and it is very peaceful, which is a great change to what it used to be in 1916.Then the Hun used to shell our trenches at Hooge very badly! Things are looking much more cheerful here too because it's summer and the trees are in leaf and we are having fine weather. I went round the trenches with Lt. Webb (Jimbo or 'Our Jim') and they are most excellent ones. We first went up Oxford Street, along which Fritz can see you from Hooge and then turned right into Rosslyn Street, past some ruined farm houses called Yeomanry Post, and then into Wellington Crescent, which is very deep and has overhead streets so you have to bend all the time. Hilton, who is at present O.C. A. Coy.

"Daily Mail" WAR PICTURES

68. YPRES AFTER TWO YEARS OF WAR.

OFFICIAL PHOTOGRAPH. CROWN COPYRIGHT RESERVED.

Figure 29. Ypres in ruins. (Author's collection)

(during Taylor's absence on leave) has his H.Q. in it. We then came back to Oxford Street and turned right into Leinster Street to O.C. C Coy's H.Q. (Warre-Dymond), and continued along it to O.C. D Coy.(Tetley) whose H.Q. is on the Menin Road at the Birr Cross Roads, then came home. All these trenches are nice and dry and well revetted. In previous days the trenches were nothing but mud holes and he has only fired about six shells at our trenches, so peaceful! Looking back at Ypres from our trenches the Cathedral and Cloth Hall have been greatly demolished during our absence, in fact, all the city seems in a more ruined condition.

Sunday 20.5.17.

We were relieved last night by the N. Staffs, after six days in. They were very peaceful ones, only had three men hit, and the weather was fine. Two of our Coys. have gone to Ypres into the Cavalry Barracks, one in Ritz Street and one in Maple Street up near Maple Copse, and our H.Q. is just alongside Halfway House. There have been some very exciting aeroplane fights and in all our airmen seem to be the top dogs. There is a great deal of mining going on, on our immediate left in Y and Railway Woods, with the result a few camouflets[3] have been blown, which don't half shake the ground! I am not feeling too fit so am going to bed, got Influenza and sore throat. Oh, I do hate being ill!

Monday 28.5.17.

We are still at Halfway House, as supporting Battalion, but go out to-night to Hopoutre, which is just beyond Poperinghe. We are to be relieved by the 19th King's Liverpools, 30th Div., and I will be glad to get away from Ypres for a bit for the mere name of Ypres makes me fed up and depressed. Still, we can't grumble because the Hun seems to shell all around except here. We have been in just fourteen days but during that period he has become more and more aggressive each day by shelling. The Batts. on our right and left and all round and in Ypres have had a bad time with his shelling but so far we have escaped. Unfortunately, I have had two of my stretcher-bearers wounded, Ptes. Allen and Huband (not badly though), Wain was also hit but very slightly and didn't go away. We got a message from Brigade to say 'the Huns were to attack Hill 60 on our right with gas, so to be on the alert'. Last night the Huns shelled that area very heavily and a message came through 'he was releasing gas', so we were all up but it afterwards proved he hadn't done so. We should have relieved the N. Staffs in the front line on Friday night but they volunteered to stay up till relieved. I was in bed two days last week with 'Flu' and sore throat, but am O.K. again. This morning a Boche aeroplane was flying over Poperinghe when our planes went after it and brought it down. It began to fall over and over at about 10,000 feet, just like a leaf, quite slowly, then to our great surprise, when about 1000 feet up it suddenly righted

3   Explosive charges designed to damage enemy mine galleries.

itself and just managed to fly into its own lines. I have never seen a plane come down like that before.

Tuesday 29.5.17.

We had quite an exciting time coming out last night. The Kings were very late in relieving us and we only got away at 2.30 a.m. and our train from the Asylum at Ypres was to go at 3 a.m. It was a cloudy night with a moon but it was light enough to see. Lts. Webb, Thomas, Picton and I set off at a deuce of a pace to try and catch the train down the China Wall, past Gordon Farm to the railway cutting, crossed it and on to the Menin Road at the school. There, we outpaced Thomas and Picton, Webb and I got in amongst a lot of ammunition wagons which were going like fury and as we reached the Menin Gate the Huns shelled us with whizz bangs which luckily just passed over our heads. When we got into Ypres we walked like blazes and trotted through the squares as it's no place to linger. Ypres is more in ruins than ever. When we reached the prison we found two dead horses just been killed and at the Asylum it was ghastly, crowds of dead horses and smashed wagons and a dead man, all killed by shell fire. When we reached the Asylum the train had just gone five minutes before (that was 3.5 a.m.). However we met Capt. Ward, our Staff Capt., and he said 'another train was coming down from Ypres' so we waited and got it to Brandhoek. Then we stopped C and D Coys. who had also missed the train at [to?]Brandhoek and we all got a train from there to Hopoutre and marched from there to our tent camp, about two miles away. It was a huge relief to get away from Ypres, as the Hun has been shelling that area very heavily lately, and the transport on all the roads have been having a very bad time. We don't know how long we are to be here. This afternoon the O.C., Colonel de la Fontaine and I rode into Poperinghe and had tea and a bath. He said to me he was very disappointed I hadn't got an M.C. for my work on the Somme and if he hadn't been wounded at Delville Wood he would have seen that I did get one, but on the first chance he would strongly recommend me for it – so I hope I survive the coming battle to be able to win it.

Thursday 31.5.17.

This afternoon Whiteman, Hilton and I drove over to our old billets at Noote Boom near Meteren, to see the Devos people we were billeted on before going to the Somme last July. Marie and Germaine and the parents were there alright and we had a great reception and spent a very jolly afternoon. When we got back, travelling via Berthen and Boeschepe, we found our camp struck and the Battalion gone. We found out it had gone to near Busseboom on the Poperinghe-Reninghelst Road so we followed them up and found them pitching their camp. It was a filthy piece of ground so we moved to a nice grass field, 400 yards further on. The men are to work for the X Corps R.Es. who have a huge dump just next to us. The other two Battalions of the Brigade are training near Steenvoorde for the coming battle. Jove it's to be some battle and our guns are going hard at it, smashing up the Hun trenches. We saw the Prince of Wales in his car the other day.[4] For the coming show I have had to increase my bearers to 32 from 16 so am busy training the new ones.

Wednesday 6.6.17.

The time is getting near for the battle and the bombardment preparatory to it is terrific. A number of raids have been done and the 12th E. Surreys[5] took five prisoners who were absolutely demoralised with the shell fire but the Huns from the intelligence are all expecting an attack between Ypres and Armentières so it will be a huge struggle. On Sunday afternoon I rode down to Reninghelst to see the A.D.M.S. to hear about the Medical arrangements. Just after I left R. the Hun began to shell it. Besides working for the X Corps R.E. we have had men working up behind the trenches and in spite of being shelled by Fritz we only had three casualties. It has been extremely hot the last few days. I have got all the new bearers trained and ready for action. I am taking six bearers per company into action and leaving two per coy. behind as reserve. Last night we shifted from our tent camp at the X Corps R.E. Dump to Scottish Lines Camp which are huts. We are supposed to be here another day and then move up to Mic Mac camp and then into action.

Thursday 7.6.17.

Last night we marched from Scottish Lines Camp via Ouderdom to Mic Mac Camp which is near Hubertshock. We spent the night there but got very little sleep as the guns were going hard. At 3.10 a.m. this morning our attack in the Battle of Messines began with a terrific hurricane of guns and the ground shook with the mines going up along the whole front. It was a beautiful morning for the battle and towards 7 a.m. prisoners began to come in. They were a very mixed lot and seemed glad to be prisoners. After lunch we moved to Ségard Château via Dickebusch and Café Belge. The rest of the Brigade are round here too and we are in reserve to the whole of the X Corps. We saw a tank going up to the line this morning. It's a weird looking object. We are in dugouts at the Château and are very comfy. We are surrounded by heavy guns and the noise is the limit. The whole battle has been a complete success everywhere.

Sunday 10.6.17.

We have been at Château Ségard the last three days, lying in reserve, ready to move up to wherever we are needed most. It has been very hot up here. The days have been quiet except for a few 5.9 shells. To-morrow we move up to Rudkin House in front of Ypres as reserve. It is a very hot spot as it's just to the left of the battle.

---

4   The future King Edward VIII was serving on the staff.
5   In 41st Division.

Tuesday 12.6.17.

Here we are at Rudkin House and it's absolute 'Hell' in this region. Last night we left Château Ségard at 8 p.m. and marched via Swan Chateau, Shrapnel Corner, to Transport Farm where we picked up our guides. Fritz was shelling the road but we came up B Route, a cross country path through Zillebeke Village and all went well till we reached Valley Cottages when he began to whizz bang us. When that stopped on we went up the road to Stafford Trench on which Rudkin House stands and just as I reached the trench an S.O.S. rocket went up on the right and then he poured shells into that area around Valley Cottage and Rudkin House. Simmons, the O.C.'s servant and Bish, the Adjutant's servant were killed and one of the transport men wounded, otherwise we had no casualties. I can't understand how we escaped so lightly considering the whole Batt. was out in the open with all that shelling. They have been shelling the life out of us in Rudkin House with 5.9s and 8 inch armour-piercing and put one of the latter clean through into our deep dugout and killed two men so we are shifting up to the big tunnel dugouts in Winnipeg St. to-morrow. This is a poisonous area!

Wednesday 13.6.17.

The O.C. and I went up to Winnipeg Street this morning to get a place for H.Q.s. All was nice and quiet going up and coming back. We went up New Cut and Davidson Street, and returned by St. Peter's Street. After lunch we all shifted up and feel much safer up here.

Figure 30. A German 21cm ('8 inch') *Mörser* firing at night. (A.R. Lucas collection)

Tuesday [Thursday] 14.6.17.

This morning the O.C. and I went along to Mount Sorrel to arrange about our taking over from the N. Staffs to-night. We were shelled a bit going there but it wasn't far to go. When we got back to Winnipeg Street we heard B. Coy. had a lot of men buried in a tunnel leading from Stafford Trench to St. Peter's Street, so Picton, Thomas and I went down and got them out – 11 were killed and 28 wounded, crushed and shaken, including four of my bearers, one of which was killed – Baldwin, a real topper. The Hun was very merciful as he let us get them out and then began to shell us. The Battalion moved into the line in front of Mount Sorrel to-night. H.Q. is in Mount Sorrel dugout but I couldn't have my dressing station there as there is no room so it's in Hedge Street Tunnel which is an extension of Winnipeg Street system.

Monday 18.6.17.

Here we are back in a tent camp by the Dickebusch Lake. It's absolute heaven back here. We had a most trying time up these last four days. D Coy. suffered badly, including their O.C., Capt. Tetley, who has had to have his right foot off. It was an awful job getting the wounded out as the whole country was shell-swept. My bearers carried from the front line to me at Hedge St. and then the R.A.M.C. bearers from me down through Armagh Wood to Fosse Wood and thence by light railway to Zillebeke village; Armagh Wood was an awful place, nothing but stumps of trees and shell holes and the bearers could be seen the whole way. The R.A.M.C. bearers were simply splendid under Sgt. Martin, D.C.M. Allam, Rand, Mountford and I came out this morning at 4.20 a.m., via St. Peter's Street, Zillebeck Street, Maple Copse, Zillebeke village to Transport Farm and down the road to Shrapnel Corner. All was beautifully quiet till I got to Transport Farm, then they began to shell the dugouts at the lake so we stepped out for all we were worth and reached Shrapnel Corner at 5 a.m. It was strewn with dead horses killed the night before. Then we turned left to Woodcote House and thence across country past Swan Château and Ségard Château, Café Belge to our camp. We were absolutely bathed in perspiration when we reached camp at 6.30 and had a thirst fit to drink a lake dry. I had a bath, in a basin and it was topping, then breakfast and slept soundly all morning. We had a violent thunder storm this afternoon which has cooled the air.

Tuesday 19.6.17.

It rained again in the night. This after-noon the O.C., Adjutant, Lt. Hilton and I rode over to No. 2 Canadian C.C.S. to see Capt. Tetley at Poperinghe. He had had his right foot amputated but was over the worst and was very cheery. That is the third time he has been wounded. After seeing him we had tea in Pop. at the officers' club. We got back at 7 p.m. and at 8 marched to Mic Mac Camp by the overland route to Reninghelst past Dickebusch village. Shortly after we got here the Huns shelled the area around us with a high velocity naval gun which rather put 'the wind up' us but did no damage. He kept up this desultory shelling all night. It rained heavily this morning at daybreak and has laid the dust.

Wednesday 20.6.17.

This afternoon Capt. Clark, Lt. Hilton and I rode into Poperinghe via Ouderdom and Busseboom and had tea at Skindles[6], then went to a show called 'The Tivolies' which was most excellent and we had a real good laugh. After it we had a great dinner at Skindles with champagne. Really, it does one a world of good to have an outing like that. Col. de la Fontaine, our O.C., is acting Brigadier General at present while General Sweny is on leave so Major Swanton is O.C. at present.

Thursday 21.6.17.

The Battalion was addressed to-day by our new Divisional Commander, Major General Bols, D.S.O., C.B. He seems a very nice fellow and has seen a lot of service.[7]

Saturday 23.6.17.

On Thursday evening Major Swanton gave us a champagne dinner as it was his dinner. It went off O.K. and we had cock fighting afterwards which was great fun.[8] It rained like fury yesterday morning, but it is very warm to-day and the roads are drying very well, they were seas of mud. Oh, Belgium is the limit for mud!! We go up to the trenches again to-night in Battle Wood which is in front of Hill 60. We do three days in the front line and three in close support and then come out for a rest. I sincerely hope it isn't such a hot spot as our last place. I do hate the Ypres Salient for the shelling is awful. We march up via Dickebusch, Voormezeele, then across country to the Spoil Bank on the Ypres Comines Canal and then to the old Hun front line where my Aid Post is.

Sunday 24.6.17.

Mountford, my servant and I set off last night at 7.15 p.m. from Mic Mac Camp and I rode as far as Scottish Wood via Dickebusch. Then walked from there to Voormezeele across country. Just as we reached Voormezeele Fritz was shelling it with 5.9s. We waited a bit till he stopped and then by luck we managed to catch a motor ambulance

6   The famous establishment at Poperinghe.
7   Louis Bols, born 1867 son of a Belgian diplomat, had commanded 84th Brigade at Second Ypres, then been Major General General Staff of Third Army, but had been found wanting in the Battle of Arras. He moved to Egypt in September 1917, where he proved a great success as Chief of Staff to General Allenby. He became a Lieutenant General.
8   According to a contemporary photograph at the Powell-Cotton Museum, this game involves tying hands to legs with a wooden bar and then trying to push your opponent over.

from there to the Spoil Bank on the Canal. Just as we reached the canal he began to shell the Spoil Bank so we had to run for it and took shelter in the F. Amb. dressing station. After it quietened down Corp. Fry of the R.A.M.C. guided us via Ravine Wood Hedge Row over our old front line trenches, across No Man's Land to the old Huns' front line where the Aid Post was. I relieved Capt. Fulton of the 13th Middlesex Regt. It was pretty quiet till about midnight then the Hun shelled all the area along our old front line and our little concrete dugout rocked with each burst of the shells but none landed near by. To-day has been fairly quiet and have had very few casualties through my hands. We are in the line which runs through Battle Wood and is just to the right of Hill 60. We get a most wonderful view of the country ahead of us. Crowds of large towns can be seen, Menin, Warneton, Wervicq and Comines. Our heavy guns are shelling them. They also set on fire three Hun Ammunition dumps. 2/ Lt. Yonge was wounded to-day – luckily not badly.

Monday 25.6.17.

It rained last night and everything is muddy and wet but it has cleared up again. The day has been quiet up here but the Hun has shelled our back areas a lot. At present I am afraid our airmen are far from being masters of the air. The Hun planes do just as they like.

Tuesday 26.6.17.

Rained again last night. Lt. Webb and I went over to Larch Wood dugouts at 4 a.m. this morning to reconnoitre the water. It isn't far from here, just on the other side of the railway cutting and bang alongside Hill 60. On our way back we had a look at the Caterpillar Crater which is on the right of the railway. It was blown on the 7th, the day of the battle. Jove it's some size.[9]

Wednesday 27.6.17.

The Batt. was relieved by the 1st N. Staffs. last night and our H.Q. shifted into Larch Wood dugouts. The relief went off without a casualty. We are very comfy down here and the whole place is lit up with electric light.

Saturday 30.6.17.

Here we are back in Mic Mac Camp. We were relieved last night by the 10th West Ridings, 30th Division and were lucky to have a quiet night for the relief. I was jolly glad to get back here at 4 a.m. We came back via the Railway Cutting which was full of water, past the Dump, along the bottom edge of Ravine Wood, to the Spoil Bank

---

9   It was the location of one of nineteen huge mines blown by the British at the start of the Battle of Messines.

(where a few shells dropped), thence by road to Voormezeele and then picked up our horses at Kruistraat Cabaret and rode back via Café Belge corner and Dickebusch. When we got in we had some coffee and went to bed for a few hours. We march off presently to catch the train.

Sunday 1.7.17.

We arrived at our billets this morning at 4.30 a.m., feeling very tired and fed up. We marched off from Mic Mac Camp yesterday at 1.15 p.m., in pouring rain via Ouderdom and Reninghelst to Reninghelst Siding at Busseboom and entrained at 4 p.m. We came via St. Omer and were to have detrained at Lumbres but on reaching there, were ordered to go on to Desvres. Really, the staff ought to be shot for if we had got off at Lumbres we would have had eight kilometres to march whereas by detraining at Desvres we had about fifteen kilometres to do. We started marching from Desvres at 11.30 p.m., got to our billets at 4.30 a.m., absolutely fagged out as we had only had had a few hours sleep in 48 hours. We at once had something to eat and then went to bed and slept like logs. The four companies are extremely spread out in little hamlets but this is a most beautiful part of the country and so very peaceful.

Monday 2.7.17.

I rode into Lumbres this afternoon to see the A.D.M.S. about getting a staff job and he has sent in my name for a D.A.D.M.S's appointment which I hope I get. The weather is topping again to-day.

Wednesday 4.7.17.

I am off on leave to-morrow from the 6th to the 16th and feel jolly glad to get home for a change as it's eight months and a week since I last had leave. Still, it's not nearly so long as some of the poor men who have been out eighteen months. The O.C. goes on leave to-morrow also, so he has borrowed a motor from the Division Headquarters to take us down to Boulogne. We are only 20 kilometres from Boulogne. I had dinner with 'Baby' and his officers at D Coy. this evening. I am awfully glad to get away for a bit as Major Swanton[10] has been making my life a misery in the mess. He's a prize outsider.

10   Swanton was wounded in August and returned briefly in October 1917. He was then locum C.O. for two other battalions. He then fell out of favour, being summoned to the War Office and subsequently made Chief Instructor in an officers' convalescent hospital as acting Major.

Thursday 5.7.17.

I did the sick parade this morning at 7 a.m. before I left. Capt. Falconer from the 74th F. Amb. is taking my place while on leave. The O.C. and I had a fine run down in the car this morning and got here, Boulogne, in about 40 minutes. It was a splendid road. The O.C. went off to Paris by the 2.30 p.m. train. I tried to cross with the afternoon boat but it was useless, they wouldn't let me cross, so am just waiting till to-morrow. I met a fellow Parsons of the M.G.C. [Machine Gun Corps] whom I know and he introduced me to a Lt. Ffrench of the Suffolks attached R.F.C. so we two are crossing to-morrow.

Friday 6.7.17.

Had a very fine crossing to-day and got to Victoria Station at 2.30 p.m. Ffrench and I went and got a room at the Regent Palace Hotel. I went to Dege the tailor in Conduit Street at once and am to be fitted to-morrow. I saw Oscar Ashe and Lily Brayton in 'Chu Chin Chow' at 'His Majesty's' theatre this evening. It was splendid.

Saturday 7.7.17.

While I was at the tailor's this morning the Huns raided London with twenty aeroplanes and bombed the place. There was fearful excitement and 'wind up'. After the tailor's I took a taxi to Eastcheap in the City to see 'Baby's' father. He was very shaken as most of the bombs were dropped on the City.[11] In the afternoon I went to see 'Smile', a revue at the 'Garrick' which was splendid. We couldn't get a seat this evening in any theatre so Ffrench and another Flying man and I just had dinner together.

Sunday 8.7.17.

It's raining like blazes to-day. This morning I went to see Lt. Manning, one of our officers who was wounded at Ypres. He's in Lady Bassey's [Brassey's?] Hospital, Upper Grosvenor Street; he's doing well. This afternoon I went to see Mrs. Cowper, the wife of one of our officers. She's awfully nice.[12]

To-night I go up to Edinburgh.

---

11 This was the second daylight raid on London by German Gotha aircraft. Twenty-two reached the target and caused, for the time, some spectacular damage and around 250 casualties in the City and East End. Public confidence was badly shaken and there were riots in the East End and Questions in Parliament, leading to withdrawal of fighter aircraft from France.

12 Her husband was Charles Cowper, born 1884, a South African farmer. Commissioned in 1915, he served with 9th East Surrey from August 1916. He was severely wounded later in 1917 and awarded an M.C. He died suddenly in 1920.

15.7.17.

I have to catch the train to London to-night and cross to France to-morrow. I am not keen on going back this time, still, duty calls and it must be done!

16.7.17.

I managed to get a sleeper down to London last night but my train got in too late to catch the leave train so came down by ordinary train to Folkestone and crossed by the evening boat. I have been unable to get a car back so am going by the wretched slow leave train which reaches Lumbres at 3 a.m., an awful hour. One blessing, we had a splendid crossing.

Tuesday 17.7.17.

Here I am back with the Regiment, fed up and dead beat. When I reached Lumbres at 3.30 a.m. I found the Regt. had marched off back at 3 a.m. towards the line but luckily our F. Ambulance hadn't gone so they gave me some food and a horse and I marched off with them at 5 a.m. from Lumbres. It was a glorious morning. We marched via Wizernes, Arques and outskirted St. Omer, to a very nice village Renescure. It was about 15-20 miles and reached our destination, at 10 a.m. The latter part of the march was very hot. I hate these early morning starts but it's splendid for marching. At the end of the march I rejoined the Regt., had lunch and began my sick parade and foot inspection but oh, I was dead beat after it and slept like a log till 7 then had dinner and am off to bed again for we have to be up at 2.30 a.m., and march off at 4 a.m.

Wednesday 18.7.17.

I was sleepy when wakened up this morning and loathe to get up. However it was nice and cool and got here, Caestre, a village near Bailleul, at 9.30 a.m. After breakfast I went to bed at 10.30 and slept like a rock till 4 p.m. After tea did the sick parade. It has been raining heavily all day. We only have a short march to-morrow, about three kilometres to Eecke.

Thursday 19.7.17.

We knocked off the march in no time to-day and are most comfortable in this village. I put the Battalion through gas helmet drill to-day and am beastly hoarse. This afternoon Whiteman and I drove over to Noote Boom to see our old billets with the Devos. We had a jolly afternoon with them. To-morrow we start early again and march to near Reninghelst.

Friday 20.7.17.

We were up at 3.30 this morning and marched off at 5. It was a most beautiful morning, fine for marching. The country is looking lovely, some of the crops are quite

Figure 31. Memorial plaque sent to Captain Pirie's next of kin. (© Michael Hall)

yellow and all the hay is mown. We marched via Godewaersvelde and Boeschepe to a tent camp near Reninghelst. This afternoon I put the Batt. through gas helmet drill again and they are quite good at it now. To-morrow we move to Mic Mac Camp, near Ouderdom. One of my Stretcher-bearers, Pte. Rolls, of D Coy. has been awarded the Military Medal for bravery. He is a very good fellow.

Saturday 21.7.17.

We only marched off at 8 a.m. this morning as there was only four miles to do. We came via Reninghelst and Ouderdom and are back in our old camp. I am not looking forward to going into the line to-morrow night. It's a beast of an area. C and D Coys. go up to-night and A and B and H.Q. Coys. to-morrow night. I hear Lt. Royal has been invalided out of the army with consumption. Jolly rotten luck.[13]

---

13   In fact, James Royal returned to the Battalion in April 1918. It was Captain Anslow who was to be invalided out through consumption, i.e. tuberculosis.

Appendix I

A chronology of the service of Captain G.S. Pirie, R.A.M.C.

1914
(14 December Pirie commences the first diary.)

1915

2 January	Commissioned in the R.A.M.C. Special Reserve.
16-30 January	Training.
5 March	With No.15 General Hospital leaves England for Mediterranean.
14 March	Arrives Alexandria, Egypt.
7 April	Transferred to 89th F.A., formerly 1st Highland F.A. (Territorial), serving 86th Infantry Brigade, 29th Division.
22 April	Temporarily transferred to the hospital ship S.S. *Aragon*.
25 April	Witnesses landings at Helles, Gallipoli, and tends wounded from same. Wounded conveyed to Alexandria and Malta.
15 May	Goes ashore at Helles to rejoin 89th F.A.
20 May	To 2nd Hampshire, 88th Brigade, 29th Division as R.M.O.
4 June	Third Battle of Krithia.
14 June	To 2nd Royal Fusiliers, 86th Brigade, 29th Division as R.M.O.
28 June-5 July	Battle of Gully Ravine.
6-7 August	Allied diversionary attacks at Helles.
20 August	To Suvla with 2nd Royal Fusiliers.
21 August	Battle of Scimitar Hill.
4 September	Wounded at Suvla.
10 September	Arrives Malta.
23 September	Arrives Southampton, then to Osborne, Isle of Wight.
29 September	Arrives Edinburgh. (Pirie closes first diary)

13 November	Medical Board concludes he is fully recovered from his wound.
11 December	Mentioned in Dispatches by General Sir Ian Hamilton.
13 December	Joins 9th East Surrey, 72nd Brigade, 24th Division at Tournehem, France, as R.M.O.

1916

7 January	9th East Surrey to Hooge trenches, Ypres.
(18 March Pirie commences the second diary.)	
27 March	9th East Surrey to Wulverghem trenches, near Ypres.
6-15 April	On leave in U.K.
30 April and 17 June	German gas attacks at Wulverghem
26 June to 4 July	At 12 C.C.S. for a rest.
8/9 July	9th East Surrey to Ploegsteert trenches.
13 August	9th East Surrey to trenches near Guillemont, Somme. (Attacks on Guillemont followed by Delville Wood action early September.)
2 October	9th East Surrey to trenches near Vimy.
25 October	9th East Surrey to trenches near Loos/Hulluch.
31 October-10 November	On leave in U.K.

1917

1 January	Granted regular commission in R.A.M.C. as Lieutenant, temporary Captain. (He had been promoted Captain in the Special Reserve by September 1915.)
6 January	Transfers to 74th F. A.
9 February to 12 February	With 73rd F. A. (temporarily.)
2 March	9th East Surrey to trenches at Cité Calonne facing Lens.
14 March	Returns to 9th East Surrey as R.M.O.
14 May	9th East Surrey to trenches at Hooge, Ypres.
(9th East Surrey in reserve for Battle of Messines commencing 7 June.)	
10 June	9th East Surrey to trenches near Klein Zillebeke, Ypres.
6-16 July	On leave in U.K.
(21 July second diary ends.)	
24 July	Pirie killed by a shell near Hill 60, Ypres.
7 November	Posthumously Mentioned in Dispatches by Field Marshal Sir Douglas Haig.

Appendix II

29th and 24th Divisions – Orders of Battle

I   Infantry of 29th Division, August 1915
86th Brigade
2nd Royal Fusiliers, 1st Lancashire Fusiliers, 1st Royal Munster Fusiliers, 1st Royal Dublin Fusiliers.

87th Brigade
2nd South Wales Borderers, 1st King's Own Scottish Borderers, 1st Royal Inniskilling Fusiliers, 1st Border.

88th Brigade
4th Worcestershire, 2nd Hampshire, 1st Essex, 1/5th Royal Scots (T.F.)

II   Infantry of 24th Division, 1916-17
17th Brigade
8th Buffs, 1st Royal Fusiliers, 12th Royal Fusiliers, 3rd Rifle Brigade.

72nd Brigade
8th Queen's, 9th East Surrey, 8th Royal West Kent, 1st North Staffordshire.

73rd Brigade
9th Royal Sussex, 7th Northamptonshire, 13th Middlesex, 2nd Leinster.

Pioneer Battalion
12th Sherwood Foresters.
(Among 24th Division's other units were 106th-109th Brigades, R.F.A.; 103rd, 104th and 129th Field Companies, R.E.; 194th- 197th Companies, A.S.C.; 72nd -74th Field Ambulances, R.A.M.C.)

Appendix III

Letter from Captain Pirie to Second Lieutenant J.L.B. Denny regarding the Somme fighting

---

'B.E.F.
12th Sept. [1916]

Dear Denny,

Ever so many thanks for your epistle I'm sorry I couldn't answer it before as we have had a H---s own strenuous time & much moving about but we are now thank goodness away back out of sound of guns & noise. It's heavenly. We're away down near where Charles [Cuthbert?] joined us. Peaceful isn't the word for it.

I had a most pathetic letter from Charles' Fiancée yesterday I replied at once. I ought to have written her long ago, but Denny I funked it, & so never wrote before, you can't imagine how I miss old D. Coy, its too sad for words. Royal is O.C. D. Coy now, Harvey 2/command, & the rest are all new fellows. Collins & Hyland [two N.C.Os.] have survived the whole show wonderful isn't it, 3 goes up. Sgt. Chipping is your only Sgt. left. He has been excellent & is up for a decoration. Poor old Rivers was killed by a 4.2 which burst alongside him, & Lillywhite & C.S.M. [Company Sergeant Major] Tanner in a C.T. going up to the left of where you were hit near a wood in the early morning. He died at once. L White [Lillywhite] was badly hit & Tanner slightly in the neck. That left Monro in the Coy so Royal took over D. Coy., mind you Monro's first trip in too.[1]

I very nearly was with Rivers, had just gone ahead as there was a stoppage so went on to see what it was about. Then that trip up Hilton was peppered about the face & arms with whizz bang splinters but has rejoined us again. He's our [life?] & hope now!!! We <u>were</u> glad when we got out the 2nd time & went back to a decent village for a week where we got more officers & a few men, but up we went again, & oh H---, it was H---, much worse than the previous events, your attack[2] was nil to it. I have never seen such shelling. We were on the edge of a wood [Delville] & of course had our line

---

1   Whilst James Royal had been with the Battalion since December 1915, J.D. Monro had only arrived in July 1916.
2   At Guillemont on 16 August.

taped. We were up when the village [Guillemont] was taken, your old objective is no more now. It was a very successful day.

The O.C. was shot through both lungs, leading a bombing show & we all thought at first he would die, but his grit & determination has pulled him through, & he is doing very well indeed. He was magnificent the way he led those tired men, they were irresistible. Poor Parker Ingrams was killed well forward in the attack. He was O.C. B Coy. Monro was also wounded knee & arm & is home now. Gold slightly wounded, Castle badly, Urban, Haines & Major Ottley our 2/command killed by direct hits of shells. Sgt. Fruish is now C.S.M. of D. Coy B. Coy C.S.M. White is killed. You wouldn't know the old Regt now tons of new officers, only Clark & I survive who have been up each time & I don't know how we did. You can expect to see Clark an M. Cross winner for leading a bombing party to the line through H--- s own barrage. He was great. Tetley rejoined us the day of the attack was only ½ hr up when over he went & survived. He was magnificent. Sgt Summers still exists- marvellous. He's up for decoration again. Matthews was detached with some men to work with the REs & he was horribly knocked about on a working party, but is doing well. I can't give you any more news about poor old Pip O'Brien. He seems to have been wounded by a bomb before getting into the trench.[3] Our numbers are very seldom [sic.] now, it's it's d--- d sad.

All officers who have been in it are being given 48 clear hours leave in Paris. Buggy Picton & Schofield went yesterday Baby [Hilton] and I go next, what a time we'll have!!!! The men are being sent to the seaside for 48 hrs & they can do as they like.

Pully [Pullan] was lost in the wood one night for 2 hrs & then a crump broke his thigh so he'll never fight again. Even on the stretch[er] he had a tin of stinkers [cigarettes] in his hand & smoking hard – typical isn't it!!!![4] Schofield is now M.G. officer. He has been away on a course .Tetley is O.C. bombers. Capt. Taylor is O.C. A & Lt. [Warre-] Dymond O.C. B. Baby O.C. C. Our new O.C. Lt. Col. Tew comes from the 1st Bn very quiet & dry & slow but awfully decent. Capt. Jackson is 2/command. Ah well Denny must stop I have heaps more to write so Cheerio. hope this will interest you Whitebait [Whiteman] & Birch, etc. send love

Yours v. sincerely
G.S. Pirie
We took 1 officer & 19 men prisoners. Royal took the officer.'

Editor's note

I found this letter in Colonel Lillywhite's papers at I.W.M. (ref. 76/19/1). It seems likely that Denny and Lillywhite were in hospital together and Denny passed the letter to Lillywhite. I have corrected some spelling mistakes.

---

3   Francis O'Brian had in fact been killed in the 16 August attack at Guillemont.
4   Cyril Pullan, with a shortened leg, lived to 75.

Appendix IV

War Office telegram notifying Pirie's next of kin of his death.

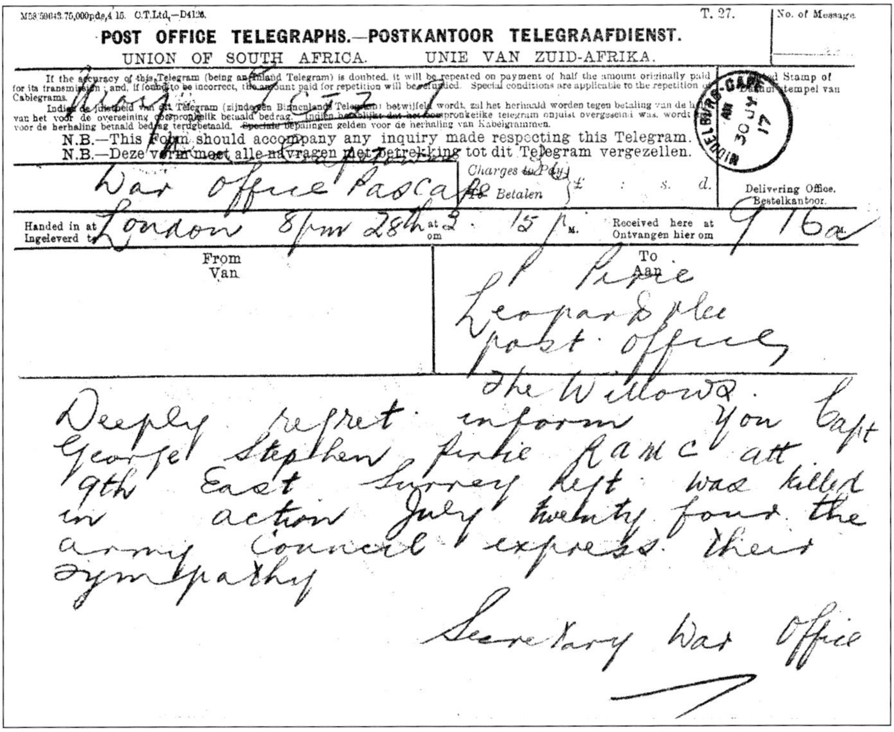
T. 27.

No. of Message

POST OFFICE TELEGRAPHS.—POSTKANTOOR TELEGRAAFDIENST.

UNION OF SOUTH AFRICA. UNIE VAN ZUID-AFRIKA.

If the accuracy of this Telegram (being an Inland Telegram) is doubted, it will be repeated on payment of half the amount originally paid for its transmission; and, if found to be incorrect, the amount paid for repetition will be refunded. Special conditions are applicable to the repetition of Cablegrams.

Indien de juistheid van dit Telegram (zijnde een Binnenlandsch Telegram) betwijfeld wordt, zal het herhaald worden tegen betaling van de helft van het voor de overseining oorspronkelijk betaald bedrag. Indien het blijkt dat het oorspronkelijke telegram onjuist overgeseind was, wordt voor de herhaling betaald bedrag terugbetaald. Speciale bepalingen gelden voor de herhaling van Kabelgrammen.

N.B.—This Form should accompany any inquiry made respecting this Telegram.
N.B.—Deze vorm moet alle navragen met betrekking tot dit Telegram vergezellen.

Stamp of Datumstempel van: MIDDELBURG-CAPE 30 JY 17

War Office

Charges to Pay / Te Betalen £ s. d.

Delivering Office. / Bestelkantoor.

Handed in at / Ingeleverd te: London 8pm 28th at 3.15 p.M.

Received here at / Ontvangen hier om: 9 16a.M.

From / Van

To / Aan: P Pirie Leopards Vlei post office The Willows.

Deeply regret inform you Capt George Stephen Pirie RAMC att 9th East Surrey Regt was killed in action July twenty four the army Council express their sympathy

Secretary War Office

Figure 32. War Office telegram notifying Pirie's next of kin of his death.
(© Peter Strasheim)

Appendix V

Letters of condolence to Pirie's family

A number of these are set out below, in full, or in part, as throwing some light on how others regarded him and something of his personal life. None survives from Lieutenant Colonel de la Fontaine, possibly because he was, himself, killed on 5 August 1917.

From Chaplain G.D.B. Poole, 9th East Surrey, 25 July, 1917 to Pirie's sister, Alice

'Dear Mrs. Ormsby,
I am very sorry indeed to write this letter. Your brother Capt. Pirie the M.O. of this Batt. was killed yesterday in the trenches. He was working in his aid post when a shell burst right in the entrance & killed him instantly. It is impossible to put into words what his death means to the Batt. He was a splendid M.O. sympathetic to a degree & yet at the same time firm. We all most deeply feel his loss. May I send you most heartfelt sympathy. I know all the men would wish to join in the message. During all these months he & I had got to know each other well & by his death I know I lose a true friend but the loss must be immeasurably greater to you & others to whom he was so close. We buried him reverently in the Military Cemetery behind the line. May he rest in peace.'

From the same correspondent, 27.7.17 [sic.] to an unidentified friend or relative

'Dear Miss Lawson,
Owing to circumstances it was not possible to write to you in time for the first anniversary of Capt. Pirie's death, but I hope you do not think that we have all of us forgotten him or it.

Those of us who still remain who knew him often speak of him, & to us he is still the model M.O., the doctor loved by both officers & men.

We should all like to send you a message of sincere sympathy in a loss which cannot but be still fresh to you.'

From Brigadier General W.F. Sweny, 72nd Brigade, 7 August 1917

'Dear Mrs. Ormsby,
I have wanted so much to tell you how sorry we all are to lose one of our very best when your brother was killed.

A more gallant cheery fellow never lived and somehow I never thought of him being taken. He was always so full of life & help for others.

I don't think he thought much of himself & when he was killed he was doing other people's work, putting up some sandbags that had been knocked down. We in my Regt. the Royal Fusiliers especially were fond of him as he had the most open and avowed love for us all. He was with one of the Batts. in Gallipoli. Please believe me his example was worth a lot to all who knew him & makes his sacrifice well worth it to his country & ourselves.'

From W.A. Robinson, formerly Pirie's housemaster, Saint Andrew's College, Grahamstown, Cape Colony, 17 November 1917 to Georgina (Nina), another of Pirie's sisters

'My dear Nina,
There were days when I used to call you by your Christian name & so I hope you will not be offended that I do so once again.

It was very kind of you to write me such a long letter on the 24th net [?] telling me such a lot about George. It seemed to me that the breaking off of his engagement must have affected him very much. Fancy him repeating a remark I made about 'Pip'. I can't remember the incident but it must be true & I can well imagine both he & you being amused. It has grieved Mr. Cornish & myself very much that the Obituary notice that appeared in our magazine was so totally inadequate. He was one of the staunchest & most loyal Andreans who ever passed through my hands but it is for his real sterling character & goodness of heart that I shall always treasure him in my memory,

If you have a spare photo I should much like to have one.'

From an unknown correspondent to an unknown recipient at an unknown date

'I think old George knew he was going to be killed, for the last visit he gave me was such a mixture of joy & sadness. I can not quite describe how apart from all things trivial, George had become.

In some way he seemed calm & expectant, & very close to God. He told us, & that so simply & truly, life was impossible in the 1st line without God. He said to us that God had become a living reality to him. Dear old George, one of our best & dearest friends, we mourn for him selfishly, because I'm sure all is well with him. He told Dr. Jardine when he said 'Goodbye' that he would never come back again. A shell struck his dug out (dressing station), and death must have been instantaneous.'

Bibliography

Manuscript sources

Imperial War Museum (I.W.M.):

P191 (Abraham); P1/6/ 20/1 (Billman); 88/18/1 (Lambert); 76/19/1 (Lillywhite); 66/304/1(Lodge Patch); P472 (Tower).

Kingston Grammar School:

Memories of Active Service by R.C.Sherriff.

Liddle Collection:

S.C. Liddle – GS 1590, L.C. Thomas interview.

National Army Museum:

2001-03-36 Diary of B.R. Mitford 1916-17.

Pirie family collection:

Transcript of G.S. Pirie's diary, letters of condolence, photographs.

Powell-Cotton Museum:

V.A.D. hospital photographic collection.

Surrey History Centre (S.H.C.):

2332 and 3813 – correspondence and papers of R.C. Sherriff; and ESR series, papers of the East Surrey Regiment and its officers and men.

The National Archives (T.N.A.):

WO95 series war diaries, WO339 and 374 series files on officers, WO363 'Burnt' Records for O.Rs.,WO364 'Pension' records for O.Rs.; WO 372 medal cards.

Printed sources

Books

Anon., *The Army List*, London, various dates.

Anon., *Field Service Pocket Book (1914)* David & Charles, Newton Abbot, 1971.

Anon., *Officers Died in the Great War 1914-19*, H.M.S.O., London, 1919.

Anon., *Soldiers Died in the Great War 1914-19 Part 36 The East Surrey Regiment* Hayward & Son, Polstead, 1989.

Anon., *Who's Who*, London, 1897-2000.

Ashworth, T., *Trench Warfare 1914-1918: The Live and Let Live System*, Pan, London, 2000.

Aspinall-Oglander, C.F., *History of the Great War Military Operations Gallipoli Volume I – Inception of the campaign to May 1915*, William Heinemann, London, 1929.

Aspinall-Oglander, C.F., *History of the Great War Military Operations Gallipoli Volume II – May 1915 to the evacuation*, William Heinemann, London, 1932.

Astill, E., *The Great War Diaries of Brigadier Alexander Johnston 1914-1917*. Pen & Sword, Barnsley, 2007.

Behrmann, F., *Die Osterschlacht bei Arras 1917, I. Teil: Zwischen Lens und Scarpe*, Verlag Gerhard Stalling, Oldenburg and Berlin, 1929.

Chambers, S., *Battleground Europe Gallipoli – Gully Ravine*, Pen & Sword, Barnsley, 2003.

Creighton, O., *With the Twenty-Ninth Division in Gallipoli*, Longmans, Green London, 1916.

Davidson, G., *The Incomparable 29th and the 'River Clyde'*, J.G. Bissett, Aberdeen, 1920.

De Ruvigny, Marquis, *The Marquis De Ruvigny's Roll of Honour: A Biographical Record of His Majesty's Military and Aerial Forces who fell in the Great War 1914-18*, n.p., 1922.

Duffy, C., *Through German Eyes The British and the Somme 1916*, Phoenix, London, 2007.

Edmonds, Sir J.E., *History of the Great War Military Operations France & Belgium 1916 Vol. I – Sir Douglas Haig's command to the 1st July: Battle of the Somme*, Macmillan, London, 1932.

Erickson, E.J., *Gallipoli: The Ottoman Campaign*, Pen & Sword, Barnsley, 2010.

Gibbon, F.P., *The 42nd (East Lancashire) Division 1914-1918*, Country Life, London, 1920.

Gliddon, G., *The Battle of the Somme: A Topographical History*, Alan Sutton, Stroud, 1996.

Graves, R., *Goodbye to All That*, Penguin, London, 1963.

Gruson, E., *Das Königlich Preussische 4. Thuringische Infanterie- Regiment Nr.72 im Weltkrieg*, Verlag Gerhard Stalling, Oldenburg, 1930.

Hamilton, R.G.A., *The War Diary of the Master of Belhaven,* John Murray, London, 1924.

Hart, P., *Gallipoli,* Profile, London, 2011.

Hitchcock, F.C., *Stand To – A Diary of the Trenches 1915-1918,* Naval & Military Press, Heathfield, n.d.

Holmes, R., *Tommy, The British Soldier on the Western Front 1914-1918.* Harper Collins, London, 2004.

Jünger, E., (trans. Mottram, R.H.) *The Storm of Steel*, Chatto and Windus, London, 1941.

Le Fleming, H.M., *Warships of World War I*, Ian Allan, London, 1970.

Lucas, M.J., *The 'Journey's End' Battalion – the 9th East Surrey in the Great War*, Pen & Sword, Barnsley, 2012.

Makoben, E., *Geschichte des Reserve-Infanterie-Regiments Nr. 212 im Weltkrieg 1914-1918.* Verlag Gerhard Stalling, Oldenburg, 1933.

McPherson, W.G., *History of the Great War Medical Services General History Vol. III,* Naval & Military Press, Uckfield, n.d.

Messenger, C., *Call to Arms the British Army 1914-1918.* Cassell, London, 2006.

Miles, W., *History of the Great War Military Operations France & Belgium 1916 Volume II – 2nd July 1916 to the end of the Battle of the Somme,* Macmillan, London, 1938.

Moore-Bick, C., *Playing the Game – The British Junior Officer on the Western Front 1914-18,* Helion, Solihull, 2011.

Moran, Lord, *The Anatomy of Courage* Constable, London, 1945.

Pearse, H.W. and Sloman, H.S., *History of the East Surrey Regiment Volumes II and III,* Medici Society, London, 1924.

Philpott, W., *Bloody Victory: The Sacrifice on the Somme*, Abacus, London, 2010.

Scotland, T. and Heys, S. (ed.), *War Surgery 1914-18*, Helion, Solihull, 2012.

Scott, M. *The Ypres Salient – A Guide to the Cemeteries and Memorials of the Salient,* Naval & Military, Uckfield, n.d.

Sheldon, J., *The German Army on the Somme 1914-1916,* Pen & Sword, Barnsley, 2005.

Spagnoly, T. and Smith, T., *A walk around Plugstreet South Ypres section 1914-1918,* Leo Cooper, London, 1997.

Stedman, M., *Battleground Europe – Guillemont,* Pen & Sword, Barnsley, 1998.

Westhorp, C. *The Wipers Times – The Famous First World War Newspaper*, Conway, London, 2013.

Articles

The British Medical Journal – various obituaries.

The Times – various obituaries.

Anon. 'To the Last Man and the Last Round', *Queen's Royal Surrey Newsletter*, May 1972.

Butcher, B., 'Army Medical Services on the Western Front' *Stand To!* January 2013.

Cohen, D., 'War Art' *Stand To!* January 1996.

Hannan, H., 'Loos reflections', *Queen's Royal Surrey Regiment Newsletter*, November 1981.

Lucas, M.J., 'Walter Summers, Film Director & 9th Battalion East Surreys.' *Between the Lines, Newsletter of the Western Front Association's East Kent Branch*, Summer 2009.

Sherriff, R.C., 'My Diary', *Journal of the East Surrey Regiment* Vol.1 Nos.1-4 and Vol.2 Nos.1-2 New Series, 1936-1939.

Websites

Commonwealth War Graves Commission at http://www.cwgc-org/

Great War Forum at http://1914-1918.invisionzone.com/forums/index.php

The London Gazette at http://www.london-gazette.co.uk

Queen's Royal Surreys at http://www.queensroyalsurreys.org.uk/war diaries/war diaries_home.shtml (for access to 9th East Surrey war diary on line).

Index

INDEX OF MILITARY UNITS

INDEX OF PEOPLE

INDEX OF PLACES

INDEX OF MISCELLANEOUS TERMS

Related titles published by Helion & Company

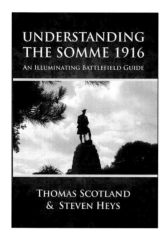

*Understanding the Somme 1916: An
Illuminating Battlefield Guide*
Thomas Scotland & Steven Heys
ISBN 978-1-909384-42-2 (paperback)

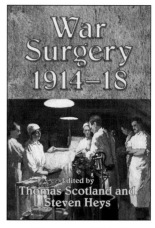

War Surgery 1914–18
Edited by Thomas Scotland & Steven Heys
ISBN 978-1-909384-40-8 (paperback)
ISBN 978-1-909384-37-8 (eBook)

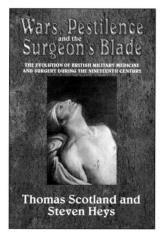

*Wars, Pestilence and the Surgeon's Blade: The
Evolution of British Military Medicine and
Surgery during the 19th Century*
Thomas Scotland & Steven Heys
ISBN 978-1-909384-09-5 (hardback)

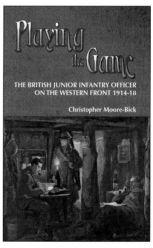

*Playing the Game: The British Junior Infantry
Officer on the Western Front 1914–18*
Christopher Moore-Bick
ISBN 978-1-906033-84-2 (hardback)

HELION & COMPANY
26 Willow Road, Solihull, West Midlands B91 1UE, England
Telephone 0121 705 3393 Fax 0121 711 4075
Website: http://www.helion.co.uk